# 3·DIMENSIONAL ILLUSTRATION

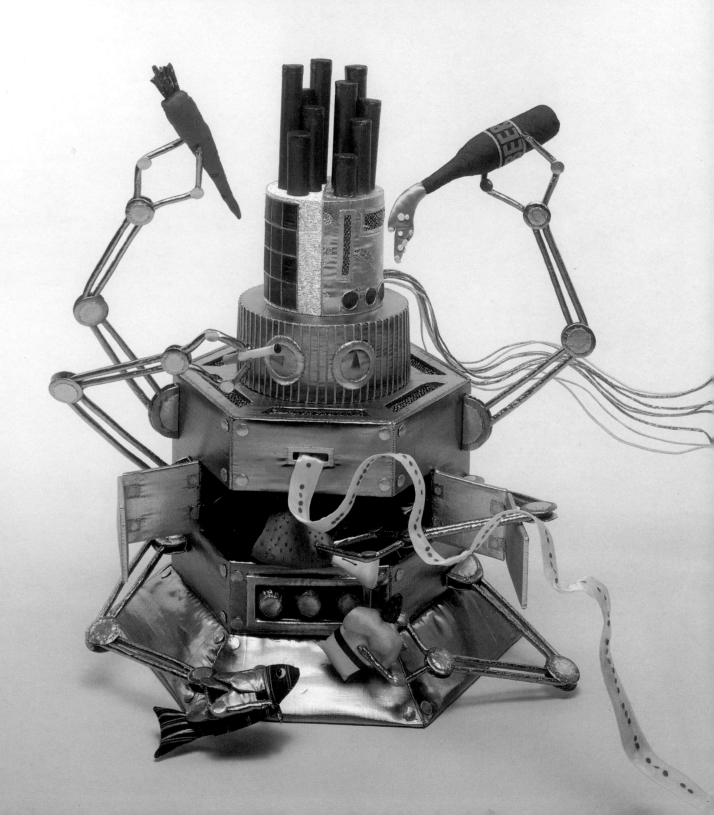

# 3·DIMENSIONAL ILLUSTRATION

## ELLEN RIXFORD

WATSON-GUPTILL PUBLICATIONS/NEW YORK

HALF-TITLE:
*Chikako Tomita*, Machine Having Lunch
*soft sculpture, for the cover of* Quark *magazine.*
*(Photographer: Akira Matsui)*

FRONTISPIECE:
*Gerald McConnell*, Mennen Assemblage *exhibition piece,*
*for permanent installation in the Mennen Museum.*
*(Photograph © Cosimo)*

PAGE 6:
*Four dimensionally illustrated interpretations*
*of the human heart. Clockwise from top left—*
*Blake Hampton*, Tired Heart,
*for an advertising series for a heart medication*
*(photograph courtesy of Wyeth Ayerst Laboratories);*
*David Epstein*, The Heart *illustration,*
*with steel wire representing electrical currents*
*in the heart (photographer: David Epstein);*
*Blake Hampton*, 6,000,000 Fewer Beats per Year,
*for an advertising series for a heart medication*
*(photograph courtesy of Wyeth Ayerst Laboratories);*
*Caspar Henselmann*, Normal Heart,
*for an advertising brochure cover*
*(photograph courtesy of Pfizer Inc.)*

PAGE 8:
*Ellen Rixford*, The Goddess of Earth *two-sided*
*self-promotional puppet, done in the Japanese Bunraku style.*
*(Photographer: Ellen Rixford; pupper mechanisms done*
*with the assistance of Mari Tobita)*

Edited by Paul Lukas
Designed by Bob Fillie
Senior Editor: Marian Appellof
Graphic Production: Ellen Greene

First published in 1992 by Watson-Guptill Publications,
a division of BPI Communications, Inc.,
1515 Broadway, New York, NY 10036

**Library of Congress Cataloging-in-Publication Data**
Rixford, Ellen.
    3-dimensional illustration: designing with paper, clay, casts, wood,
assemblage, plastics, fabric, metal, and food/Ellen Rixford.
        p.   cm.
    Includes index.
    ISBN 0-8230-5367-9
    1. Models and modelmaking.    I. Title    II. Three-dimensional illustration.
TT 154.R58 1992                          92-11619
741.6—dc20                               CIP

Manufactured in Singapore

First printing, 1992

1 2 3 4 5 6 7 8 9 / 99 98 97 96 95 94 93 92

**ACKNOWLEDGMENTS**
This book is dedicated to the dimensional illustrators who made it possible. Without their help, both as technical advisers and as friends, I would never have been able to write the book. I am especially grateful to the illustrators who prepared the how-to photos of their own work, generously sharing their hard-won technical knowledge with others. This selflessness and kind-heartedness are typical of the spirit of cooperation and mutual support that exists within the field of graphic design and illustration, especially within the dimensional illustration community.

I also want to acknowledge the kindness of the photographers who allowed their photos to be used in this book, and of publications, notably *Step-by-Step Graphics* and *Threads* magazines, which permitted me reprint how-to series and final art that originally appeared in their pages.

Most of all, I want to say, "Hats off, and three cheers!" to the Graphic Artists Guild, a tireless supporter of artists' rights and an indefatigable helper of illustrators and artists struggling to run their own businesses and remain true to their work. Artists—all artists, in all fields—should stick together, share with each other, support each other, and defend each other in a society where art is not supported and defended. This book, whatever its faults (and there are plenty of them), is an attempt to share knowledge, and to celebrate the artists who have made our field grow and blossom.

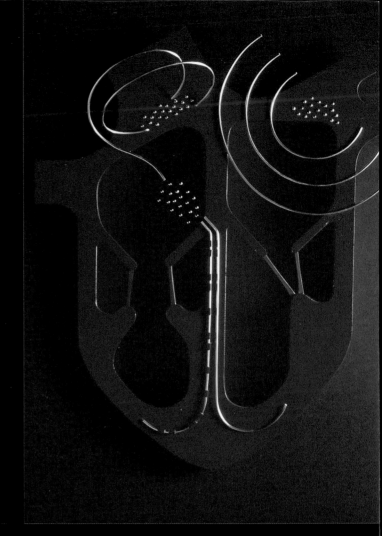

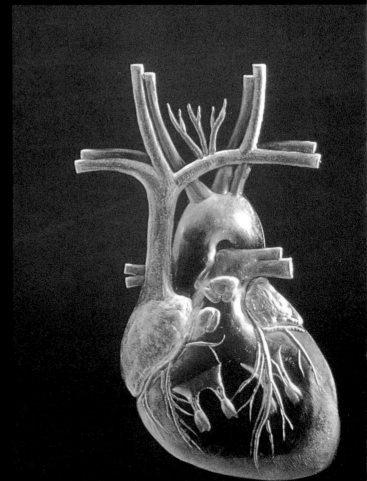

# CONTENTS

# INTRODUCTION

**T**his note is for those of you who are opening this book for the first time—those who have either bought the book (thank you) or are considering whether to do so.

In the area of illustration, dimensional illustration is a frontier. There is an infinite number of possibilities and discoveries yet to be made, of media and styles to be explored. Yet dimensional illustration is an underpopulated area—underrepresented in general illustration books and annuals, and its practical applications underutilized in both publishing and advertising. The reason for this is ignorance. Art directors, art buyers, creative directors, and producers are not introduced to most sculpture media in art school. Curricula in most graphic design and illustration departments include almost nothing in the way of three-dimensional work, focusing 98 percent of course content on two-dimensional media. Until now, there have been no technical books on dimensional illustration. And until the recent advent of Dimensional Illustrators Inc., which does a beautiful annual show of the best in dimensional illustration each year, together with gorgeous books on each year's show, there was only one book on dimensional illustration.

This book, therefore, is an attempt to fill an enormous void. And because the field *is* enormous—at least a dozen media and an limitless number of styles—the book is, by necessity, a compromise. It really should have been several books, each devoted to a major medium or group of media, or it should have been much larger. Indeed, my original manuscript would have filled three books this size. Unfortunately, for reasons of practicality and manageability, the project had to be pared down, so that the book now concentrates on areas of sculpture in illustration not covered well elsewhere, while techniques that are adequately handled in other sources are described much more briefly. Foundry casting and wood joinery, for instance, are thoroughly discussed and well illustrated in many books on metal- and woodworking, but there is no book with an extensive treatment of soft sculpture, so I devoted more attention and space to the latter than to the former.

I also have tried to pay attention to the needs and limitations of the average student, illustrator, or art director who will be using this text as a handbook for planning, fabricating, and purchasing dimensional illustration. I have concentrated on media and techniques that are accessible to most artists, are not extremely hazardous, and require a modest amount of space and widely available or reasonably obtainable tools. If a technique is very specialized, or requires unusual, expensive, and/or industrial facilities (electroplating or heavy-duty welding are good examples), the process is described in sufficient detail for readers to get a good idea of how it works, after which they are directed to seek a cooperative arrangement with a professional facility. Such cooperation is necessary in any case for these techniques, and the hands-on experience of watching a professional do the work is a necessity for the novice, as these processes can be dangerous to the unskilled. And I have tried to focus on media that are likely to remain in demand and to be of real practical use for illustrators and clients alike.

With luck, this book will encourage the production of other volumes, perhaps including media-specific books with much more exhaustive treatments of their respective media than I have been able to give within the confines of these 176 pages. As artists and their clients share experience and expertise, more artists will be encourage to try sculpture as illustration, and more clients will ask for it. In turn, more art schools will begin to consider sculpture illustration as a valid course subject in its own right, so that a new generation of educated professionals will emerge. Then sculpture will come into its own in illustration, and illustration—and art generally—will be the better for it.

ELLEN RIXFORD
Dante's Divine
Comedy *paper pop-
up-style diorama,
for Christmas
windows at Gucci,
1990, with Inferno at
bottom, Purgatorio at
center, and Paradiso
at top, with silhouette
of Dante at left,
Beatrice at right.
Canson and
Fabriano colored
papers over
cardboard structure.
Height: 6′ (1.8 m).
Client: Gucci.
(Photographer:
Ellen Rixford)*

# 1 | PAPER SCULPTURE

**P**aper sculpture is two dimensions frozen in the act of metamorphosing into three. Although it can be complex and detailed, its charm and power lie in its elegant reduction of infinitely complex natural forms to a finite number of flat, folded, or curled shapes juxtaposed or layered upon each other. This relationship of carefully designed and expressive shapes is the essence of paper sculpture. Its clean, precise look makes it equally appropriate for rendering hard-edged objects like city buildings or for simplifying soft-edged objects like human faces. It is excellent for caricature and for humorous illustration—its ability to transform the face and figure into a few eloquent lines and shapes allows it to distill the essence of a character. The same economy of means makes paper sculpture ideal for medical illustration, since it can fuse the clarity of a diagram with the richness and subtlety of a work of art.

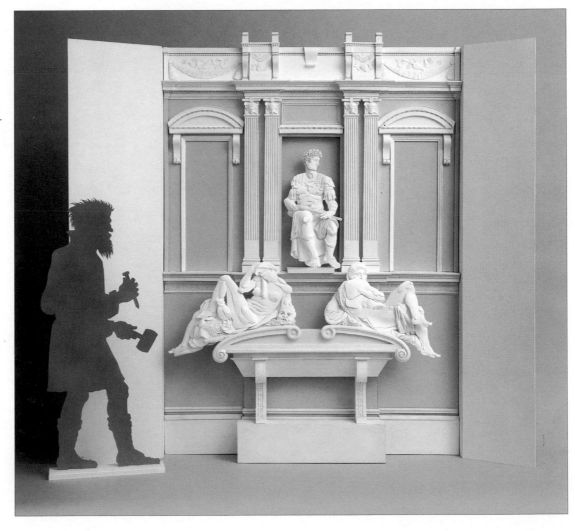

ELLEN RIXFORD
Michelangelo's Tomb of Giuliano de'Medici *paper sculpture pop-up-style diorama, for Gucci Christmas window, with silhouette of Michelangelo at left. Strathmore Bristol, Stonehenge, and foam-core boards. Details of tiny beads and basswood model-making strips. Width: 4' (1.2 m). Client: Gucci. (Photographer: Ellen Rixford)*

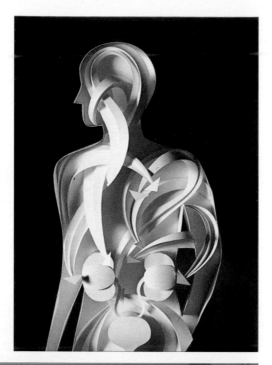

DAVID EPSTEIN
Body Infection *sculpture.*
*White bond paper.*
*Holding the severe bends*
*and curves in place was*
*difficult, but Elmer's glue*
*and slivers of transparent*
*tape did the job on this*
*version of a systemic*
*infection. The color*
*chemistry of the film was*
*used to advantage on this*
*all-white construction.*
*Dimensions: 12 × 18″*
*(30 × 46 cm). Client:*
*Winthrop Laboratories.*
*(Photograph: David*
*Epstein)*

Paper sculpture is among the most accessible media in dimensional illustration. It neither requires a large space or special tools, like wood or metal sculpture, nor produces toxic fumes requiring special venting and filtering equipment, like cast resin sculpture or some of the solvent-softened casting materials used in display and puppetry. For the most part, it is a tabletop activity, easy to clean up and comfortable to live around. Moreover, since it has a long, wide history, most art directors have seen numerous examples of it, and familiarity with a medium is reassuring to client and art director alike, particularly when facing a tight deadline. Paper sculpture is also fairly fast, and can render large groups of things quite well. If you need to make crowds of people, a cityful of buildings, flocks of birds, or schools of fish, and you need to get them done in a hurry, paper sculpture is a good bet.

Because paper comes in so many different weights, textures, colors, and forms, and is so versatile, accessible, and easy to work with, paper sculptors considerably outnumber those working in clay, wood, fabric, plastics, metal, or other media. This great number of practitioners has led to a number of different approaches.

Paper sculpture first appeared in the form of movable or mechanical children's books, forerunners of today's pop-ups, with the earliest of these appearing in the 1700s. The genre flowered in the 1890s with the advent of mass-production techniques, which made it possible to print and distribute large numbers of the books, especially in Europe. After a long period of neglect, occasioned first by the devastation and hardship of World Wars I and II and then by a lack of imagination in the publishing industry, pop-up, or *paper engineering*, as it is now often called, had a renaissance in the mid-1960s and has been growing ever since.

*Pop-ups*—so named because most of them are designed to lift up and out of a book, magazine, or greeting card when it is opened and fold flat when it is closed again—can have other features: disappearing and reappearing images, parts that move back and forth imitating human gestures, or parts that make surprising noises as the page is opened and closed. While this last form is rarely used in magazine illustration or ordinary print advertising because of the

RAY AMEIJIDE
*Opposite page:*
Cast of Barney Miller,
*for* TV Guide *cover art.*
*PANTONE paper.*
*Dimensions: 10 × 15″*
*(25 × 38 cm).*
*Client:* TV Guide.
*(Photographer: Matt Sultan)*

AJIN
Dolly Parton
*paper sculpture.*
*Dimensions: 15 × 20″*
*(38 × 51 cm). Client:*
Penthouse Letters *magazine.*
*(Photographer: Ajin)*

prohibitive costs of die cutting the paper and gluing or grommetting it into place, it is found in a wide selection of children's books, some of the pricier greeting cards, and special promotional pieces.

The next form of paper sculpture to appear was *bas-relief*, which dates to the 1930s, when it appeared principally as exhibition stands, wall constructions, and window displays. Paper sculpture mannequin forms replaced ordinary mannequins, and when these displays were photographed and used as advertisements, the first paper sculpture illustrations came into being. In the 1940s and 1950s, although paper sculpture became more popular and its applications wider, more creative, and more complex, it was still limited primarily to display art, only occasionally appearing in magazines and newspapers. Gradually the form gained more print visibility, and today it is the most common form of dimensional illustration.

Paper sculpture bas-reliefs tend to be semirealistic to semiabstract, with exaggerations, simplifications, and distortions added to provide interest, clarity, and humor. They can be done white on white, white on monochromatic background, white plus subtle tints of color (or with color added through the use of colored gels or reflective screens during photography), or in full color. They can be executed in one kind of paper only or in several kinds, playing surface textures and patterns off against each other. One sculptor, Ray Ameijide, has pioneered the use of colored felt, glued on a backing of bristol board, to give a softer, fuzzier look to his humorous work. Others like Blake Hampton and David Csicsko often incorporate found papers and found objects, such as doilies, wrapping paper, patterned paper cut from magazines, embossed foils, and even fake gems and bits of fur and cloth, into their pieces.

A more recent development is the arrival of *freestanding paper constructions*, which can be freely moved about a staged environment. These forms are much more difficult to make, and thus rarer, but offer the advantage that backgrounds, lighting, and relative positions of the pieces can be changed easily.

Paper sculpture, either bas-relief or full round, is sometimes surfaced with various shapes of cutout paper. In sculpture collaged in this way, the object itself is chosen or constructed, and the

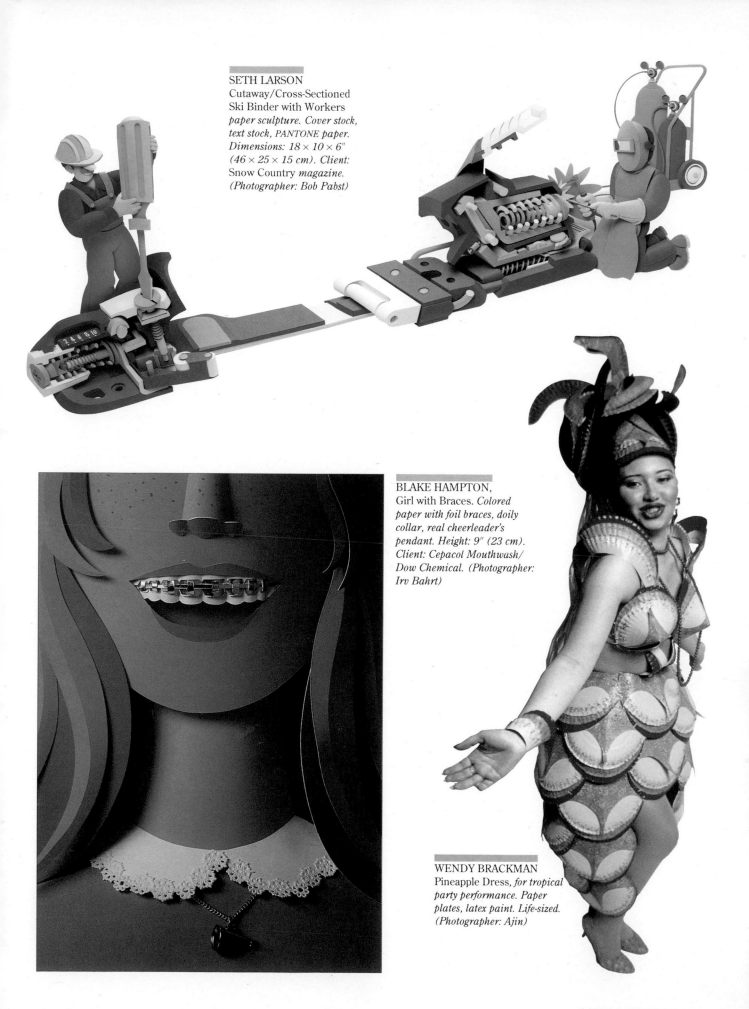

SETH LARSON
Cutaway/Cross-Sectioned
Ski Binder with Workers
*paper sculpture. Cover stock,
text stock, PANTONE paper.
Dimensions: 18 × 10 × 6″
(46 × 25 × 15 cm). Client:
Snow Country magazine.
(Photographer: Bob Pabst)*

BLAKE HAMPTON,
Girl with Braces. *Colored
paper with foil braces, doily
collar, real cheerleader's
pendant. Height: 9″ (23 cm).
Client: Cepacol Mouthwash/
Dow Chemical. (Photographer:
Irv Bahrt)*

WENDY BRACKMAN
Pineapple Dress, *for tropical
party performance. Paper
plates, latex paint. Life-sized.
(Photographer: Ajin)*

# MATERIALS AND TOOLS

## PAPER

If you look at a piece of paper under magnification, you see a flattened mass of interlaced fibers, which is precisely what paper is made from: cellulose fibers. The first piece of paper was probably made in A.D. 105 in China, most likely from a mixture of mulberry bark, hemp, rags, and water. The fibers were beaten into a pulp and the water was pressed from the resulting mat, which was then dried in the sun.

Paper remained expensive and scarce until the invention of the first paper-making machine—the Fourdrinier—in 1799. Most papermaking machines now in commercial use are much faster and more efficient, but the slower Fourdriniers are still in use, as are the old handmade and moldmade paper-making techniques. These procedures produce a much finer surface, better working qualities, and a stronger, more stable sheet.

Handmade paper is made on a framed screen, which gives the paper its deckled edge. The screen is shaken slowly as the water solution drains out, and the paper fibers arrange themselves in a random pattern and have plenty of time to interlock, producing a strong, grainless sheet. This paper will accept folding in any direction without cracking or *curdling* (many small breaks in the fibers).

Moldmade paper is made on a cylinder mold that picks up the pulp and shakes it in a wide side-to-side motion, resulting in a slightly perceptible grain, while Fourdrinier-made paper is formed on a rapidly moving screen conveyor belt, which gives the fibers less time to interweave. This paper will have evident grain, because most of the fibers lie along the belt's direction of movement. When folding this kind of paper, fold in the same direction as the grain, because folds at right angles to the fibers will cause tiny breaks.

Papers made in high-speed commercial mills have the most grain of all, making the slower-produced hand- and moldmade papers a better choice for any work involving curved folds. These papers also resist buckling when exposed to water—a distinct advantage for sculptors using water-based glues.

Chemically, the cheaper commercially made papers have an additional disadvantage. Depending on the source

CALVIN NICHOLLS
Snowy Owl *paper sculpture,
for limited-edition print.
Dimensions: 18 × 21" (46 × 53 cm).
(Photographer: Calvin Nicholls)*

of the paper's fibers, various chemicals may be added to the water bath to give the final product its desired quality. But these acids ultimately react with the paper's fibers and with the moisture and pollutants in the Earth's atmosphere, causing complete destruction of the paper's integrity in a little over a decade.

Artists seeking to safeguard their works should therefore use *archival-quality* paper—paper that has been made completely of alpha cellulose fibers, is free of acids, alum, and whiteners and brighteners, and has had buffering compounds, such as calcium or magnesium carbonate, added to it. These buffers will keep paper at a neutral acid–alkaline balance and maintain an alkaline reserve to combat the acidity in the atmosphere.

A paper's surface qualities will affect its ability to accept forming, embossing, curling, bending, and creasing. There are two major surface-quality variables, the first of which is the *mechanical treatment* of the paper surface. All paper is made on some sort of screen, which is used to drain the water bath containing the pulp fibers. Depending on the process used, the screen can leave an impression. A woven screen, for example, will leave an impression like the warp and weft of cloth; a screen consisting of many fine wire strips or rods laid in one direction and held together by crossing threads will have a laid finish. Some papers clearly reveal these characteristics when held up to the light. The same principle gives us watermarks, which are wire designs on the screen that leave little dents in the paper, where pulp settles around them. Watermarks help us identify the "right" and "wrong" sides of the paper, when the side facing the screen (wrong) is perceptibly different from the side facing up away from the screen (right)—when we are looking at the right side, the watermark is also right-side-up.

The right side is also known as the "felt" side, a reference to the techniques of drying handmade paper by placing it between layers of felt and drying machine-made paper on rollers that may be covered with felt, synthetic fiber, or metal—either highly polished for a smooth finish or rough-surfaced for embossing a rough finish on the paper. For many papers, there is no appreciable difference between the screen and felt sides, because the rollers impart their own surface characteristics to the paper. Hot-pressed paper is subjected to more heat and pressure during the drying process than cold-pressed, ironing down and flattening the fibers, and giving the sheet a harder, shinier finish. Paper sculptors tend to prefer the cold-pressed or slightly rough finishes (also known as "kid" finishes), because they can be more easily formed and do not create distracting reflections or shiny spots.

The second major surface-quality factor is the *chemical sizing compounds* with which the sheet is made. These compounds are added to the pulp bath to help the pulp fibers stick together and keep one damp sheet from sticking to another when stacked or rolled. The more sizing, the harder, slicker, and more water-resistant the paper will be. Almost all papers have some sizing in them, or else they could not be used with inks or paints. Sizing is also added to some papers after the sheet is formed, which gives us the hard, water-resistant papers. And special papers can also be treated with clay, pigment, lacquers, and varnishes. Such papers are fun to work with occasionally because of their rich colors and interesting surfaces, but they cannot withstand much forming and do not cooperate when shaped into anything but the simplest curves or folds. The best way to use this sort of sheet for paper sculpture is to try laminating a thin sheet of coated shiny paper to a sheet of heavier paper, like Stonehenge or Strathmore Bristol.

*Color* is another concern of paper-makers and paper sculptors. For most paper sculptors, today's variety of colored papers is an enormous time-saver. But the only way to be sure that a richly colored paper will not fade or crumble away is to paint or airbrush an archival-quality paper with watercolor or acrylic paint, which defeats the whole point of colored paper anyway. The internationally known paper sculptor Leo Monohan works almost exclusively in Strathmore paper airbrushed in acrylic paints, a technique that enables him to subtly change colors in beautiful gradations within the forms.

Most current color papers incorporate aniline dyes, but recently a few paper mills, notably the Mohawk Mills in Cohoes, New York, have changed over to alkaline-compatible dyes, ensuring the integrity of their colored paper over time.

There is, however, a tradeoff: Aniline dyes are more lightfast, especially under ultraviolet and fluorescent lights, than the alkaline dyes, leaving the artist to choose between imperfect solutions. Certain colors, like earth tones, are more stable than others; reds and purples tend to fade fast. How do you choose the right paper? By asking questions of a knowledgeable salesperson, by asking for any available literature describing the papers, and by some judicious home testing.

Certain papers are particularly popular among paper sculptors—they make smooth curves, accept scoring and folding without tearing or cracking, and keep their shape when curled, formed, or embossed (a quality called memory). Strathmore Bristol, which is 100 percent cotton rag, is acid-free, very cooperative, and comes in five convenient weights, from one-ply—the thinnest, for small delicate shapes like facial features and curling hair—up to five-ply, the thickest, for wide, flat, or gently curved areas that might buckle if the paper is too thin. The plies are actually laminated together, so two-ply is twice as thick as one-ply. Strathmore comes in two kinds of finish: plate, which is smooth and shiny, and kid, or matte.

Stonehenge, though it comes in only one weight and finish, is certified as archival-quality, and readily takes acrylic, gouache, and other paints. It is a bit softer than Strathmore, making it better for embossing. These and other similar papers hold most adhesives, and can serve as a backing for colored felt or colored papers, such as the PANTONE or Color Aid papers. These colored papers have an enormous range of rich colors but are neither archival nor acid-free. For those who want a very high-quality, long-lasting colored paper, Canson Mi-Teintes is an all-purpose, medium-weight, 65-percent-rag uncoated color stock, available in 33 lightfast colors. Other quality colored charcoal, pastel, and cover papers include Canson Ingres, Strathmore Charcoal, and Fabriano Ingres.

The thickness, or "weight," of your paper or board will affect its working qualities substantially. The American system of expressing a paper's weight as the number of pounds of 500 sheets of a standard "parent size" can be misleading, as standard parent sizes differ for different paper types: Ordinary 8½-by-11-inch writing or bond paper's parent size is 17 by 22 inches; book paper's parent size is 25 by 38 inches; cover stock is 20 by 26 inches; and newsprint and wrapping paper is 24 by 36 inches. So it is virtually impossible to compare the weight of one kind of paper to another under this system.

A far better way is the metric system, used almost everywhere except America. Under this method, which is universal for all papers, the paper's weight is measured in grams per square meter of paper, expressed as *gsm*, or $g/m^2$. Another clear, consistent way of measuring paper is by thickness rather than weight, expressed in caliper points, with one point equal to 1/1000 of an inch.

Mat and illustration boards are usually measured as single-thick (or ¹⁄₁₆-inch), double-thick (or ⅛-inch), or triple-thick (or ³⁄₁₆-inch).

## TESTING PAPERS

Different paper sculptors naturally differ in the qualities they feel are most important in paper. Some like to work with light, thin papers, and some like theirs heavy and substantial; some do not care for permanence in their work, while others will use nothing but archival-quality materials; some love an abundance of rich color, and others like white on white. But even in the face of this diversity I recommend a few tests

you can apply when considering a paper purchase, whatever your artistic preferences:

❑ Fold it in several different directions and make some complex curved folds to see how much grain the paper has and how well and evenly it handles sharply curved folds.

❑ Form it into several different bends and curls and see how well it holds these. A paper with good memory will form easily and will retain its form stably.

❑ Steam the paper a little and then emboss it with a round-ended tool until you get a shallow double curve. For deep embossing, you may need a great

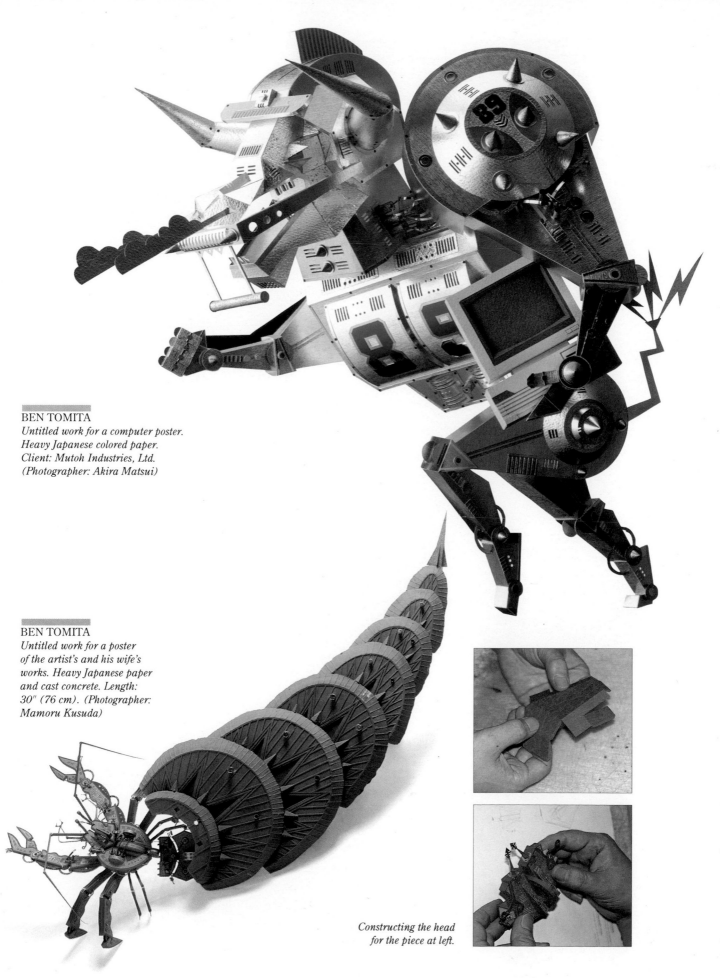

**BEN TOMITA**
*Untitled work for a computer poster.*
*Heavy Japanese colored paper.*
*Client: Mutoh Industries, Ltd.*
*(Photographer: Akira Matsui)*

**BEN TOMITA**
*Untitled work for a poster*
*of the artist's and his wife's*
*works. Heavy Japanese paper*
*and cast concrete. Length:*
*30" (76 cm). (Photographer:*
*Mamoru Kusuda)*

*Constructing the head*
*for the piece at left.*

This sequence shows Meg White's process of paper-sculpting
the gymnast Kurt Thomas.

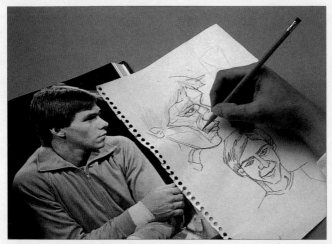

White watched gymnastics videos to get the pose she wanted, after
which she made sketches. She also consulted a book, which gave
the basis of facial sketches.

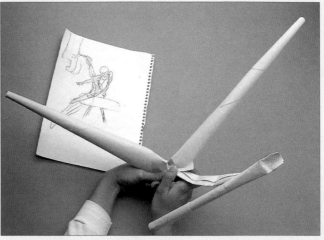

White uses a Canson Mi-Teintes colored paper, which she rolls and
shapes to form the structure of the piece.

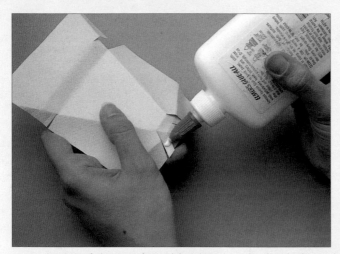

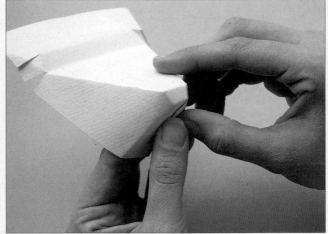

Using sketches of Thomas's face, White begins to develop the basic shape and glue it together.

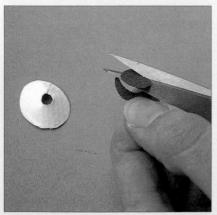

The eyeball and iris were formed by cutting out circles of paper and pulling the ends together to create a rounded surface. Each iris was then
wrapped with tiny strips of paper to create more of a feeling of depth. Attaching the eyeballs to the face.

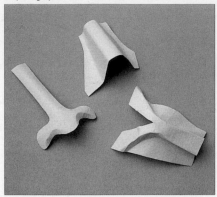

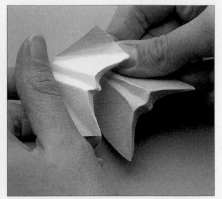

*Note the several different shapes that make up the nose. These were pieced together, and the finished nose was then compared to the reference photo.*

*The upper lip and the cleft below the nose were formed separately and then glued together.*

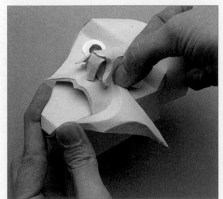

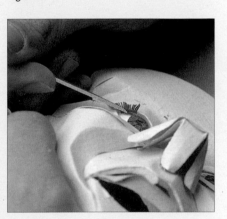

*White again referred to her photo in order to cut and form the shape of the cheek, which was then glued onto the face.*

*Cutting and attaching the lashes.*

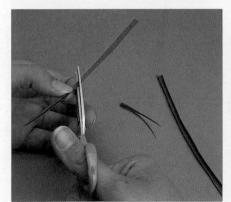

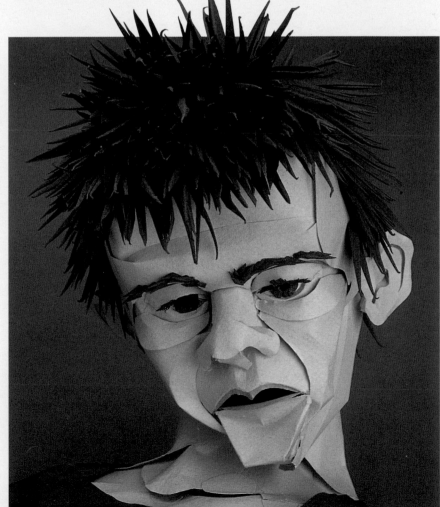

*To make the hair, White cut a strip of paper and folded it in two. The folded-over piece was then cut at a long angle and cut again at the hair's end at a short angle.*

*Close-up of face after application of hair.*

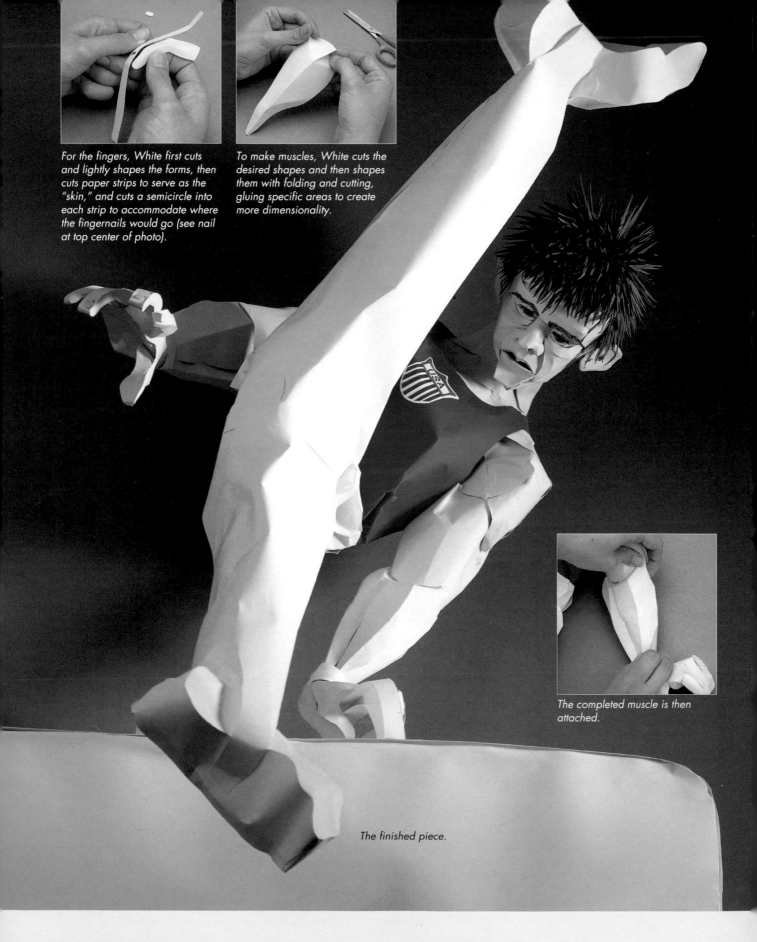

For the fingers, White first cuts and lightly shapes the forms, then cuts paper strips to serve as the "skin," and cuts a semicircle into each strip to accommodate where the fingernails would go (see nail at top center of photo).

To make muscles, White cuts the desired shapes and then shapes them with folding and cutting, gluing specific areas to create more dimensionality.

The completed muscle is then attached.

The finished piece.

## POP-UP

The process of producing a pop-up or mechanical book is difficult and exacting. There are no schools that teach it, and the few accomplished specialists in the field are all self-taught.

The idea for a pop-up book usually begins with the designer, who roughs out a storyboard containing the sketches for illustrations and ideas for how they will move. The illustrations and paper mechanics normally take precedence over text, which is kept to a minimum. To minimize production costs, book size is limited to between one and two press sheets (which corresponds to a page count of between four and eight book spreads).

The designer and paper engineer work together to decide which parts of the picture will move and how various technical problems will be solved. The various assembled mechanisms must be able to hold up under constant use by children—if a piece will eventually tear, lose its spring, or bend the wrong way, it must be discarded, no matter how clever it is. The insert pieces—everything that must be die-cut and glued onto or into the pages—must fit into the area of the press sheets, along with the flat pages of the book, a process called *nesting*.

After the mechanisms are designed and the press sheet layout is planned, a blank, unillustrated dummy or "first-cut" version of the book is assembled, hand-glued, and sent to the illustrator with instructions on how to do the pictures. When the illustrations are completed, this blank dummy serves as the master for the assembly process.

Once the art has been color-separated, the next step is the printing and assembly of the book. The press sheets are printed and die-cut, and the die-cut pieces are then collated with their pages. The assembly of a single book can occupy as many as 60 people gluing, folding, inserting tabs, and making sure the mechanisms are properly aligned and functioning smoothly.

The best way to learn pop-up is to practice some of its basic mechanics. Once mastered, they can be endlessly varied and combined. Although pop-up pieces are flat, the necessary tools are essentially the same as for paper sculpture: scissors, a small knife, a cutting surface, a ruler, a triangle, compasses, dividers, pencils and erasers, and a tracing pad are useful; in addition, graph paper makes it easier to measure and plan your mechanisms. Use a fairly substantial weight of paper, so that your pieces will remain crisp and rigid; two- to four-ply Bristol board is good. Because you are simply making a design for a mass-produced item, don't worry about archival materials. Papers with a definite grain are sometimes preferable because they are more rigid in one direction than the other, which helps keep the mechanism working smoothly. These papers are more flexible if curved or rolled from side to side, rather than lengthwise.

Creasing and scoring should be done against the grain (the opposite of bas-relief). Pop-up's inherent bending and hinging makes creasing preferable to scoring since scoring weakens the paper and a scored fold can only fold away from the scored side, while a crease is a much stronger joint and can bend both ways.

When developing an idea for a mechanism, start by designing a rough but functional model. Focus on how well it works, not how visually appealing the illustration is. Once you have mastered the movement, you can alter proportions and sizes, design the page layout, and finish the illustration. As you put together the model, consider a nonpermanent adhesive, like rubber cement, so that you can reposition pieces—even slightly inaccurate placement of a pivot, tab, or hinge can gum up the works. When you are sure of where your pieces should go, glue them down permanently.

ROBERT CROWTHER
*Pages from the* Most Amazing Pop-Up Book of Machines, *by Robert Crowther. This spread is a series of sliders, some making parts of the illustration flip over (the dump truck and excavator), some making illustrations appear to bend (the legs of the pneumatic drill operator), some turning a flat shape into a box (the 18-wheeler), and some tilting illustrations back and forth (the police car). Copyright © 1988 by Robert Crowther. Used by permission of the publisher, Viking Penguin, a division of Penguin Books USA Inc.*

In preparing to make these simplified models of basic pop-up movements, I disemboweled many of my own pop-up books, trying to break down the complex mechanisms into their simplest forms. Although several different mechanisms are often combined in one spread, you will be better off by mastering each movement one at a time. It's helpful to group different sorts of related mechanisms together. Shown here are a few basic groupings; there are many variations.

One of the most common pop-up forms is the **V-fold.** In most cases, the fold of the V lies along the main fold of the book. Its two sides are glued on facing pages in a V, the angle of which determines how sharply upward or downward the V will go—an acute angle results in less popping up than an obtuse angle. These images show folded and unfolded views of a simple V-fold and a V-fold with an additional reverse fold on the top. The simple V is nice for monster mouths, giant bird beaks, and alligator jaws; the one with the reverse fold is the basis for wonderful hooded cobra heads and sea serpents rising from the deep. Cutting the straight center fold of the V a little so that it curves along the spine yields a curved (and more realistic) beak or jaw.

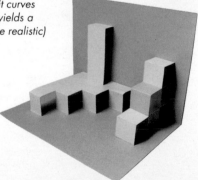

Another family of pop-up mechanisms is based on **stair-step** construction. Whereas V-fold spreads are viewed with the book in a horizontal position, vertical, stair-step pop-ups vary—some such mechanisms function best vertically, some horizontally, and some are best laid flat. The classic version, shown here, is fully opened with the book's pages forming a right angle. This works nicely with the book held horizontally or vertically, making it possible to create stairs, series of pop-out buildings or structures, or multileveled scenes resembling little stage sets—a favorite for greeting cards.

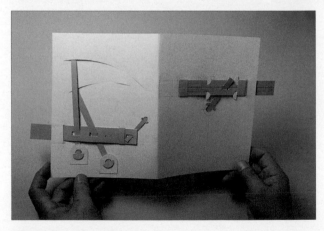

**Sliders and swingers** enable the reader to make things move across the page while the book is held stationary.

Top: The right page features two simple slides; the left page has a more complex one, using a piece of string attached to the back of an object to slide the object up. When the slider is pulled down, the string, traveling up through a hole in the page and down to its anchor point on the slider, moves the object.

Center: The little boats swinging across the page are attached to pivoting arms anchored at the bottom of the page—not to the slides—and are swung back and forth by the motion of the slide.

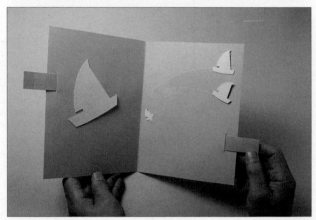

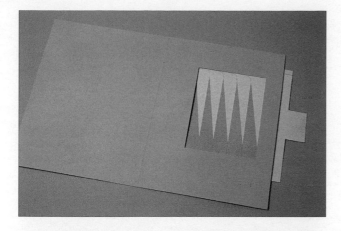

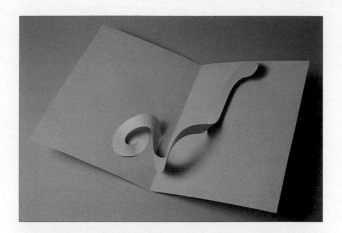

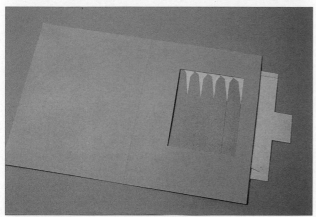

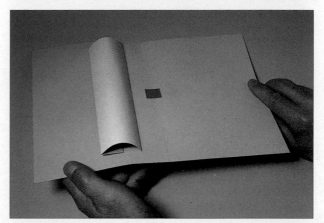

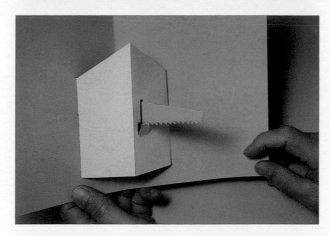

**Disappearing pictures** operate on either slides or pivots; when activated, they give the appearance of one image dissolving into another. For this model, in which two slotted shapes fit into each other and slide back and forth, I've painted the sliding panels very distinct colors to emphasize shape and structure. In a real book, the backgrounds would be painted the same color, making the different foreground images "disappear" very convincingly, because it would be hard to see how the similarly colored panels slid apart and together.

Another type of disappearing picture, not shown here, employs a much simpler mechanism: the changing picture is painted on a rotating disc, with the spindle point at one side of a window in the page. As the reader turns the disc edge, which is exposed at the side of the page, the scene in the window changes.

A few delightful mechanisms don't fit into any particular classification: The **snake** (top) is a spiral with its ends attached to opposite page—when the book is opened, the spiral opens out. This is very effective for octopuses and perhaps Medusa's curls. The **tree trunk** (center) is flat when the book is closed. It rounds up because the side farther from the book's spine is attached to a slider whose other end is attached to the opposite page. When the book is opened, the slider pulls the side of the trunk toward the opposite page, pulling it into a curve. The **saw** (bottom), my personal favorite, is, strictly speaking, a stair-step design. Two sides of a box are attached to opposite pages; slits cut in the box accommodate a little tab shape that can bend out and in, and a saw-blade shape is attached to the page directly behind it. As the book is opened, the teeth of the saw hit the little tab, making a loud rat-a-tat-tat.

# 2 CLAY AND MODELING MATERIALS

lay is the most straightforward, accommodating material available to the dimensional illustrator. It is both additive and subtractive—it can be built up or carved down—and you can see exactly what you have as you work. Trying out different effects is easy: You can push a nose this way or that, make it bigger, smaller, pointed or bulbous, alter its proportions and features—all with no danger of spoiling your piece. Clay is ideal for the beginner because it allows so many experiments and a joy for the experienced professional because it permits any changes a client may request. Moreover, modeling materials are, for the most part, predictable, so there are usually no last-minute disasters to scuttle a deadline.

I say "for the most part" because occasionally things can go wrong. Air-dry clay, for instance, can crack if one area is too thick, another too thin, and it is dried too quickly or too slowly. Thick and thin areas can also be a problem with oven-bake compounds—one part can burn while another is left soft, the same as with cookies. And modeling compounds are sometimes incompatible with certain paints. But if you read package directions and ask questions of the manufacturer and a colleague or two, you should be able to avoid unpleasant surprises.

Clay is soft and fluid. It is poorly suited for precise architectural models or technical illustration, where wood and paper sculpture excel, and it cannot take advantage of existing colors, patterns, and textures, as illustration in fabric, paper, and assemblage can. But for showing emotions and capturing likenesses, clay has no peer. It is used most often (and most effectively) to portray people, or animals and objects that look like people, making it the preferred medium of portraiture and caricature. While it can render the full range of human emotions beautifully, today's clients are much more likely to ask for humor than for pathos.

Clay first escaped the bounds of fine art and went public in the late 1950s and early 1960s with the prototypes for Poppin' Fresh (the Pillsbury Doughboy) and Speedy Alka-Seltzer—animated figures used in television commercials. Clay and figures cast from clay models were later used in movies as stop-motion animation, and then made their way into print. The scandal-ridden years of the Nixon administration, the continuing financial difficulties of New York City, and the Burt Lance affair during Carter's presidency were a dream come true for caricaturists, many of whom incorporated other molding materials into their work: For *Time,* Stan Glaubach used newspaper clippings to collage a head of Nixon and chrome-plated a forbidding bust of John Mitchell; at rival *Newsweek,* chief art director Robert Engle produced some hilariously comic portraits of history makers of the 1970s in brightly painted plasticene. The ordinary citizen became a popular subject too, as seen in Carol Anthony's papier- and linen-mâché figures of old folks, little kids, and everyone in between. By the late 1970s, clay and modeling materials had become accepted as an all-purpose illustration medium by the editorial and advertising worlds. And as the materials market responded to these changes, illustrators found a growing number of commercially available modeling materials to choose from.

MARK STEELE
*Left:* The Discovery of Talent, *commissioned illustration for* Print *magazine. Self-hardening clay, plaster, and acrylics. Dimensions: 3 × 3 × 3' (91 × 91 × 91 cm). Client:* Print *magazine. (Photographer: Ken Clark)*

ROBERT ENGLE
*Above:* Ford and New York *cover art. Acrylic-painted plasticene. Approximate dimensions: 12 × 12" (30 × 30 cm). Client:* Newsweek *magazine. (Photographer: Newsweek— Matt Sultan)*

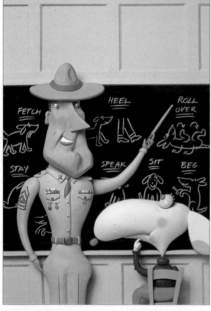

RICHARD McNEEL
*Above:* Training Your Dog *cover illustration. Sculpey, acrylics. Dimensions: 9 × 12" (23 × 30 cm). Client: Whittle Communications/ Pet Care Report (Photographer: William G. Wagner)*

fibers, and don't use the family cooking pots and bowls to prepare the mix with water. When carving, filing, and sanding down any compound or clay, don't breathe in the dust. If you are heating plasticene over a burner and mistakenly drop some of the compound on the flame, don't breathe in the fumes. And be careful when baking up your oven-cured compounds, which can emit nasty fumes and gases. Illustrators who use Sculpey don't use the family oven to cure their work—at least not without giving the oven a good washing and airing afterward. If your work is not too big, use a separate toaster-oven in your workshop instead, and maintain good ventilation.

## ARMATURE MATERIALS AND MODELING TOOLS

While it isn't always necessary to use an armature or a form, especially if you're working small, making compact pieces, or working in bas-relief, in most cases it is helpful. There are four reasons for this:

❏ Armatures allow you to sculpt the delicate, attenuated shapes that clay is unable to hold by itself. The slender legs of insects, a gesticulating hand, a pointing finger, flying drapery—each of these requires an armature.

❏ Armatures make the final piece much stronger and less prone to stress cracks and outright breakage. A famous puppeteer whose puppets were made of Sculpey found that in midperformance their fingers would break off and go flying across the set. Armatured fingers might crack, but at least they stay on—I have dropped several armatured puppet hands made of ordinary Sculpey from a considerable height, and they were fine.

❏ Armatures save clay and time. If you have to make a life-sized mask, it's easier to start with a wig form nearly the correct size and then build about an inch or so out from it than to do the whole 6- to 8-inch diameter form of clay.

❏ Armatures lessen the inherent technical problems of a thick area falling next to a thin one. Thick and thin areas together mean uneven drying time for air-dry clays and uneven baking time for oven-cured clays. And large globs of clay have a tendency to droop over time, distorting the original form. If an armature is built with the final sculpture's form in mind, such distortions are minimal to nonexistent. For example, if you are sculpting a portly fellow with spindly legs, use an armature

to strengthen the legs, and anchor the feet so he won't keel over. Fill out the body with a light, compact material, so you won't need to worry about a big mass of heavy clay in the middle of the figure.

Armatures are best made of different gauges of either half-hard galvanized or soft aluminum armature wire. Ordinary half-hard wire from the hardware store,

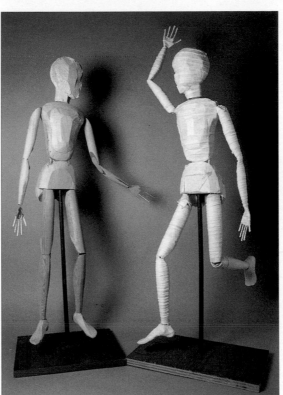

*Two very elaborate wood-and-wire armatures wrapped in cloth for a large clay sculpture. Height: 36″ (91 cm). (Armatures and photograph: Ellen Rixford)*

which is less expensive, will eventually snap after extensive bending, but it's fine if you won't need to bend and rebend your armature. Whatever wire you choose, use a gauge appropriate to the size of your piece and the weight of clay the armature will have to bear. Some sculptors working at life size make armatures of plumber's pipe, with standard L and T connections where the figure bends.

A figure can be given added bulk with bunched-up aluminum foil, old paper tied with a string, wood, Styrofoam, or any other material compatible with your clay. Styrofoam is unsuitable for oven-bake clays because it vaporizes in the oven, emitting horrible fumes, but it is

very good for large figures made of air-dry cellulose-based clays, especially if the figures must be lightweight. For the bodies of his figures, Lee Sievers uses a glue-impregnated cloth called Craft-Drape, made by Fibre-Craft Materials Corp. in Chicago; similar brands work just as well.

As for tools, a few simple ones will suffice. I use only two favorite ones myself: a spatulate shape I carved from a piece of dowel rod for shaping and smoothing, and a little loop shaped like a teardrop for carving. I have a few auxiliary tools—some rods with little round balls stuck on the ends for modeling concave areas, a set of small files for finishing the hardened piece—and also a few different grades of sandpaper. And I make good use of my thumbs.

Some artists also like dentist's tools and the special shaped auto-repair files you can buy in a machinist's shop. If you are using compounds that need to be mixed with water, add a set of mixing basins and cheap surgical gloves to keep the stickier mixes from gumming up your hands.

## STORING AND CARING FOR YOUR WORK

There's no getting around it: Unless your work is very small, this medium takes up a lot of space. If your pieces are made entirely of hard clay or compounds, there isn't much of a problem about keeping them clean— you can just wash them or wipe them off. Clay pieces made using real clothes would benefit from dust-free storage—a glass case, if you can afford it. Some sculptors coat or dip real clothes with varnish or thinned-down white glue, which makes cleaning the sculpture much easier. Plasticene pieces are very difficult to keep in good condition because they are so fragile and soft; if you want such a piece to be permanent, consider casting it in something harder and more durable after completion. If you don't display a piece, a strong cardboard box and soft wrappings will protect it.

# WORKING PROCESSES

There are as many styles of working in clay as there are artists. Sculptors have their own ways of conceiving and executing a piece, their own unique sets of procedures: Richard McNeel meticulously plans his layout and composition in careful drawings before beginning; Gordon Swenarton eschews drawings in favor of three-dimensionally "sketching" in clay, capturing gestures and interactions between characters and then refining the piece and body to a finished state; Bob Selby, caricaturist for the *Providence Journal* and a teacher of two- and three-dimensional illustration at the Rhode Island School of Design, begins with the right eye and builds his figures in sections, so he can transpose heads and hands at will. The infinite variety of specialized techniques notwithstanding, there are some basic approaches we can examine here.

## BAS-RELIEF

McNeel works in bas-relief, and therefore finds a working drawing, the same size as the finish, to be a convenient way of laying out the composition so that the client can see exactly how it will look. He needs little in the way of supporting structures, because his forms all lie on a background. But sometimes he will use other materials, like wood or paper, as a base or as details for his Sculpey forms. He sculpts his forms with great care for details and smooths them down as much as possible before baking. After baking, he sands them to a perfect finish. Such handling works well with his rather cartoony but elegant style. The wit and charm of his work come in great part from his simplification of the natural into the graceful and almost semiabstract, and from his unfailing sense of humor—eyes are reduced to little balls, noses are pointed triangles.

Many of McNeel's elements are made separately and glued together after priming and painting. He uses Liquitex Gesso because it gives the smoothest coat, free of grain and brush marks. If a shiny metallic surface is called for, McNeel either uses an acrylic metallic or seals the Sculpey with gesso or another primer before using enamel-based paint. Enamels react with Sculpey, remaining sticky and refusing to dry, so the primer is essential here.

McNeel makes his pieces in sections. Most sections are sculpted, but some, when appropriate, are cut from paper or board, painted, and then assembled with the dimensional pieces. When it's time for the photo, he arranges all the elements on a table in the studio, where they are shot with a camera pointing straight down at them. Because the pieces can be disassembled, storage is fairly simple: The pieces are wrapped in tissue, slipped into zip-lock bags, and then put in boxes coded by job number.

KATHY JEFFERS
Food, the Vital Meeting Ingredient, *for a magazine cover. Sculpey. Figure heights: 8–10″ (20–25 cm). Reprinted from* Meetings and Conventions *magazine, February 1985, © by Reed Travel Group. (Photographer: Jerry Finzi)*

Left: Baking and airbrushing one of the workshoes. (Photographer: Bill Miller)

Above: The final shot for the ad. (Photographer: Walter Wick)

Jeffers plants the grass and the grubs. At right: The final shot of the grubs feasting in the grass for the ad. (Photographer: Walter Wick)

Mark Steele's step-by-step sculpting of British Prime Minister Margaret Thatcher is a nice example of using air-dry clay.

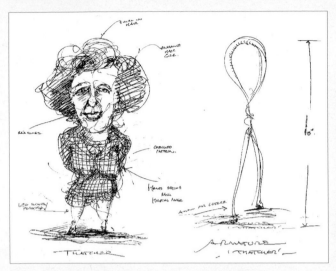

*Above: At left, a rough sketch created to give the figure a sense of gesture and attitude; at right, a sketch of the armature design.*

*Right: Tools, photos, and clay in the beginning stages of clay buildup. Strips of clay are pushed into the armature, which was created from ³⁄₁₆-inch aluminum wire wrapped in ¹⁄₁₆-inch aluminum wire.*

*Secondary head buildup. After determining general placement of facial features, the development of the eyes, nose, and mouth now starts to crystallize.*

*Layering clay in strips to loosely define the figure's overall gesture and the legs, arms, and hair.*

*Front view of the fairly well-resolved form. The head is becoming strongly defined at this stage.*

Working the final stages of the head. The hair is formed, the face smoothed. Because the clay is water-based, it remains workable as long as it is kept wet.

Once the piece is dry (about two days), gesso is applied over the entire surface.

After the gesso, acrylic paint is used to color the sculpture and define the features.

The dress and all related clothing details are added.

The finished piece.
Height: 12" (30 cm).

ROBERT W. SELBY
"Tip" O'Neill.
*Acrylic-airbrushed
No. 2 Roma
Plastilina with real
false teeth, glass eyes,
clothing, and smoke .
Slightly larger than
life-sized. Copyright
1991 the Providence
Journal Co. Used
with permission.
(Photographer:
Richard O.
Benjamin)*

ROBERT W. SELBY
Don Zimmer Talks
Baseball. *Acrylic-
painted No. 2 Roma
Plastilina, real
baseball. Zimmer
chews big wads of
tobacco, hence the
visual pun. Height:
18″ (46 cm).
Copyright 1991 the
Providence Journal
Co. Used with permis-
sion. (Photographer:
Richard O.
Benjamin)*

## CELLULOSE-BASED CLAY

Bob Selby's preferred medium is a
cellulose-based mash—he divides his
loyalties among Celluclay, Claycrete,
and Sculptamold, all fairly common
products, and essentially interchangeable as far as working characteristics go,
though he likes Sculptamold best. These
clays come dry and are mixed with
water. Since they tend to harden pretty
fast, make some advance preparations
before starting. These materials tend to
seal up the outside surface, leaving the
interior damp—especially in large
figures, where there is substantial
volume—so advance preparation of an
armature that closely resembles the
finished piece is a must. Selby tells of
one figure, made without such an
armature, that hardened up outside
while the inside was still soggy, leading
to a messy gutting operation. To avoid
this problem, Selby builds up the
masses of the figure with cardboard and
masking tape, even making the nose,
eye sockets, and jaw. Over this he wraps
plaster gauze bandage. Having prepared
this very complete skeleton figure, he
makes a paste of 50-percent-plus acrylic
modeling paste and 50-percent-minus
acrylic gel medium and dips paper strips
in it. Any paper will do for building up
the basic forms of the body and
clothing—Selby routinely uses blank
newsprint and even typing paper. But
because these papers bend in only one
direction, he switches to paper toweling,
which bends in all directions, where he
needs to build up a smooth surface on a
face or simulate complex folds in fabric.

The cellulose-fiber mash, which Selby
describes as having the consistency of
wet oatmeal, is used primarily in
modeling the face and hands, where the
paste-and-paper application won't give
the required detail. But the paste plus
small pieces of paper towel are handy
for filling cracks and building up facial
jowls, bags, and folds.

In his early figures, Selby used real
glass eyes and even real false teeth.
Now he casts his eyeballs from the glass
ones by covering them with a plastic
bag, putting paste plus paper towel over
it, smoothing that, and finally pulling the
glass eye out from inside when it is dry.
The eyeball is then painted and
varnished. Frayed red thread pressed
into the wet acrylic matte varnish makes
very realistic eye veins. The eyes are
given a last coat of clear lacquer dripped
for a wet look. Lids are made with paper

# 3 | MOLDMAKING AND CASTING

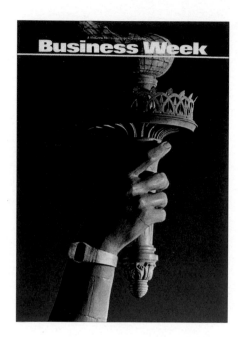

**T**here are three reasons to use moldmaking and casting: First, they allow the artist to make things from materials that are not easily sculpted on their own, like casting resins; second, they enable the artist to make multiple forms from the same basic form or prototype—a population of little people from one generic body, for example; and third, they permit the artist to cast from life, saving the time and trouble of imitation.

Molding and casting techniques are used all the time by special effects people (who make monsters and artificial heads to get blown apart in the horror movies), modelmakers (who make elaborate props for television and print ads—giant aspirins, transparent lungs, and so on), toy prototype people (who produce the final models of Barbie dolls, G.I. Joes, and the like), and natural-history museums (to create realistic dioramas). But illustrators don't use them much. Why? Because illustrators are usually asked to make a form only once, not in duplicate; because most illustrators don't have the facilities or the expertise to produce the difficult resin castings that would justify the extra step of making a mold; and because illustrators are generally not required to work at life size, or to produce an exact imitation of a natural form. In short, the time and effort required for these techniques are too substantial to make them worthwhile for the average illustrator. There are, however, a few illustrators who specialize in moldmaking, because they find it the best way to get the kind of image their clients want.

The first dimensional illustrator to adopt casting as a modus operandi was Nick Aristovulos. He became acquainted with polyester resin while repairing his surfboard with it, and went on to use it as a sculpture medium, producing his first cast piece in 1971. As he became more adept, he began to produce perfectly transparent or delicately colored polyester resin sculptures, often of heads, sometimes embedded with symbolic objects. Sometimes he works full-round, but often his pieces are flat in

back—a much easier approach that requires only a one-part, open-backed mold. A transparent, flat-backed sculpture focuses light around its perimeter, giving Aristovulos's sculpture its characteristic halo effect.

Another illustrator using moldmaking and casting is Jim Haberman, who since 1980 has been using Moulage molds and casts made of its companion material, Posmoulage, to create props for a series of surreal and satirical postcard images. In some of the images, Haberman claims a debt to René Magritte; others are purely Haberman's wry view of American culture.

Haberman's initial inspiration was a gift from a friend of 25 mannequins. Living in the same space with a bunch of recycled body parts led him to make some of his own, so he began experimenting with Moulage—a sort of "gelatinous goo," as he puts it—which can be melted in a double-boiler, cooled to a little above body temperature, and then poured over the model. It gives very detailed impressions as it cools to form a mold, but the mold tends to degrade after one or two castings, so Haberman remolded the body parts in latex rubber and produced groups of feet, hands, and ears, around which he developed his striking images.

Haberman's trademark "mouth-body" people, affectionately known as "the Mergatroyds," were inspired by another gift—a set of perfect false teeth from a dental hygienist. Using a combination of room-temperature-vulcanized (RTV) urethane rubber molds and the Posmoulage for the casts, Haberman has created a population of frighteningly real beings.

NICK ARISTOVULOS
*Left:* Conception. *Polyester resin and Speedstone (a type of casting stone similar to the Hydro-Stone). The two faces cast are Linda and Gary, who have never actually met. The faces were embedded in a block of clear polyester resin. The sperm cells were carved into a ½-inch-thick panel of Plexiglas suspended in front of the sculpture and filled with transparent resin dyed pale blue. Dimensions: 8 × 4" (20 × 10 cm). Client:* Science Digest *magazine. (Photographer: Shig Ikeda)*

ELLEN RIXFORD
*Above:* Ms. Liberty's Arm with Watch, *for a story on the return of the digital watch industry to the United States. Plaster cast of human arm, resculpted to look like Statue of Liberty's; torch is carved wood with paper railing; piece is painted with acrylics. Life-sized. Client:* Business Week *magazine. (Photographer: Fred Burrell; art director: John Vogler)*

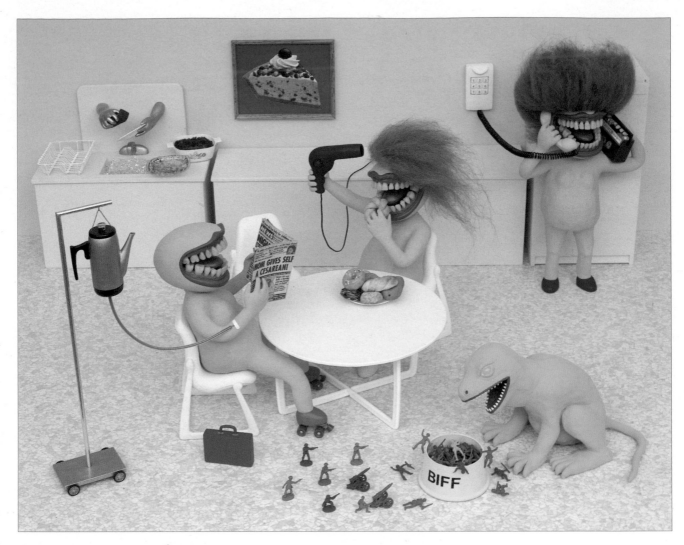

Some illustrators use moldmaking as a supplementary or secondary technique. Tim Young, who does a great deal of clay sculpture and animation, uses moldmaking to make parts, like teeth and eyes, for his modeled pieces, and derives part of his studio income from making toy prototypes, which are modeled in sulfur-free plasticene clay and then cast in plastic using silicone molds. He frequently uses wax to cast fine delicate details.

I first began experimenting with moldmaking by casting from life when a few jobs called for an arm, a face, or a whole body, often using my own face and body as the models. I worked largely with plaster bandage, Moulage, and Jeltrate (an alginate mold). Eventually I learned to build puppets with heads cast of a material called Celastic. (Although puppets are occasionally used in illustration, puppet-making itself is far too broad a subject to be covered in detail here.)

**JIM HABERMAN**
*Left:* Morning Madness
*Mergatroyd scene, for a
postcard. Wax casts of teeth,
plus assorted other props.
These characters are made
from three wax casts: the upper
teeth, the lower teeth, and a
generic adult or child body.
Gum areas are painted onto
the teeth casts, and a tongue is
made from a polyester-filled
balloon. The wax body is
warmed in hot water, so it is
pliable enough to position the
arms and legs in whatever
gestures are required.
Approximate heights of figures:
8–9" (20–23 cm). Client:
Postcards published by Jim
Haberman, distributed
through Fotofolio, New York.
(Photographer: Jim
Haberman, © 1987)*

**TIMOTHY YOUNG**
*Bottom left:* Wild Cherry,
*from the "The Flavor's Gonna
Hit You!" series of fruit characters created for liquor store
point-of-purchase ads. Body is
Super Sculpey; teeth are casts
of the artist's teeth. Young
bought alginate and dental
casting plates, took impressions
of his teeth, made plaster casts,
and then made silicone molds
of them so that he could make
as many plastic casts as he
might need. The eyes are casts
of plastic hemispheres. Young
often makes molds of extra
forms such as these with
leftover silicone from larger
pours. Height: 18" (46 cm).
Client: Seible/Mohr.
(Photographer: Bruno
Benvenuto; art director:
Gary Blake)*

**ELLEN RIXFORD**
*Right:* "Reader's Digest
Readers Unmasked" masks, for
*Reader's Digest advertise-
ment. Clockwise from top:
Uncle Mo the Accountant;
Hayseed Farmer; Everybody's
Ditzy Aunt; New York City
Cabbie; Housewife in Pink
Curlers. Celastic modeled over
plasticene prototypes. Life-
sized. Client: Reader's Digest.
(Photographer: Ellen Rixford)*

# TERMINOLOGY, TOOLS, AND MATERIALS

Molding and casting are highly detailed and technical subjects—a full examination of all the principles and materials involved would be a book in itself. What follows here is an overview, admittedly brief, of the major concepts these techniques entail. Readers who want more information are encouraged to consult *Sculpture Casting* (Crown, 1972), by Dennis Kowal and Dona Z. Meilach, and *Sculpture in Plastics* (Watson-Guptill, 1978), by Nicholas Roukes.

## MOLDS

A mold is defined as a cavity or matrix, into or onto which casting material is put, and from which the casting material takes its form. While most molds are based on a positive–negative relation-ship in which the mold is the negative form and the cast is the positive, there are casts made positive-to-positive, in which the matrix is a positive form and the casting material is formed in a "skin" over the matrix.

Molds can generally be divided into two types: hard and soft. Common materials for *hard* and *rigid molds* include plaster, plaster bandage (plaster-impregnated gauze) and its more modern cousin, fiberglass casting tape, resins (polyester, epoxy, and poly-urethane), metal, and clay. Plaster is most common among illustrators because it's cheap, fast-setting, easy to work with, and nontoxic. Metal molds are used mostly in big industrial runs of toys, masks, or doll parts.

Common *soft* and *flexible mold* materials are latex rubber, urethane and silicone RTV rubbers, Moulage, and alginate. These last two are specially designed for casting from living models.

Mold configurations can be *one-part* (usually used to cast bas-relief or flat-backed forms), *two-part* (usually for full-round forms that can be divided in half easily), and *three-* or *multipart* (for forms that are too complex to be cast properly with a two-part mold). There is also the *glove mold*, a flexible, usually thin mold that comes in one part but is used for casting full-round forms. After casting, the glove mold is pulled off the cast piece, like a glove. Related to this is the *overcoat mold,* which has a slit up one side that is closed up when casting.

Using hard molds entails no danger of the mold distorting or losing its shape. A soft mold, however, particularly a thin-walled, flexible one, should be encased in a *mother mold,* a hard outer mold layer that protects the inner mold from damage and keeps it in its proper form. Mother molds can be made of plaster alone or plaster reinforced with strips of fabric; they can also be boxes built of wood, cardboard, or rigid foam.

The last kind of mold—used if you need to reproduce your original only once—is a *waste mold.* Often made with plaster, which is cheap and easy to crack off the original with a hammer and chisel, waste molds are sometimes used to reproduce clay forms quickly in polyester resin or other resins.

## CASTS

A cast is a reproduction of a form made either by pouring a free-flowing material into a mold and letting it harden with or without the application of heat, or by applying a flowing or easily formed material to the surface of a prototype and allowing it to assume that form and harden onto it, with or without heat.

Common casting materials are plaster, soft rubber, hard rubber (a mix of soft latex rubber solution with a slurry or suspension of clay particles), casting foam, wax, and various resins, which are solid or semisolid organic or synthetic products, including polyester, epoxy, and polyurethane.

## PROTOTYPES

The prototype, or model, is the original from which the mold is made. Discrepancies between prototype and final casting are usually due to shrinkage of the mold, in which the mold becomes smaller after casting, or of the casting material. Depending on the material, such shrinkage can be as much as 10 percent. In positive–negative casting, the cast is usually the same size as the prototype or a little smaller; in positive–positive casting, because the casting material is applied over the model surface, the cast is always a little bigger than the prototype.

A major consideration in planning the procedure for making a mold and choosing molding and casting materials is the number and type of *undercuts* the prototype has. An undercut is a part or form of the model that joins onto the model's main mass and is larger at its projecting end than at the part joining

the main area. For example, if casting an arm, the hand is wider across the palm than the wrist—an undercut. A portrait bust from shoulders up has an undercut situation, as the head is larger than the neck. Parts that project and curve at sharp angles make undercuts too, like inwardly curved fingers on a hand.

A model's number and degree of undercuts will determine whether you should use a flexible or hard mold, or a flexible or hard casting material, and whether you should make a one-, two-, or multipart mold. When using hard molds and hard casting materials, any undercut will get stuck, so plan the mold carefully. If you won't need to use the mold again, you may want to make a waste mold. Going beyond the simplicity of a one-part mold is another way to solve undercut problems—the hand and bust examples could perhaps be cast in

Not all men dream of castles.

MARK YURKIW
*Above:* Chivas Sandcastle *advertisement. Plaster and sand, cast in an RTV silicone mold, sandblasted lightly, and touched up with sand color. The type on the bottle was first engraved photographically on a metal plate, then the plate was fitted into the original bottle cast. Another mold was made of this combination in sand and plaster in order to get the final result, which is the same size as an actual Chivas bottle. Client: Chivas Regal. (Photo: Bruno Benvenuto)*

JIM HABERMAN
*Opposite page:* Laundry Time *postcard image. Cast hands and feet, real clothing. The artist made casts of his own hands and feet using Moulage and Posmoulage, and then made latex rubber molds of each, so he could make multiple copies in Posmoulage. Life-sized. Client: Postcards published by Jim Haberman, distributed through Fotofolio, New York. (Photographer: Jim Haberman)*

two-part molds, divided along the outline of the hand and the sides of the head.

## ANTI-ADHESIVES
Prototype, molding, and casting materials usually have to be prevented from sticking (and occasionally reacting) to each other. *Sealers* close the material's pores, lessening the tendency toward adhesion. Plaster and wood prototypes are usually sealed with shellac and then sprayed with clear polyurethane varnish; plaster is sometimes shellacked and then given several coats of wax.

*Release agents* and *mold releases* are lubricants applied to prototypes and molds. They keep prototypes from sticking to molds, molds from sticking to casts, and mold parts from sticking to

each other. Green soap (a special mold soap, available in sculpture supply and crafts outlets) is often used for plaster, and Vaseline is essential when casting from life with plaster bandage.

*Barrier coats* are sprayed- or painted-on layers applied to the *inside* of the mold before casting, and they later stick to the *outside* of the cast. They are used to protect the mold surface and to give the cast surface a "primed" layer to precede painting. If a barrier coat is applied in conjunction with a mold release, the release agent is applied to the mold first; then the barrier coat follows.

If you're unsure of whether a given material will react properly with a given release or barrier coat, or whether your prototype, mold, and cast materials are

compatible, do a patch test. Mix a small amount of material, apply the coatings you've chosen, and see what happens, right through to a complete cure. This sort of dry run can save a lot of aggravation, not to mention money. Some casting and molding materials are inhibited by substances found in other materials, resulting in incompletely cured molds or casts, not to mention one hell of a sticky mess. For example, the sulfur in plasticene inhibits silicone molds, so you have to use a sulfur-free modeling clay; water inhibits some urethane casting materials, so a plaster mold used with it must be thoroughly dry and well sealed.

## CURING
Both the initial step of making the mold and the further step of casting something into it involve a curing process, during which the material undergoes a chemical reaction to go from free-flowing to solid—hard or soft, but no longer capable of flowing into a different form. The most common chemical reactions are vulcanization for rubber molds and polymerization for resins. These processes are accomplished by the use of catalysts—chemical enablers, often called *curing agents* or *hardeners*, that generate a chemical reaction when mixed with a given material, usually called a base. Mixing must by very thorough, or the material will not cure evenly or completely. Once the stuff is mixed, the reaction begins. The duration until complete curing, which can very from a few minutes to a day, depends on a number of factors, including the chemical nature of the material, ambient temperature, the presence of inhibitors (chemicals that slow or stop the reaction), and humidity, which can itself act as an inhibitor for some substances.

## SUPPRESSING AIR BUBBLES
Sometimes molding and casting materials are prepared for pouring by

LOU BORY
Stress from Within, *for a medical journal advertisement. Plaster-impregnated gauze applied to live clothed and wigged model. The hollow plaster shell was filled with insulating foam. The foam beneath the chest plaster was removed and replaced with a red light to create the internal glow. Life-sized. Client: Lederle Laboratories. (Photographer: Klemtner Advertising)*

NICK ARISTOVULOS
Hands Holding Disc
with Cloud, *for the
cover of* Beethoven's
Ode to Joy. *Polyester
resin, Speedstone. The
hands were molded in
aginate, cast in
Speedstone, tinted with
a flesh-toned wash, and
then embedded in a
block of clear polyester
resin. The disc shape is
a ½-inch-deep trench
carved in front of this
clear polyester resin
block and filled
with yellow-tinted
transparent resin.
Dimensions:
15 × 15 × 6″
(38 × 38 × 15 cm).
Client: RCA Records.
(Photographer:
Carl Flatow)*

being put in a *vacuum chamber* or an *autoclave* to suppress air bubbles, which are a nuisance if they settle on a mold surface. They're even worse if they appear in what was supposed to be a perfectly clear, transparent resin casting.

The process of vacuum degassment involves subjecting the mold or casting material to enough of a vacuum to pull the air bubbles out of it. The material will expand up to 300 percent under vacuum, then return to its original size, minus the bubbles.

The autoclave works the opposite way: It applies pressure to a material, rather like a pressure cooker, compressing bubbles to an invisible size.

Better still, choose materials of low viscosity. Such materials flow freely, like water, rather than like molasses, and usually allow bubbles to rise and pop out of their own accord (or you can skim them off if you see them collecting). The more viscous the material, the more likely it is to trap air.

An alternate de-aeration method is to place your mixed material in a container suspended above the pour area and punch a little hole in the bottom, allowing a thin stream to fill the pour space. This will take care of most entrapped air. Do not use this method unless your material takes a reasonably long time to set up or gel—otherwise it will thicken too much to pass through the hole before all of it can pour. And of course, don't use a material that is very viscous to begin with.

## FILLERS AND COLORANTS
Casting resins are often mixed with *fillers*, which can be just about any inert material that will sit still and let itself get stirred into the pot. Obviously, you can't use a filler if you want to achieve a clear or transparent effect. But fillers are useful for opaque casts because:

❏ They're cheaper than resin.

❏ They can make casts a lot lighter or a lot heavier.

❏ Most resins emit heat while gelling—sometimes enough to cause cracks—and the filler can act as a heat sink, stabilizing the reaction.

❏ They can make the resin look like something else—stone, bronze, wood, or whatever. Stone powder–filled castings can either be polished to resemble smooth stones, like marble, or sandblasted to look a bit rough, like sandstone. Metal powder–filled castings can be buffed and polished to look like real metal.

Common fillers include plaster, baking soda, ground nut shells, wood dust, stone dust, metal powders, glass microspheres (tiny hollow glass balls), and Cabosil, or fumed silica, a very popular lightweight inert substance.

You can also add *colorants* to resins. Clear or translucent resins can be delicately tinted, deeply colored, or made opaque; opaque resins can be tinted or colored as well. Fillers will impart their own color to a mix, so this must be considered when planning the final color of the resin.

## CASTING APPROACHES
There are several approaches to making a positive—negative cast once you have prepared your mix and stirred in your filler. The casting material can simply be poured into the mold up to the brim and left there to cure—a solid cast. Or, if the material is thick, it can be spread or "buttered" all over the mold interior, making a ¼- to ½-inch-thick layer. Two halves of a two-part mold can be spread with material and then closed up, with additional material applied to the parting line through the mold's open "neck." This can be done with many types of resins; since many resins of fragile, reinforce them with fiberglass mat, pieces of fiberglass cloth, or pieces of strong, absorbent fabric. Wet down these materials with the resin and apply them in one, two, or several layers inside the cast. A third option is the slush mold: The cavity is filled about one-fourth full with material, which is slushed around until the mold interior is evenly coated and then poured out. This is repeated until a sufficiently thick layer of material is built up

Some resins will foam when additional components are added. They can be slush-molded as a pure layer of hard, smooth, dense resin and then transformed into foam of varying densities, which can be poured in to fill the rest of the mold cavity. The hard outer layer is called a *gel coat* or *print coat,* because it gels before the next layer is poured in and is imprinted with the details of the

mold surface. The cast's outer surface will be a fine, hard, perfect form, but the whole cast will be light and strong. Modelmakers put a lot of stuff inside castings to use up space and save money—old rags, cardboard, chunks of Styrofoam, wood, and so on.

## FINISHING THE CAST SURFACE
When the cast is complete, you can do many things to the surface to get the finish you want. For clear casting resins, like epoxies, polyesters, or EZ Clear, if the cast surface is rough, as it might be after casting in a plaster mold, you can rasp, sand, and ultimately polish it to a glasslike finish with white jeweler's polishing compound. You can buff and

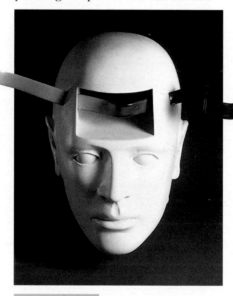

NICK ARISTOVULOS
Face with Open Forehead, *for a magazine cover showing the process of free thought running through a person's head. Polyester resin. About 75 percent life-sized. Client:* Psychology Today *magazine. (Photgrapher: Carl Flatow)*

polish metal-filled castings too, and sandblast stone-filled ones to look weathered and rough. Most cast materials can be painted, though some need to be primed first to ensure paint adherence and some, like the super-flexible cast foams, must have special paint that can stretch and flex as much as the surface does. As most materials work best with certain surface coatings, a patch test is a good idea.

## TOOLS AND EQUIPMENT
The scope of casting and moldmaking tools is far too broad to be addressed here—a full inventory with descriptive

analysis would merit a chapter of its own. A simple listing of the basics will have to suffice, along with the promise that many of these items' functions and applications are described in the procedures section that follows.

That said, the needed equipment breaks down like this:

❏ *Mixing vessels and tools:* Vessels and spatulas of all sizes, including cardboard, metal, glass, and plastic. For mixing plaster, be sure to have flexible containers, as they are much easier to clean.

❏ *Mold boxes, mother molds, and reinforcements:* Plaster and/or resin outer forms to keep flexible molds in place, or boxes built to contain flexible molds. Box materials include wood, strong cardboard boxes, and foam-core board; to put them together, have on hand a hammer, nails, strong T-pins (for foamcore), tape that works with your mold material, and clay for sealing joints. To hold molds together, use clamps, industrial-size rubber bands, or nylon belts with special tightening clamps.

❏ *Tooling and finishing equipment:* Rasps, files, sandpaper, and, if you plan to do any finishing work on resin casts, a buffing wheel, some white polishing compound, and a flexible-shaft tool, grinder, electric drill, or moto-tool to turn the wheel.

❏ *Measuring tools:* A triple-beam balance scale (see photo on page 64).

❏ *Air-removal tools:* A Jiffy Mixer (a nonaerating mixer blade), a vacuum-degassment unit, or—less effective but simpler—a vibrating table with a pneumatic vibrator.

## MATERIALS
Even professionals in the field have not been able to keep up with the huge range of molding and casting materials that have appeared in recent years, and new ones continue to appear. The trend now is toward increased safety, a happy development, as casting and molding supplies, particularly the resins and the solvent-softened display materials, can be quite toxic. I'll mention here some of the most commonly used substances, and a few of the good newcomers. All of the manufacturers listed are cooperative about sending product information, and will field questions over the phone.

Plaster of Paris is commonly used for mother molds and for rough waste rigid molds. But for good-quality models, a harder, finer-textured and stronger sculpture and craft plaster is Hydrocal, sold in art supply stores. Rock Hard Water Putty, a cheap, cream-colored powdered putty sold in hardware stores, can be mixed with water to any consistency, and hardens very hard. It is dimensionally stable, makes good, strong casts, and can be easily carved, like soap, before it dries.

Plaster bandage, long a favorite for simple life casting, now has a stronger, more modern form: fiberglass casting tape. Both are available from surgical supply places. Alginate, which gives excellent detail, is a soft, flexible material for casting from life, and can be bought at dental supply places. Moulage, a flexible life-casting material, is reusable, and can be bought at big art supply and craft stores. Like alginate, it is safe for artist and model.

Flexible molds are normally made either of RTV urethane rubber or RTV silicone rubber, which costs three times as much but lasts longer and features some special properties. Some silicones, for example, can be used with very hot casting materials, like low-temperature-melt metals. Smooth-On is one of the better sources for urethane rubbers, and Silicones Inc. makes several good silicone products. Many RTV rubber molds are inhibited by sulfur, so be sure to use sulfur-free modeling clays for your prototypes. They are made by Chavant and Zeller International.

Among display materials used for casting large figures, puppets, and masks, the once-popular Celastic is no longer made, as the chemicals used in it poisoned plant workers and artists alike. Among its replacements, Aquaform is a milky liquid that can be used to stiffen any receptive fabric or soft paper to give a strong, hard cast. It tends to heat-soften under temperatures above 110° F, but can be protected with a sealer coat of paint or varnish. Form Fast is the brand name for a number of display materials made by Plastics Adhesion Technology in New Jersey. Some of them are solvent-softened, much like Celastic, but now a good water-softened Form Fast material has been developed, as well as a thermoform product. Unnatural Resources, another New Jersey company, also makes several very interesting thermoplastic sheet materials, which give good detail for positive–positive casting.

Casting resins can be extremely toxic.

BRAD WILLIAMS
Centipede *body puppet, built for a television advertisement. Celastic molded over clar forms and worn like a suit of armor. Life-sized. Client: Atari Video Games. (Photographer: Spencer Jones, © Schillaci/Jones 1985)*

Several new low-toxicity resins are available now, two of the best made by Zeller International: EZ Plastic, a two-component cream-colored resin, gives beautiful casts, and can be machined and tooled; Proto Plastic is more expensive, but is much more versatile. Other good casting resins are made by BJB Enterprises, which specializes in urethanes, and by Alumilite, whose resins mix well with metal powders.

A big problem with resins is getting a perfectly clear water-white cast. Both epoxy and polyester resins can be clear-cast, but the casting process is tricky, and these materials are quite toxic. Nontoxic clear resins are being developed by Zeller International and Alumilite; BJB makes a clear resin that is less toxic than polyester and epoxy, but it can't be polished or tooled. This is an area for future product development, so try to keep up with the market.

Finally, we come to flexible casting materials, which are used for sculptures that must flex and bend, and for casting "skins" for armatured characters that must move. BJB makes Skin Flex, a reliable and versatile product, and Zeller makes Fleshtex, also excellent.

# WORKING PROCESSES

Here I will concentrate on fairly simple techniques that are accessible to illustrators, most of whom are not professional moldmakers. Rigid molds are common in industry, but their use in illustration has considerably diminished in favor of flexible RTV rubber molds, which are able to cast much more complex forms, so we will focus on flexible molds here. If you are interested in pursuing the subject of casting in further detail, *Sculpture Casting*, by Dennis Kowal and Dona Meilach (Crown, 1972), is a good resource, as are various brochures available from Smooth-On and Ciba-Geigy.

## FLEXIBLE ONE-PIECE MOLDS
For this type of mold, start by mounting your model on a strong, flat backboard, filling in any edges between the model and the board. Apply the appropriate sealer coats and release agents. You can choose between making a poured mold using a liquid rubber or making a brush-on or butter-on mold using a rubber thickened enough to hold its shape once applied to the model. For a brush-on or butter-on mold, start with a thin coat and be careful of pinhole bubbles, which can form on the prototype's surface as the rubber is applied. After this initial coat cures, apply one or two thick coats of thickened rubber over it, reinforcing if you wish with a few pieces of open-weave fabric embedded in the rubber.

Because the mold material is flexible and can't hold its shape by itself once the model is removed, it will need a hard mother mold to keep its contours in place. After the rubber mold has completely cured, apply a thick coat of thickened reinforced plaster. When the plaster mold is hard, separate it from the rubber mold. Then peel off the rubber mold from the model. Clean the molds up if necessary, apply appropriate release and/or barrier coats, and make your cast.

If you use liquid rubber for the mold, you'll need to provide an enclosure for your mold material. The simplest way is to build a wood, cardboard, or foam-core box around the model, with a hole in the box to pour in the rubber. The backboard on which your mold is mounted will be the floor of the box, and the four sides will enclose the model; when the box is poured full of mold material, the space between the model and the box interior will ensure that the mold walls are thick enough to hold their shape without tearing or distorting. Seal the cracks with clay or tape and apply mold release. Mix the rubber, watch for bubbles, pour the mold, let it cure, and remove the mold from the box and the model. You can use the box as a kind of permanent mother mold after this. Then cast as already described.

## FLEXIBLE TWO-PIECE MOLDS
There are several approaches toward making a flexible two-piece mold, but the trickier ones tend not to be used by illustrators; the easiest is the simple box mold. While it does not save material the way a mold contoured to the form of the model does, it is the simplest, most straightforward kind of mold to do, and this is crucial for an illustrator working under great pressure and tight deadlines.

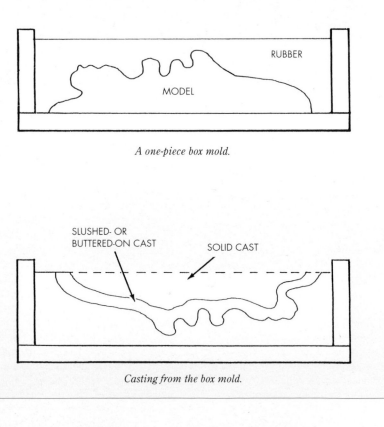

Diagrams: Lenor Robinson

HARD MOTHER MOLD

RUBBER BUTTERED-ON MOLD

PROTOTYPE

*A flexible one-piece mold.*

RUBBER

MODEL

*A one-piece box mold.*

SLUSHED- OR BUTTERED-ON CAST

SOLID CAST

*Casting from the box mold.*

**TIMOTHY YOUNG**
Marilyn Banana, *from the "The Flavor's Gonna Hit You" series of fruit characters created for liquor store point-of-purchase ads. Body is Super Sculpey; teeth are casts of the artist's teeth; eyes are casts of plastic hemispheres. Height: 18" (46 cm). Client: Seible/Mohr. (Photographer: Bruno Benvenuto; art director: Gary Blake)*

Here are the steps taken by illustrator Timothy Young for making a two-piece silicone mold for casting a puffin.

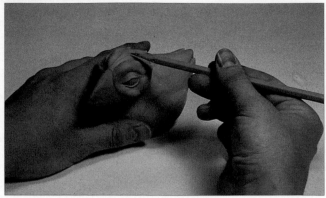

The necessary tools and materials, from left: respirator, wooden stirring paddles, triple-beam balance scale with mixing container on it and weights alongside, silicone, catalyst, and rubber gloves.

Young examines his Sculpey model, measures it, and adds the thickness of his desired mold wall on either side to get the dimensions of the box for the mold. Young decides on a wall thickness of 1 inch, locates the division line (where the model would most naturally be divided in half), and chooses a spot for the pour spout (an unobtrusive location). Because this model is simple and compact, no venting channel is necessary.

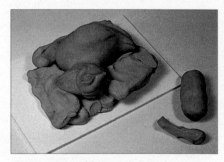

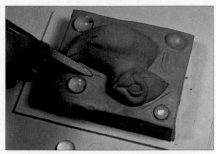

Using a piece of foam-core board, Young builds a square base of nonsulfuric modeling clay and places the model in it. The clay bed comes right up to the division line and is a bit bigger than the box will be.

Young cleans up the edge next to the model with small modeling tools, making sure that the model is level, that the parting line divides it exactly in half, and that the clay bed forms a right angle (or something very close to it) with the sides of the model.

After cutting the bed to the dimensions of the mold box, Young keys the mold, using plastic hemispheres pressed into the clay. These will register as depressions on the first half of the silicone mold; when the second half of the mold is poured, it will have corresponding hemispherical bumps fitting exactly into the depressions.

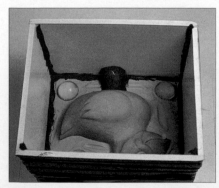

After pinning the box around the clay bed and sealing the joints with soft clay, Young builds a pour spout on the bottom of the model. He then wraps several rubber bands around the box and sprays mold release onto the model and clay bed.

Young measures his silicone and catalyst on the scale. He is working with GI 1000, an easy-to-use Silicones Inc. product that mixes in a catalyst-to-silicone ratio of 1:6. He stirs well to achieve a complete blend.

Young pours the silicone into the mold, slowly pouring toward the outside of the box so it flows around and over the model, preventing air bubbles from being trapped next to the model surface.

Silicone should sit undisturbed for the manufacturer's recommended time period—18 to 24 hours, in this case. When the mold has cured, Young turns it over and removes the clay bed, being careful not to loosen the model from the silicone. He then cleans any clay off the model with alcohol and removes the keys. The first half of the silicone mold is now on the bottom, and the uncast half of the model is facing up, ready for pouring. Young now secures the box around it, making sure there are no gaps. Next, he replaces the clay plug for the pour spout, sealing it against the model and box wall. Finally, he applies release agent—a crucial step, as uncoated silicone sticks to itself.

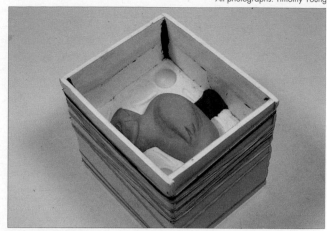

Young mixes another batch of silicone, and pours it into the second half of the box. After pouring the second half of the mold and letting it cure, he removes the foam-core box (but saves it for the casting process). Grasping the silicone firmly, he gently pries the two halves apart, removes the model, and cleans it with alcohol.

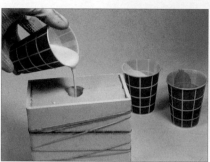

After turning the mold so that the pour spout is at the top, Young recuts the box to fit it and puts on the rubber bands. The casting material here is EZ Plastic, an easy-to-use-, nontoxic, 50–50 two-component resin made by Zeller International. Young makes a slush (or hollow) cast by pouring in enough plastic to thickly coat the inside of the mold—about 25 to 35 percent of the mold's volume—and by rotating the mold on all axes until the plastic sets up or gels.

The opened mold showing the completed cast. The pour spout can be cut away with a hacksaw and the resulting rough area sanded smooth. To fill the hole, Young mixes about 2 tablespoons of plastic, pours it into the hole, puts a piece of tape over it, and positions the cast with the hole facing down. After the plastic hardens, the spot is sanded smooth.

Three finished rubber duckies, made by the same process just demonstrated. The pieces were used in a commercial for Regina Home Spas. Young used a Dremel Moto-Tool to carve out areas of the faces in order to resculpt the expression changes with Sculpey, and used Microtool body putty, a model filler putty purchased from a hobby shop, to fill the cracks. He ultimately air-brushed the ducks with enamel paints. Client: MS 25 Model-making, Nicolella & Company Film Productions for Regina. (Art director: Mark Stein)

## CASTING FROM LIFE WITH PLASTER BANDAGE

The main problems in casting from a living model are that a live person doesn't want to stay still very long while a mold cures up and that living skin is sensitive to a lot of moldmaking solvents. Moulage and the alginates are comfortable for the model and allow a high degree of detail, but take a bit of practice to master. Beginners may prefer plaster bandage, which does not capture as much detail but is simple enough for anyone. It captures basic forms very accurately and can produce casts of the whole body with relatively little trouble. It softens up and gets very cooperative when dipped in water, so you can shape it around almost anything. It then hardens into an eggshell-thin but fairly rigid form. If you want it to flex some, use about two or three layers; if you want more rigidity, use more, or reinforce it with plaster.

For this medium we can use a face casting—a life mask—which offers a combination of smooth, large areas and small details. For such a mask, I'd cut about 30 2-by-3-inch pieces, 30 1-by-2-inch pieces, and 20½-by-1-inch pieces of bandage; the smaller the piece, the more detail it can be used to achieve. It's best to cut the pieces before beginning to work, as the plaster sets very fast.

Plaster bandage sticks to the skin and tends to pull out little hairs, eyebrows, and eyelashes if the model isn't greased up, so apply Vaseline in a thin coat on the skin, and put plenty on eyebrows and lashes. Cover mustaches and beards with thin plastic held on with surgical tape; you can sculpt these areas later by hand. Cover hair with plastic if you intend to mold this area of the head.

Plaster is messy, so wear a smock and cover the parts of your model that you don't want to cast with a smock or plastic bag. Starting with the forehead, lay pieces of bandage smoothly on the skin, rubbing slightly to work the plaster onto the skin surface so it makes a smooth layer. Overlap the pieces by a half to a third as you work your way down from the forehead. Don't leave any one area too long, as an edge of plaster bandage can dry out and curl up and away from the skin if left too long without the next wet piece laid over it.

The model's eyes will be closed, of course—you can carve them open on the cast later. But the nostrils should be left open so the model can breathe. Put the smallest pieces of bandage around the nostrils and smooth them partway into the nostrils with a chopstick or a small dowel. If you wish, you can mold the whole face down to neck. If you want to mold the ears, do only the front sides—anything more creates undercuts.

When you've finished the first layer, do another layer or two for strength. Allow the mold to harden up for five minutes or so, and then have your model wiggle his or her face around inside the mold. This loosens the skin from the plaster, so the mold can come off easily. Most models prefer to pull the mold off themselves, as hairs occasionally get stuck despite all your precautions.

After the mold dries, you can cast from it. Remember to plug up the nostrils with clay or a little plaster. If you want to save the mold, apply a few coats of shellac to the interior mold surface, followed by a coat of clear-gloss polyurethane varnish. You can use almost any casting material—plaster and Rock Hard Water Putty are common, but you could use resins too. But remember that the inner surface of this mold is going to be slightly rough and imperfect, so your cast will need plenty of sanding and polishing. For a perfect resin cast, do a plaster bandage mold first, then cast in an easily sculpted medium, like plaster or Water Putty. Clean up this cast and do any necessary resculpting; then make an RTV rubber mold from that, and use it for the resin.

ELLEN RIXFORD
Mermaid *life-sized body cast. Papier-mâché with wig, wooden trident, sequin scales, and green lace "seaweed." The body was originally molded in plaster bandage, then cast in Water Putty, and finally cast positive–positive in papier-mâché applied in a thin skin over the putty form. The papier-mâché was then removed, sanded, and painted with acrylics. Client: Private collection. (Photographer and model: Ellen Rixford)*

## CASTING FROM LIFE WITH ALGINATES

Alginate, used to make dental molds for braces and prostheses, is a jellylike material derived from seaweed. It needs no release agent next to the skin and is harmless if swallowed. It is not reusable, and is more expensive than plaster bandage, but if you need very exquisite detail, showing every pore and wrinkle, and want a fast-setting and very comfort-able mold material, it is very good.

Be sure to get regular Jeltrate, not fast-setting. It will set in 5 to 10 minutes, depending on how much water you mix with it, which should give you time to make whatever adjustments you need. I've found the proportion of water to Jeltrate suggested on the package is too low—I use about one part Jeltrate to two or three parts water by volume. You can experiment for yourself with small amounts, casting a fingertip or the palm of your hand to get comfortable with it.

Alginate is quite fragile and tears very easily, so it is hard to get more than one or two casts from an alginate mold; if there are severe undercuts, the alginate will rip apart no matter how gentle you are with it. If you need multiple castings, use the cast made from the alginate as your prototype, and make another mold from it with a flexible RTV rubber.

### CASTING AN EAR

Here is a step-by-step procedure of casting an ear by Jim Haberman, who frequently uses life casting in his work.

All photographs: Jim Haberman

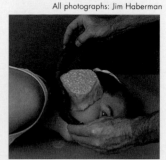

Haberman starts by making a fence of modeling clay around the ear to contain the alginate. The clay must be blended into the subject's skin to make a watertight seal, so no alginate can leak out. The ear canal is protected with a little wad of cotton.

The volume of the enclosed area is measured to determine the correct amount of material needed to cover the ear to the depth of at least 1 inch, and the alginate is mixed—three level coffee measuring scoops to each 7-ounce cup of water. Red food coloring has been added for photographic purposes.

After Haberman mixes the water and powder, the alginate is slowly poured to the side of the ear to avoid trapping air bubbles. If possible, the subject should be gently jiggled to release any air that might be trapped, especially at the surface of the skin.

A minute or two after pouring, the alginate begins setting up; it is pretty well gelled in another few minutes. When it sets, Haberman takes off the clay fence and carefully lifts and removes the mold, taking care not to tear it.

Haberman then turns the mold upside-down on a sheet of wax paper for pouring. Again, a modeling clay fence is built around the mold to contain the casting material—plaster. The fence is sized to avoid pinching the mold but is sufficiently snug to keep the plaster from leaking. A release agent—vegetable oil, in this case—is brushed on the clay so the plaster won't stick to it when set.

The plaster is mixed to a liquid consistency so it will pour easily and harden slowly. Haberman pours it into one end of the mold so air can escape; after pouring, he vibrates the table to bring any air bubbles to the surface.

The mold is removed from the plaster cast.

The completed casting.

## POSITIVE–POSITIVE CASTING WITH CLAY AND OTHER MATERIALS

Artists often use display casting materials that are softened by solvents, water, or heat. These materials, most often used for puppet heads and masks, make light, hollow casts that are ideal for setting mechanisms into—a big help for puppet builders. The materials are much stronger than traditional papier-mâché, stand up well to wear and tear, and last a long time.

ELLEN RIXFORD
The Queen of Heaven, *detail of unmasked face. Face is vacuum-formed styrene, hands are acrylic, body is foam, mask is Celastic, and costume is fabric. The use of vacuum-formed sculpture makes it possible to achieve the effect of readiating light, like the dawn. The puppet mechanism was done with the assistance of Japanese master puppet builder Mari Tobita. Height: 54" (1.4 m). (Photographer: Ellen Rixford)*

ELLEN RIXFORD
The Goddess of Storms *(the reverse side of* The Queen of Heaven*), detail of figure, holding mask. Face is Celastic, hands are jointed wood covered with fabric gloves, body is foam, costume is fabric. Note the light behind the eyes, as well as the eyes' changing color. Height: 54" (1.4 m). (Photographer: Ellen Rixford)*

# 4 | CARVING AND ASSEMBLAGE

**O**f all dimensional illustration media, illustration in carving and assemblage has the closest relationship with traditional gallery- and museum-oriented sculpture; given the type of work illustrators are now producing and the commercialization of gallery work, this distinction is now dubious at best anyway. The lines began to blur during the 1960s, as illustrators experimented in all directions, some of them taking inspiration from artisanship and folk art, and in the process invented completely original working styles and modes.

Fred Otnes began as a realist painter, but he found the mode dull. He felt that collage and assemblage could be a bridge between abstract and realistic art. Freeing himself from accepted illustration rules but incorporating enough specifics to make his subjects recognizable, he began creating "illustrated" collages that quickly became popular. In some of them, he included found objects and photographed them, rather than submitting the compositions as flat art. The response was enthusiastic, and he found himself, along with other illustrators, haunting antique shops, flea markets, and yard sales. The unwanted contents of America's attics had become assemblage.

As the 1976 bicentennial approached, Otnes was bombarded with assignments to do historical subjects. He built pieces with an antique look, distressing surfaces and giving them patinas to make them look old, and filled his box constructions with faded pictures, tiny flags and pennants, old photos, and toy parts. The images were magical and seemingly effortless, but they concealed an enormous amount of thought and work.

Although Otnes no longer builds boxes, which he considers rather dated, he continues to use assemblage, and employs sophisticated equipment to reproduce the images he selects as his subjects. In Otnes's technique, photographs and drawings are combined with transfer color keys, a process in which the picture surface—paper or canvas, for example—is sensi-

tized, and color, black lines, or tone is transferred to it. Images are reproduced, often layered together, and combined with collage and assemblage elements, all resulting in an arresting yet dignified effect.

Gerry McConnell got into dimensional illustration at the suggestion of one of his clients. Eventually he became known as a problem solver for unique assignments, as he and his clients discovered that it was much easier and cheaper for a client to have a miniature set built to illustrate a scene than to go on location and shoot a real place. Because his lifelike sets were small, he could do all sorts of outrageous things with them that would be impossible working life-sized. His business, now managed mostly by his former assistant and present partner Mark Borow, specializes in print advertising and television commercials for a wide range of corporate clients.

Joan Steiner has taken imaginative, concept-oriented miniature environments to a point beyond anything else in the field. A 5-foot-long sculpture showing the route of the New York Marathon in 1984 established her reputation, and subsequent assignments for editorial and corporate clients gave her the chance to create her signature style of visual puzzles. Her particular gift is the ability to make completely believable miniature environments using everyday objects—a kind of visual punning, in which a brush holder becomes a chandelier light fixture or a hand grenade becomes a wood-burning stove fueled by

**FRED OTNES**
*Left:* Howard Pyle *poster, for exhibit of this famous illustrator's work. Clock parts, wooden balls, backs of wood type, collaged photos, negatives, illustrations, and zinc plate from photos of the illustrator and one of his well-known illustrations. Dimensions: 30 × 36" (76 × 91 cm). Client: Society of Illustrators. (Photography directed by Fred Otnes)*

**JOAN HALL**
*Above:* The Year 2000 *mixed-media box construction. Clock parts, carved antique wooden ring, velvet background, and lighting effects. This illustration was the First Award winner in an* Omni *magazine photo contest on the title subject. The visual problem was to combine old- and new-looking elements to make a fantasy space vehicle carrying New York. Dimensions: 4 × 5 × 8" (10 × 13 × 20 cm). Client:* Omni. *(Photographer: John Budde)*

cinnamon-stick logs. It is this visual tension set up between full-scale and miniature, between our real world and her small imagined ones, that make her work so seductive and special.

In contrast with these miniature sets is folk art–based dimensional illustration. Dimensional illustrator-sculptors took the modest and humble crafts of folk toys, weather vanes, whirligigs, and wooden Indians and transformed them into magical, unforgettable works for display, television, and print. Walter Einsel, one of the best-known of such artists, got his first assignment in 1962, a cover for the *Saturday Evening Post*. It was Benjamin Franklin, the magazine's founder, sculpted as part of his own printing press. The piece never ran, as the magazine folded, but Einsel continued to expand his knowledge of the mechanics of movement. His first published dimensional piece came in 1972. Commissioned by Macy's department store for a piece to celebrate its 100th anniversary, he proposed a moving sculpture of Rowland H. Macy, the store's founder, set on his store's original building, with little shoppers moving in and out of the building on tracks. The piece was hugely successful—it was used as a window display and television commercial and bought for exhibit in the corporate executive offices—and Einsel's career has flourished since.

### JOAN STEINER
*Top:* New York City Marathon *map. Paper and board, plastics, fabric, notions, and wood. The piece is built as a curved trapezoid, with the front section on floor level. The trapezoid field fits the camera field, making it possible to shoot the piece from the side and giving a nicer horizon line. A great deal of this piece, and Steiner's work in general, uses forced perspective and distorted forms to get a better photograph. Front length: 4' (1.2 m); depth: 3' (91 cm); height: 18" (46 cm). Client:* The *New York Times. (Photographer: Walter Wick)*

### McCONNELL & BOROW
Absolut Miami *print advertisement. Lacquer-painted Plexiglas cylinders, feathers, styrene and thin tapes, Sculpey, railroad grass, rear-lit interior chromes, foam-core board, Gatorboard. The full set is pie-shaped, to accommodate the angle of photography. Front width: 52" (132 cm); back width: 9' (2.7 m); approximate height: 3' (91 cm). Client: TBWA Advertising and Carillon Importers. (Photographer: Steve Bronstein)*

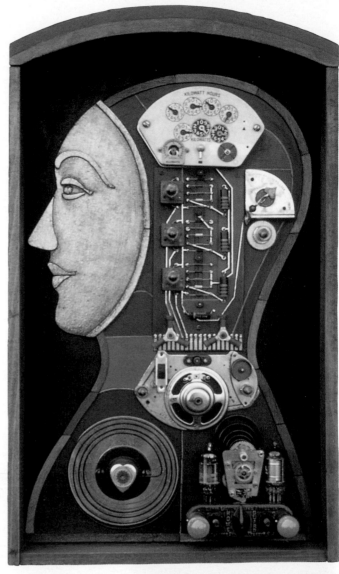

WALTER EINSEL
*Above:* Captain R. H. Macy *promotional sculpture, for 100th anniversary of R. H. Macy's. Polychromed wood (bass, birch, etc.), aluminum, glass. Height: 40" (1 m). Client:* R. H. Macy Inc. *(Photographer: Walter Einsel)*

WALTER EINSEL
Ben Franklin *magazine cover illustration. Polychromed busswood, brass. Height: 28" (71 cm). Client: The* Saturday Evening Post. *(Photographer: Walter Einsel)*

VIN GIULIANI
*Above:* Electric Grandmother *editorial assemblage, for a Ray Bradbury story. Tempera-painted balsa wood, found objects. Dimensions: 12 × 18" (30.5 × 46 cm). Client: McCall's magazine. (Photographer: Vin Giuliani)*

VIN GIULIANI
Mechanical Cat *illustration, for an article on the artist in* Graphis *magazine. Balsa wood, tempera, and found objects, including gears that whir when wound up, giving the cat a mechanical purr. Dimensions: 14 × 18" (36 × 46 cm). Client: Private collection. (Photographer: Vin Giuliani)*

BONNIE RASMUSSEN
Formby's Workshop, *for a national ad, unpublished. Four-inch-thick pine and basswood, raw linseed oil, stain, artist's oil paint, and wire glasses. Client: Thompson & Formby. (Photograph © Sauer & Associates)*

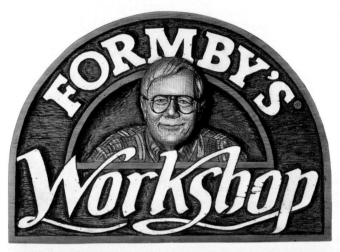

AL PISANO
Kayser Glockenspiel
*point-of-purchase advertisement. One-and-a-quarter-inch stock, acrylic-painted pine with basswood laminates. Dimensions: 17 × 22" (43 × 56 cm). Client: Seagram. (Photography directed by Al Pisano)*

AL PISANO
Dogs *book cover illustration. Oil-painted 3-inch-thick pine. Dimensions: 14 × 14" (36 × 36 cm). Client: Dell Publishing. (Photography directed by Al Pisano)*

BONNIE RASMUSSEN
Snowflake *Christmas story illustration. Basswood, artist's oil paints, and One Shot sign paint. Diameter: 14" (36 cm). Collection of the artist. (Photographer: Bonnie Rasmussen)*

STEPHEN TARANTAL
Electric Power *annual
report illustration.
Shaped canvas over
wood, painted with
acrylics on the top;
bottom pieces are of
acrylic-painted wood.
Dimensions: 3 × 3'
(91 × 91 cm). Client:
Combustion Engineering
Inc. (Photographer:
Dan Moerder)*

finishing when using cast resin, many dimensional illustrators opt for carving blocks of factory-cast acrylic instead, secure in the knowledge that it will be perfectly clear and transparent when finished. Such sculptures cannot be too thick, because acrylic plastic is usually unavailable in thicknesses beyond 4 inches, but this should be sufficient for most projects. Acrylic plastic is expensive, too—a 4-by-4-by-12-inch piece can run close to $200—but the same can be said of casting resins.

Acrylic is carved, tooled, and polished with the same kinds of tools used in finishing cast polyester and epoxy resins—grinders, cutters, rasps, sanders, and buffers normally used with flexible-shaft tools. For final polishing, a white polishing compound made especially for plastics and sold in plastics supply places works well. Don't use jeweler's rouge or colored compounds—trace amounts of them will get into the

tiny crevices in the surface of the piece and color them. Carving and tooling plastics is an exacting art, and takes a substantial amount of time to do well, which is probably why there are so few illustrators who do it. But it is a skill that is in demand, especially in pharmaceutical advertising, and is worth learning.

## MOLDINGS, TURNINGS, AND FURNITURE PARTS

These materials begin to bridge the gap between carving and assemblage. Moldings, turnings, machine-made decorative furniture parts, sometimes found on jettisoned furniture and often sold in lumberyards, are intended for cabinetmaking, but they make excellent materials for a somewhat stylized form of sculpture: Turned wood knobs make little round curls of hair; decorative composition curlicues make curly, flowing locks of hair or nice decorations for robes and gowns; a cut-down section

of table leg turns into a puffed sleeve; a whole table leg becomes a person's leg; a hunk of mantel molding becomes a swelling breast.

Lumberyard moldings and turnings are made of various kinds of wood—sometimes birch, sometimes poplar, sometimes even mahogany. Wood furniture parts can be made of anything, and can be stained or painted. Sometimes decorations or decorative moldings are made of composition, a kind of plastic material pressure-molded or -formed into the decorative shape. Since a piece made of such components will incorporate many different kinds of wood, such sculptures usually should be painted or stained to establish color uniformity.

## ASSEMBLAGE MATERIALS

This is an extremely variable area, unique to each artist. The best way to find what you need is to decide what

LENOR ROBINSON
Sugar Under Siege
by Nutrasweet
*editorial illustration.*
*Sugar cubes, silver*
*miniature teaspoons,*
*wood, paper, notions,*
*and sugar packages*
*and bags. Dimen-*
*sions: 4 × 4 × 4'*
*(1.2 × 1.2 × 1.2 m)*
*Client: Fortune*
*magazine.*
*(Photographer:*
*Chris Collins)*

kinds of images and objects you like and go looking for them well in advance of when you will need them. Finding assemblage materials is a matter of serendipity. Often you find yourself storing up stuff for years before you can use it; sometimes you never use it. It's best to have plenty of storage space and to organize your stuff.

Many once-reliable sources for memorabilia have now either dried up or become outrageously expensive. Flea markets, junk stores, antique shops, and the like now price the best wares beyond the reach of the artist. Today the best places seem to be tag sales, yard sales, garage sales, and estate sales, especially if the house owner lived in the house a long time. There are many sculptors who work only in materials found in the trash. If you're really serious, be prepared at all times—carry a bag or two, and take a screwdriver, some pliers, and a small hammer. You never know.

Don't get trapped into only one type of nostalgia—change with the times. The assemblagists of yesteryear favored what was then considered junk; it's

precious memorabilia now—too fashionable to be affordable, and plenty dated too. It's better to focus on what is considered junk *now* and make your magic with that. On Manhattan's Canal Street, for example, a modest sum of cash can fetch you such Information Age flotsam and jetsam as television and VCR innards, computer circuit boards, and machine parts. Repair shops are excellent sources, as they often have old parts and equipment they can't use anymore; check with the ones that service computers, typewriters, sewing machines, vacuum cleaners, clocks, and watches. Start a friendly relationship and explain that you'd like to have some of the junked parts that they would otherwise pay to have taken away. Then check in regularly and be willing to pay a bit for any really good finds. Since most people like to think they are participating in some sort of artistic process, send or bring them pictures of the pieces you made using their parts—this small touch can lead to more favors down the road.

Spread the word that you like collecting old things—networking

works as well for assemblage artists as for anyone else. One time I needed some telephone cable wire—the beautiful multicolored wire that comes packed in gray plastic tubes—and one of my students, the daughter of a telephone repairman, showed up a week later with yards of it.

Above all, don't get discouraged by the inevitable dry spells—rest assured, you *will* have days when you go through a whole storeful of stuff without hitting paydirt. But keep an open mind and a ready eye and you'll find something eventually.

## ASSEMBLAGE MATERIALS FROM NATURE

Nature has an unlimited supply of wonderful objects and images to offer us, free for the taking if we would bother to look. A trip to the countryside, the beach, or even the park can yield exquisite things—stones, shells, bird or animal skeletons, and every kind of plant form, from moss to seed pods. For the most part, assemblage artists don't seem to be taking sufficient advantage of what's out there. Jeannie Baker, who builds enchanting miniature landscapes using natural vegetation, is the exception. Relying on techniques like those used by natural history museums for preserving natural specimens, she bleaches and preserves the plants and then sprays them with oil paint. For a classic reference on this subject, track down *Taxidermy and Museum Exhibition* by John Rowley (D. Appleton & Co., 1925). It is an old book, and some of the materials, formulae, and techniques it refers to are probably obsolete, but the formulae for solutions for preserving plant specimens are quite good—easy to mix and very effective.

## GLUES

Assemblagists tend to use several different kinds of glue. Since assemblage materials vary, choose a glue that is compatible with both surfaces being bonded. When attaching objects to a surface without much surface-to-surface connection, try adding a mechanical connection to the glue joint—a bit of wire twisted round an inconspicuous part, or a dowel plug driven into the back of the object and then into its setting. Most gluing for wood involves laminating the pieces to make a thicker section, or adding separate carved components, like a nose and ears, to a face. Laminating gives you a strong surface-to-surface bond, but connections with small bonding surfaces may require a hidden peg or screw.

The following glues are relatively common and should be widely available. When using an unfamiliar glue, glue up a practice joint with it and test it out before using the glue on your final piece.

❏ *For wood:* Yellow carpenter's glue is a tried-and-true favorite, good for laminating and joinery. It can be sanded, and its cream color leaves little visible trace at the joint. Good brands are Elmer's, Titebond, and Franklin. Another option is Resorcinol, made by Weldwood, a resin glue composed of liquid and powder that you mix together, like epoxy. It is waterproof, strong, and durable, good for outdoor use, but its dark reddish-brown color is visible if a glue seam shows on a light-colored wood. You can also use contact cement, which, as its name implies, is applied to both surfaces, allowed to dry, and then pressed together. It's especially useful for hard-to-clamp jobs with a lot of surface-to-surface bonding, like applying

wood veneer tape to the edges of plywood. It contains toxic solvents, so you should have adequate ventilation—and a respirator, if you will be using it much. Weldwood is a standard brand.

❏ *For foam and leather:* Barge cement is made especially for these surfaces. The flammable variety, which comes in a yellow and red bottle, is strong, dries beige, and is more smelly and toxic than the slightly darker nonflammable version, which comes in a green and yellow bottle and is safer. Brown glue, which lives up to its name and is therefore quite visible, is safest—nonflammable and nontoxic.

❏ *For fabric and paper:* White glue is good for these, as it holds tightly and dries clear. Sobo dries sort of rubbery and flexible; Elmer's dries stiff. (For archival-quality paper glues, see Chapter 1.)

❏ *For plastics:* Brand names vary here, and plastics supply places often sell their own house brands. Various plastics have special glues made especially for them. For acrylic, for example, there is a thin solvent glue that is dripped into tight-fitting joints, where it slightly "melts" the surfaces, causing them to stick. There is also a thicker acrylic glue that is daubed into joints, where it fills in areas between surfaces that don't meet perfectly. The best route is to ask the plastic's manufacturer which glue is best; in the long run, you'll probably end up experimenting with a few.

❏ *All-purpose (or almost):* Epoxy glue, a good bonder for small areas, works on a lot of things, especially if you slightly roughen the surfaces to be joined. Because it is thick, it will make a setting for pieces that don't meet perfectly, filling in the gaps. Krazy Glue is just as strong but needs a perfect fit to work properly; it is ideal, however, for fixing a break with two matching surfaces. Hot glue is wonderfully fast and has enough body to hold things in position—you just apply a blob of glue, hold the part in the proper position, and it's stuck in a moment. It can melt things, though, and it pops off some surfaces, especially if they are not well-roughened. A nice feature is that it can be remelted and repositioned by applying the hot gun nozzle to a cooled-down blob.

## FINISHES, STAINS, AND PAINTS FOR WOOD

Unpainted wood carvings look good with a simple linseed oil finish or a few

coats of clear paste wax, buffed. Clear lacquer is good for a harder finish; polyurethane varnish is okay but varnishes yellow after a while. Very shiny finishes look a little *too* shiny sometimes; going over them with 000 steel wool and applying a coat of wax cuts that slick look, or just use satin-finish varnish.

Never mix oil- and water-based colorants and dyes, as they are made with different solvents. It is a pity to stain the really beautiful woods, of course, but the range of options is wide: alcohol-based stains, water-based dyes and inks, oil stains, and oil paints thinned down or applied as they are. If you want an opaque painted finish, you can use oil or acrylics over the bare wood, but these may raise the grain. If you prefer a flat, smooth, painted-looking finish, use white shellac (good brands are Hauser or BIN Enamelac) as a primer—what little grain it raises can be sanded down easily. Over this sanded-down primer coat, try a coat of acrylic gesso, or just proceed with the acrylic paint. To get a consistent, grainless sort of finish, I use a stippled finish, which I get by tapping the ends of a bristle brush or a bit of sponge on barely wet paint, thus raising tiny bumps; when photographed, this looks like a solid version of velvet or terrycloth.

## PAINTING AND COLORING FOUND OBJECTS

The paint or coloring agent will depend on the surface. Most porous surfaces will accept almost any of the colorants mentioned for woods; nearly any surface will be receptive to paint after a coat of white shellac. For plastics, roughening with 000 steel wool or very fine sandpaper will give a tooth to which primer and paint can bond; if you want to color acrylic plastic with dye, stores that sell plastics may have the dyes you need. A particularly good source for colorants is the Schwartz Chemical Co. in Queens, New York. Their Rez-N paint and dye products come in several basic, mixable colors, and the dye has a thinner that can be used to make the colors paler.

Plastic to be colored must be completely clean and free of fingerprints and other grease marks, as these result in a mottled surface. Actually, if you plan for it, the mottling is rather beautiful, somewhat resembling tortoiseshell.

# TOOLS

If you are carving, using power tools, or building anything besides miniatures, get a solid workbench with at least one attached wood clamp. To hold your work steady for carving, you will need a corner made by bolting two pieces of wood, usually two-by-twos or two-by-fours, each about 24 inches long, in a 90-degree angle. To position the work a little closer, you can slip in another foot-long piece or two of two-by-two wood.

If you work with a lot of small items, get some kind of cabinet or organizer with lots of little drawers. Another tactic is to collect glass baby food jars and screw the caps into the underside of a shelf or overhanging cabinet. When you want what's in the jar, unscrew it from the attached lid.

## POWER TOOLS FOR WOOD AND PLASTICS

Drills can be used with a lot of accessories: disc and drum sanders, circular rasp heads, circle cutters, buffing wheels, all kinds of grinders and shapers, and screwdriver points. Your drill should have variable speeds, as different tasks call for different capabilities. Get a sturdy drill stand to hold the drill vertical.

A flexible-shaft tool, which can hold all the things a drill can, is a motor connected to a handle by a long, flexible cable that translates the motor's motion to the handle. These tools are wonderful for sculpture—they save a lot of carving, sanding, and polishing time, and can access hard-to-reach spots much more easily than a drill motor can. Many illustrators also use a moto-tool—Dremel is a popular brand—a small, hand-held motor that can be fitted with all kinds of cutters and blades. A moto-tool is useful, but it tends to break down sooner than a good flexible-shaft tool.

As for power saws, I use a hand-held electric reciprocating model. Bosch is an excellent brand—very strong, and it doesn't vibrate too much. I turn the saw upside-down and grip the handle in a heavy machinist's vise, freeing my hands to steer the wood around. Choose

a saw with a universal mount, which will let you replace the standard, heavy blades with pieces of coping saw blade for fine jigsaw cutting.

If you do larger pieces and have the space, a jigsaw or band saw is good for cutting out wooden letters or pieces intended for further carving. The jigsaw has a fine blade and is meant for fine cutting and intricate shapes; the band saw blade is wider and stronger, can cut gentle curves, and is very good for cutting shapes several inches thick.

If you work with rigid foam, consider a hot wire cutter, which has a hot wire that melts its way through foam. These tools make very clean cuts and are very useful for architectural models, making thick

The Seven Deadly Sins *seven-sided box, with a mask of a deadly sin on each side. Wood, Masonite board, and decorative elements. Width: 28"(71 cm); height: 18" (46 cm). Private collection. (Photographer: Ellen Rixford)*

foam letters, and roughing out shapes for carving later. The best ones are big and expensive, but there are several cheap, small ones. Foam cutters are fine for pure rigid foam, but tend to rip and burn the paper facing of foam-core board.

Circular saws can be portable; when mounted in a table, they become table saws. They are great if you are doing a lot of long, straight cuts, as the circular blade holds a line a lot better than the narrow jigsaw or band saw blades. Table

saws can be fitted with dado blades for cutting grooves in wood for cabinet joinery, and the blade can be tilted to make all kinds of angle cuts. When I built my *Seven Deadly Sins* box, I used a table saw to cut the joining strips that hold the sides together—a tricky job, because the strips and the grooves cut into them were cut at a 51.43-degree angle (360 divided by seven).

If you need not-too-big grooves cut in not-too-big things, a router and a router table are a good alternative. Routers are hand-held portable motors that spin a cutting blade, which protrudes from a faceplate. The cutters come in many shapes: Some can make grooves of different sizes; others, called shapers, can cut lovely decorative molding—like edges. When mounted on the router table, the router is turned upside-down to free the user's hands, with the cutter protruding from the bed.

If you sharpen tools (like chipped chisels), a grinder is a big help. You can also use it to grind down the back edges of X-Acto blades, which keeps them sharp nearly forever. But you really don't need one if you get a grindstone disc and mount it on a drill or a flexshaft—just grip that in a vise and use it as a grinder instead.

I have a 9-inch bench model disc sander with an adjustable plate, which can be set at variable angles to the sanding disc. The disc can be fitted with sticky-back sandpaper circles. It's good for getting exact angles, because of the adjustable faceplate, and it's nice for sanding down and speed-shaping sculptured hunks of wood.

## HAND TOOLS FOR WOOD

Get a heavy machinist's vise and bolt it to something solid so it won't move around while you use it. A heavy woodworking vise is handy if you do a lot of woodcarving.

As for hammers, a claw hammer will do, and maybe a small ball peen hammer for shaping or pounding dents into or out of metal. Small hammers are nice for small, delicate tasks, like clouage.

## CHISELS

There are four main types of chisels—gouges, veiners, V-parting tools, and flat chisels—each with some subvariations. They come in many different sizes and *sweeps*, or depths of curve—the higher the sweep number, the deeper the curve. The workhorse tools for basic carving are the gouges—they rough out the basic forms and do most of the carving and smoothing out. Veiners and V-parting tools do detail work, fluting, and outlining. Flat chisels, particularly the skew, are also good for detail work, as is the macaroni tool. (Yes, that's its name!)

*Plain gouges have a shallow, U-shaped cutting edge and a straight shaft. They are forged in various sweeps in order to remove greater or lesser amounts of wood.*

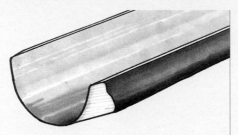

*Veiners are like gouges, but have a deeper U-shaped sweep, allowing them to make a clean, deep cut in one pass.*

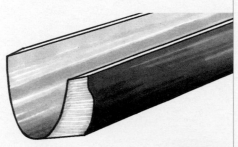

*Spoon gouges are bowl-shaped at the end. They are useful in areas where a long, straight blade would be impractical due to the detail or size of the work.*

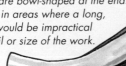

*Back-bent gouges have a reverse curve, making the cutting edge convex, rather than concave. They are used for carving or for cleaning out the underside of a carving or cut.*

*Bent gouges have a slight bend along the shaft, making them practical for roughing out and smoothing concave sections on sculpture.*

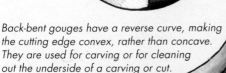

*Fishtail gouges, which flare out at the end, are good for cleaning out corners, especially when side clearance is limited.*

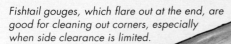

*V-parting tools have a V-shaped cutting edge. Principal uses include outlining, rounding over edges with the straight side, and adding detail.*

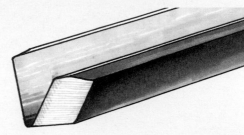

*Long-bent V-parting tools have a longer shaft and are curved, allowing them to reach into concave surfaces.*

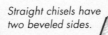

*Bent V-parting tools have a short curve at the end—good for accessing hard-to-reach spots.*

*Straight chisels have two beveled sides.*

*Dog leg chisels have a corner shape bent into the shaft, allowing for cutting into deep recesses.*

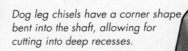

*The improved macaroni tool is not too common. Its three working edges allow it to be used as a gouge or as a V-parting tool.*

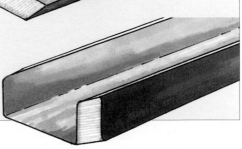

A variety of handsaws is essential. A straight-spined mitering saw is good to cut miters on corners; you use it with a miter box, which holds the wood in place and guides the saw. Get a small, all-purpose handsaw to cut pieces of wood and dowel that are too small to cut with a power saw, a coping saw for delicate cutting, and a hacksaw for cutting metals and hard plastics.

If your budget is limited, you can do without an ordinary set of pliers; instead, get an extra-large pair with jaws that can spread around the cap of a metal can of solvent. The jaws of my big pair can hold something 2¼ to 2½ inches across, and are really useful—not just for opening things, but for tightening and bending heavy things, and for holding big objects while you work on them. Also get some long-nosed pliers for delicate work— perhaps a large and a small pair, depending on the size of your work. These are good for making delicate bends in wire or working in small metal pieces for assemblage.

If you can't afford a few sizes of wire cutters, get one good big one that can cut the thickest wire you tend to work with. Many pointy-nosed or needle-nosed pliers have wire cutters built into them, so you don't need to bother with small cutters.

When stocking screwdrivers, consider what you need. In general, large and small sizes of both regular and philips-head styles will do. Very small screwdrivers, often sold in sets, are handy, but only if you will be working very small or need to fix things with little screws holding them together.

The need for clamps depends on your work. The largest of these—furniture clamps and pipe clamps—feature two jaws sliding on a length of metal bar or pipe, and are good for building large frames, boxes, and cabinets. C clamps are useful for almost everybody, and come in many different sizes.

If you are going to be doing any carving or shaping of wood, you should have a wood rasp or two. A large one (with an 11-inch blade) may be too big, unless you are doing large-scale stuff, but it is very efficient in taking down surfaces. You should also consider rifflers, or shaped sculptor's rasps, if you like a smoothed finish instead of a chisel-carved one. Rifflers come in different sizes and shapes; the handiest one for me is a curved, pointed one that enables me to get into little corners.

Wood files give a smoother, finer finish than rasps give; some artists like very small files, like machinist's and jeweler's models. Other good items include a surform tool (sort of like a rasp, but with a replaceable blade of grating, cutting metal fitted into a handle) and Dragon Skin (metal sheets, either hand-held or handle-mounted, with perforations that create a rasplike roughness).

Of course you need sandpaper, but how much and which grits depend on the kind of surface you want on your wood—some carvers, like Bonnie Rasmussen, do all or most of their finishing with razor-sharp chisels and make little use of sandpaper. High-quality sandpaper is more satisfying to work with and lasts much longer than cheap stuff.

Miscellaneous carpenter's tools that may be necessary include tin snips, dividers and calipers, awls, nail sets, and a shallow triangular cutter-grinder for countersinking screws, a spirit level, and a carpenter's square for measuring right angles and making pieces with very square corners.

ELLEN RIXFORD
Woman of Housewares *illustration, for a story on the disproportionate share of housework done by women. Housewares, including mop for hair, vent tubes for arms, sponges for jacket, and refrigerator logo for brooch. Height: 42" (1.1 m). Client:* Ms. *magazine. (Photographer: Pat Field)*

Get a few sizes of paintbrushes. Relatively cheap ones are okay, unless you are doing very delicate decorative painting, which requires artist's brushes. There are three basic kinds of bristles from which to choose: the pig-bristle stiff brush for oil paint brushes, which are built square rather than pointed, and the pointy-tipped sable and synthetic brushes for fine-line watercolor and acrylic painting. Acrylics tend to chew up sable bristles, so acrylic painters should use the nylon-based synthetic models, which are also a good deal less expensive. Sable is good for watercolor and oil colors; oil and turpentine react with and ultimately destroy the synthetic bristles. Any bristle is okay for watercolor and water-soluble inks and dyes. For artist's brushes, don't skimp on quality—the cheap ones don't hold a point, and their bristles start to fall out after a while.

VIN GIULIANI
Factory Line *editorial spread. Balsa, tempera, and found objects. Dimensions: 15 × 20″ (38 × 51 cm). Client:* Playboy *magazine. (Photographer: Vin Giuliani)*

Be sure to have some sharpening tools. Don't try to save money here—a good sharpening stone lasts a long time and is well worth the money. Although small stones are much cheaper, they don't give enough room to sharpen chisels comfortably; a stone 1 inch thick, 2 inches wide and 6 to 8 inches long is okay. Most chisels are sold unsharpened, and small carving sets don't come sharp enough either, so you'll need to sharpen your tools before using them; after that, get into a sharpening routine so your tools are always in good shape. You should have a 240-grit India stone, 500- and 900-grit Arkansas stones, and,

if your budget permits, a 1,000-grit ultrafine ceramic stone. For final honing, use a strop of thick leather with jeweler's rouge.

Finally, you'll need mallets. Wooden ones are made of *lignum vitae*, a dense, super-hard wood that sinks in water and resists chipping and cracking even after repeated blows from heavy use. The best ones have a lot of the dark heartwood; the lighter wood is softer and will chip and rip after a while. Protect your mallet by covering it with thick leather—15-pound weight, say—or by wrapping an old leather belt around it, gluing it with contact cement or Barge glue (first remove any wax that may coat your new mallet, or the leather won't stick). The leather will absorb some of the punishment inflicted on the mallet, and will also absorb noise. To keep your mallet from drying out, store it in a plastic bag.

# WORKING PROCESSES

## WOOD CARVING

Good carving is essentially a subtractive process: you take material off. Putting wood back on after you have mistakenly removed it is laborious and tricky; it also leaves a glue joint, which may show. So be slow and careful, and do lots of advance planning—more than with any other medium.

The following sequence outlines the basic carving procedure used by Bonnie Rasmussen: First, create a design appropriate to this medium—woodcarvings should be limited to forms with enough mass to give them strength and durability. A design with a lot of thin, delicate shapes, for example, might crack if done in wood.

Enlarge your design to full-scale, so you will be able to make good patterns to use as you carve. You might even want to make a full-scale clay model, especially if you are a beginner. Next, select the best wood for the job—consider the design of the piece and how it will fit with the wood's color and grain, and also whether the design will entail a lot of detail carving, necessitating a chip-resistant wood.

Buy the wood. If your design requires a size or shape of wood that you can't find in a single piece, you can have it planed, jointed, and glued up. Or, if you have the equipment, you can do this yourself. Be sure the grain is going in the proper direction. Don't use any pegging dowels or biscuits (small, thin pieces of wood inserted into wood joints) in the alignment of the joints, as you might carve into them.

When your wood blank is ready, tape the design onto the wood surface, making sure the wood grain is aligned for maximum strength and ease of carving. Grain usually runs diagonally, not perfectly straight. Always carve with the grain without pushing your chisel too deep into the wood and ripping off too large a chunk by mistake. Turn your blank around a few times and plan how it will best fit your desired form.

Transfer the design to the wood with carbon paper. As the top layers get carved away, however, the original lines will disappear, so it's helpful to have a few keyed line drawings on clear acetate, representing different carving depths; you can use these as you carve away the top layers.

DONN RUSSELL
Local Newscast. *Sugar pine, acrylics. Dimensions: 27 × 18″ (69 × 46 cm). Client: Private collection. (Photographer: Donn Russell)*

Cut out the basic shapes using whatever saws are appropriate. If you don't have a good band saw and are trying to cut out a shape in thick wood, the next best thing is to make a number of cuts perpendicular to the outline you are trying to make, either with a handsaw or a reciprocating saw, and then use a medium to large gouge to cut off the excess pieces.

Now begin to carve. Keep anything that could possibly nick your chisels—including clamps, nuts, bolts, and screws—away from your working area. As you carve, one hand will guide and push the tool; the other will control and brake it. When carving with a mallet, one hand will tap the tool as the other guides and brakes it. Take off small amounts at time, especially if you are unsure of where you are going. If you cut off a piece you did not mean to, glue it back on with the same glue you used to glue up the blank. If you carve down a piece too much, fit a new piece on; try to get the two joining faces to conform as perfectly as possible. Glue will not take paint or stain as wood does, so carve away any excess glue.

As you carve, think about which tools are best suited to the task at hand, what depth you want to carve to (use calipers to help check), and how the surface will be finished (a whittled finish? a smooth-sanded finish? a distressed "antiqued" finish?). After the carving, add any trim, hardware, or mounting devices.

Paint or finish your piece. For interior work, Rasmussen uses a liberal coat of raw or boiled linseed oil (the raw dries slower). Let it penetrate 15 minutes or so, and then rub off any excess with a soft, lint-free rag. Use artist's oil paints applied straight from the tube with a rag or brush while the wood is still wet with linseed oil; this gives a rich, transparent color that is easy to control. When the stained and painted carving is dry, you can seal areas with varnish for gold leaf, if you want it, or go on to applying oil-based antiquing glaze, which can visually unify the surface and keep the piece from looking too new. Apply glazes with a brush and wipe with a soft, lint-free cloth until you get the effect you like. This technique will remove glaze from the high spots selectively, leaving it in crevices and low spots, accenting the carving.

If your piece is for exterior use, use enamel colors. Sign Painter's 1 Shot is the best paint line, but these colors are lead-based, so be careful. If you prefer to go with paint store enamels, be sure they are high-quality exterior products.

Rasmussen notices a little drag on her carving tool—it's time to give it a fresh edge. Shown here are her sharpening materials: hard black Arkansas oil stone, honing oil, hard white Arkansas oil slip stone, and a leather strop.

Almost finished carving. The gauntlet part of the wood has been hand-sanded smooth using 80 grit sandpaper, followed by 100 and then 220 grit. Rasmussen positions the logo on the gauntlet, traces it on with carbon paper, and carves it in relief by carving away the background with a No. 11 veiner and a No. 5 gouge.

Note the variety of surface-finishing techniques: The surface of the glove hand is finished with the carving tool alone, its marks texturing the glove's working surface. Incised trim cuts emphasize the seams and sewing lines on the real glove and contrast with the smooth finish of the gauntlet. The raised lettering is smooth-surfaced and is set off by a decorative border. Rasmussen now applies linseed oil and begins to paint with oil colors, beginning with midrange hues.

Rasmussen uses colors straight from the tube, then enriches them by rubbing away color to let wood show through, or adds extra color highlights of lighter tints. Darker colors cover the mid-range hues.

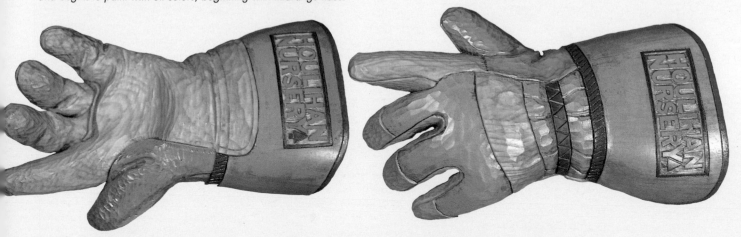

Front and back views of the finished piece, with antiquing glaze added to complete the project.

## ASSEMBLAGE

Assemblage is more a matter of composition and vision than of technique; the technique comes in planning and building a setting for the components. Further, your skill may be called upon to create pieces you need but cannot find, or to modify existing pieces. You can use anything. I was once asked to do an old-fashioned medicine chest with a little family of jointed wood dolls living in it. I was dubious of finding the proper doll family, so I carved and painted them myself. When the client saw a Polaroid of a nice square oak chest I planned to use, he frowned and asked if it could have a little decorative top and some feet. Finding it hard to match the oak's grain, I finally made the added pieces of sugar pine and faked the grain with brown and black inks and a crow quill pen.

Assemblage procedures vary enormously, but here are a few observations. Since you're making pictures, not furniture, there will be little physical strain on the pieces—super-strong wood and glue joints are unnecessary. Consider such niceties as tongue-in-groove joints only if your client asks for them.

ELLEN RIXFORD
*Facing page:* Medicine Cabinet Family, *to illustrate home remedies a family can use without calling a doctor. Real medicine chest, with wood details added, medicine bottles, jars, packages, and jointed wood dolls. Height: 28"* (71 cm). Client: Families *magazine,* © *Reader's Digest Assoc., Inc. (Photographer: Bill Sontag)*

## HOW TO BUILD A BOX

It is often better to find a box than to make one, but if you need to make one to a client's size specifications, especially one that must contain specific objects (like the client's products), you will have to build one from scratch and make compartments to fit the objects. Start by making a very precise drawing of the box from the front—not a perspective rendering but a plan drawing, showing the exact sizes of all objects and compartments—and have the client check and approve it. Then decide how you want to fasten the wooden box pieces together. Options include the following:

❏ *Nailing:* Fast, good for temporary joints or joints that will bear no strain. If the box will be painted rather than stained, use brads—nails with very small heads—and a nail set to hammer them in a bit below surface, where they can be puttied over and sanded smooth.

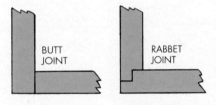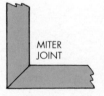

BUTT JOINT
RABBET JOINT
MITER JOINT
TONGUE-IN-GROOVE JOINT

Diagrams: Lenor Robinson

❏ *Screwing:* More solid than a nail, because screw threads hold wood tighter. Screws can be hidden by being countersunk—drill a little conical hole at the point the screw will go in. Flathead wood screws end up a bit below the surface, where they can be puttied over.

❏ *Pegging:* An old-fashioned but very nice way to fasten wood to wood. It entails drilling a hole the same diameter as a slender dowel, dipping the dowel peg in glue, hammering it in, and then sanding off the excess. The glue on the peg seeps into the fibers of the wood around it and into the fibers of the peg, holding it very tight.

Next, decide what kind of joints you want in the box. Some choices:

❏ *Butt joint:* None too elegant, but very simple to make. Not very strong, unless reinforced by screws or pegs. But if the whole piece will be painted

and the joint won't be visible, it's okay.

❏ *Rabbet joint:* Stronger, because there is more surface-to-surface contact, so the glue has more area to grip. The interlocking "shelf" on the wood can be made with a cut from a table saw, or with a router in a router table.

❏ *Miter joint:* Usually used for edges that show, particularly those with moldings or decorations, like a picture frame or box edge. It looks nice but is much stronger if reinforced.

❏ *Tongue-in-groove joint:* The strongest glue joint, because it has the most surface-to-surface contact. This does not need reinforcing with metal fasteners, and is common in good furniture.

When planning how your box will fit together, decide about fasteners and joint types and include them in your plan. The box's corners can be butt, rabbet, tongue-in-groove, or miter; the inner compartments, if you have some, can be butt, rabbet, or tongue-in-groove. Careful measuring and a willingness to make lots of little adjustments so everything will fit are necessary, especially if you attempt the more demanding furniture-type joints. For further detail, consult one of the many books on joinery or articles in various popular home-builder magazines.

Objects can be merely set into the box—a more flexible arrangement for photographic purposes—or they can be fastened permanently, a good thing to do if the client wants to buy the piece and hang it on a corporate wall. If you have plenty of surface-to-surface connection, fasten with glue; it not, use glue plus some kind of physical connection—a loop of wire in an unobtrusive spot, a small screw driven into the back of object, and so on.

## MINIATURE SETS

The miniature set is a more modern form of assemblage, and a far more demanding one than the traditional box type, because its composition and design are more open and flexible, and the choice of objects required to get the composition to work is far more demanding. Joan Steiner's assemblage methodology epitomizes the sense of wit and the powers of visual discernment this form demands.

The first stage is the sketch. Here, working from a general idea of what the set should look like, Steiner chooses a core group of items that seem to work together to establish the overall scale of the piece, and uses cardboard and ordinary studio materials to create an approximation of the rest of the set. Then she shops for objects that will be compatible with the core group. This is the most difficult stage, because it is hard to tell how various objects in a store will eventually harmonize with the core items and with each other.

After this comes what Steiner calls "the fooling-around stage"—the real work of fitting the objects together, accommodating things to each other, playing with layouts, and working out sight lines for the photo. To help herself visualize the set through the camera lens, she uses a homemade cardboard viewfinder cut to the proportions of the final photo and sketches out how the composition elements will fall within it.

The last step is the assembly. Steiner builds the set in sections; they will ultimately be assembled in the photo studio, a painstaking task that often requires repeated adjustments in lighting.

Here's how she applied this technique to creating the cover for *Step-by-Step Graphics* magazine's 1989 Designer's Guide.

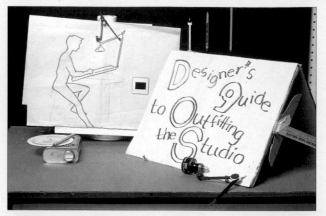

The sketch. The piece had to be constructed in three separate planes at different distances from the camera, because the items to be used in the assemblage were of differing scales. The use of three planes—foreground, middle, and background—helped to even up the scale and unify the whole.

After collecting a variety of items for potential inclusion, Steiner enters the fooling-around stage. As she works out various combinations, she secures the objects with tape so she can study their interrelationships.

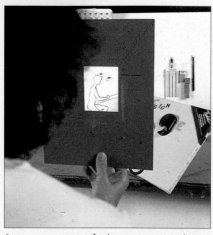

Steiner uses a viewfinder, proportioned to match the final printed image, to mock up the finished picture.

A close-up look at the viewfinder: Major elements of the three planes are indicated by lines drawn on acetate taped over the viewfinder opening; the dotted line indicates the center. As Steiner finds that objects may appear larger or smaller in the final image than she had planned, she makes revised drawings.

Steiner makes the back wall from marbleized vellum glued to foam-core board. Dividers are used as architectural details.

# 5 FABRIC SCULPTURE

ELLEN RIXFORD
*Left:* Vegetables in a Garden *illustration. Soft sculpture, mostly cotton jersey. Approximate length: 5' (1.5 m). Client: Family Weekly magazine. (Photographer: Ellen Rixford)*

SANAE AWATSUJI
*Below:* Mother's Chorus, *for an exhibition at Ginza Matsuya. Soft sculpture. Heights range from 14–18" (35–45 cm). Client: Ginza Matsuya department store. (Photographer: Mitsumasa Fujitsuka)*

Dimensional illustration in fabric has a shorter history than illustration in paper, clay, or wood, but its roots stretch far back into the traditional crafts of quilting, embroidery, and dollmaking. Its pioneer was Sanae Awatsuji, a Japanese textile designer who began by making immensely original dolls for her daughter. Awatsuji's early dolls looked primitive and demented; some only vaguely resembled human figures, and many were hilariously sexual. Her first gallery exhibition was in 1970, and she has exhibited regularly since then, building up a respectable clientele in advertising and publishing along the way.

Soft sculpture as dimensional illustration began in America in the 1970s as well. The late Judith Jampel, whose medium was nylon stocking and polyester fiberfill, did her first illustration for an award-winning feminist book. Encouraged by its success, Jampel experimented further. Within a year, she had developed a technique that produced portraits of such perfection that careless onlookers often mistook them for real people. Her technique was later adopted by Lisa Lichtenfels, who independently developed her own methods for extremely realistic soft sculpture in nylon stocking and polyester fiberfill plus cotton batting and foam. Because Lichtenfels did much of

JUDITH JAMPEL
*Above:* Emmett Kelly *illustration, for magazine advertisement. Soft sculpture in nylon stocking and polyester fiberfill, with face painted to look like clown makeup. Life-sized. Client: Ciba Geigy. (Photograph ©️ George Ehrlich 1979)*

JUDITH JAMPEL
Generalissimo Rockefeller *editorial illustration. Soft sculpture in nylon stocking and polyester fiberfill. Dimensions: 25 × 26 × 15"* *(64 × 66 × 38 cm). Client:* Penthouse *magazine. (Photographer: Klaus Lucka)*

her early work as a gallery artist, she had more time to produce her figures, and experimented extensively.

Both Jampel and Lichtenfels use wire skeletons covered with carefully modeled foam and batting, both use skull-like structures with padded wire defining such forms as nose and lips, and both skillfully work the seams of the nylon "skin" into the natural creases of the body. But Lichtenfels developed a movable skeleton and a system of manipulated control wires in the face, enabling her to alter the position and expression of facial features. Jampel used nylon and polyester fiberfill for everything in the figure; Lichtenfels

makes eyes of painted marbles coated with polyurethane varnish, and shiny hard teeth of varnished Sculpey. Most of Jampel's sculptures are human and fully clothed; Lichtenfels's repertoire includes nude figures, animals, and mythical hybrid creatures.

I began working in soft sculpture in 1969, when a friend gave me a sizable piece of red leather. I decided to make a mask out of it, but I didn't want to ruin it with an injudicious cut, so I experimented first on an old T-shirt, not realizing that cotton and leather have entirely different working characteristics. My first face was a baggy, wrinkled old grandma, and its combination of

**CATHY LAZAR**
*Top:* Peas and Carrots, *for a television commercial. Foam with fabric covering. Length of corn: 11' (3.4 m). Client: Saran Wrap. (Photographer: Michael Miller)*

**BRAD WILLIAMS**
Night Memories *goblins and ghosts, created for an original play. Inch-thick Scotfoam, dyed, folded, glued, and airbrushed. Heights: 5–6' (1.5–1.8 m). Client: National Technical Institute for the Deaf. (Photographer: Brad Williams)*

human personality and unmistakable "clothiness" suggested possibilities for a new genre. I forgot about the red leather and turned my attention to T-shirts, making young and middle-aged faces as well as old, and produced a series of bas-relief portraits. These were fitted with hinged plastic doors instead of glass, so their owners could open up the portraits and manipulate the facial expressions.

Soft sculpture generates a feeling of subtle wit and humor toward its subjects, which are almost always human or parahuman—anthropomorphic animals, insects, vegetables, or hybrids of any of these. The figures are built from the inside out, and even a small mistake in the basic form—the shape of a nostril, say—can mean starting over. Doing this work on a tight deadline requires patience, a high frustration threshold, and a good deal of sangfroid. This demanding medium is not for everyone; consider that for every 20 artists working in clay, which, like fabric, is well-suited for portraits and caricatures, there is only one working in soft sculpture.

Another form of soft sculpture is *foam sculpture*, which is often used for puppets and costumes for children's television shows and commercials. Possibilities include animals, like a giant chicken advertising a restaurant; vegetables, like Cathy Lazar's vegetable plate for a Saran-Wrap commercial; giant household objects, like Lazar's oversized shoes, peanuts, and dollar bills; and of course humans of every size and description. While many of the puppets with foam bodies also have heads made of other media, we will concentrate in this chapter on the use of foam in making their bodies. We will also examine the costumes, which are usually almost completely constructed of foam; the only other materials used in them are fabric or fake-fur coverings and stiffening materials, like foam-core board and steel boning (thin flexible rods that help keep the costume's shape).

In 1972, around the same time the first full-round soft sculptures made their appearance, Margaret Cusack introduced fabric pictures as illustration. Art directors were initially concerned that stitched technique wouldn't reproduce well in print, but after several spectacularly successful assignments, she and her medium—*fabric collage*, as she named it—found their way into the mainstream. Other artists, intrigued with the idea of using fabric and stitchery in place of paint, began experimenting with it, attracted by its warmth and its expressive qualities. Deidre Scherer, one such former painter who turned to fabric, creates portraits of old people. The multilayered richness and density of experience written upon her subjects' faces is mirrored in her sewing—pieces of cloth and lines of colored stitching layered upon each other until sometimes the needle breaks in the cloth. In contrast to Cusack's meticulously planned compositions, Scherer allows a piece to change as it progresses. Cusack glues down her fabric pieces very tightly before sewing

them, and her applique-edge stitching must be absolutely perfect, or she will rip it out—sometimes several times— and do it over. Since she uses a good deal of lettering in her work, correct spacing and positioning are essential, so nothing is left to chance. Scherer, on the other hand, "draws" freehand with the scissors and sewing machine as she works, letting the layers of cloth move as they will.

Illustrating with fabric lends itself to diversity: There are as many styles as there are artists, and this variety will only increase as clients' receptiveness to the medium grows. Some artists mix painterly skills with skillful stitchery,

dyeing and painting the fabric in their compositions. Anne Cook uses watercolor to paint in parts of her pieces, and has pushed at least one piece over into the area of assemblage by adding real rooster feathers to a fabric rooster. Cusack routinely uses fabric paint to define her letterforms, dyes many of her own fabrics, and sometimes paints in tiny details over large areas of a composition. In the *April* collage for her Avon calendar, she painted all the pink flowers on the "rainy" side of the field green.

When I first began working in this medium, what attracted me most about the form was its scope. Under a normal deadline and with a normal amount of space, it is a bit of a strain to turn out large, populated landscapes in soft sculpture. But fabric pictures, being pictures, allow this with relative ease, and the fabric itself contributes charming and lovely details of its own. It also makes the medium particularly appropriate for certain types of work; since quilting, for instance, is an American tradition, fabric pictures lend themselves to Americana and tradition-oriented themes. Clients tend to think of them this way, and use them for this purpose.

MARGARET CUSACK
Perrier *fabric collage, for print advertisement. Handmade and storebought beads, with batikwork for bubbles in the water. Dimensions: 20 × 27" (51 × 69 cm). (Photographer: Ron Breland)*

DEIDRE SCHERER
*Above:* Coleus in Blue *card series design. Fabrics, pima cotton, woven cottons, thread. Dimensions: 10 × 14" (25 × 36 cm). Client: Material-Notes. (Photography: True Color)*

DEIDRE SCHERER
*Top right:* Afternoon Sun. *Calico fabric, pima cotton, and thread. Dimensions: 22 × 26" (56 × 66 cm). Private collection. (Photographer: Jeff Baird)*

KATHLEEN LENGYEL
*Right: Untitled cover art for 1991 Women's Center calendar, to promote classes in parenting, birthing, and other family-oriented matters. Fabric collage. Dimensions: 24 × 36" (61 × 91 cm). Client: Morton Plant Hospital. (Photographer: Hans Kaczmarek)*

ANNE COOK
Bed and Breakfast
Still Life. *Watercolor
on muslin, fabrics,
thread, and batting.
Dimensions:
11 × 17" (28 × 43 cm).
Client: Yankee
magazine.
(Photographer:
Will Mosgrove)*

ANNE COOK
*Below:* Classic
Recipes. *Various
fabrics, thread,
embroidery floss, and
watercolor on muslin.
Dimensions: 14 × 20"
(36 × 51 cm). Client:
Beatrice Foods.
(Photographer:
Will Mosgrove)*

# MATERIALS AND TOOLS

## CLOTH

The most practical way to categorize fabrics is by how they behave as you work with them. The most important quality is stretch. For two-dimensional or bas-relief work, the fabric should maintain its dimensions without puckering or "walking around" in the sewing machine. If the material is stretchy, usually it is glued down or backed with iron-on backing so it will behave. For the soft sculpture artist, however, stretch is desirable—the more a fabric stretches, the more easily it can go around a double curve or be modeled into more complex forms.

The stretchiest fabric is nylon stocking. Brand names are irrelevant, because stocking manufacturers do not maintain standards of color, texture, and durability over long periods. In general, the best nylons are usually the cheapest, as they tend not to run as easily as the expensive ones. Stockings with a distinctly all-over mesh pattern and a matte finish are much less prone to running than those with a horizontal-vertical weave and a silky sheen. Finer textures are good for portraits of women and children, rougher ones for old people and men. High-weave fuzzy textures are good for simulating animal fur. Don't get stockings that have been sized (they look like a flattened pair of legs when you pull them out of the package; unsized ones look crumpled)—size is a chemical coating that keeps the stocking from stretching and resists dyes.

If you do find good stockings, buy a lot of them—queen size, if possible. Even a half-life-sized figure takes six pairs to do. For simple faces, I use castoff stockings from friends—a pair will produce five or six faces.

Most nylons come in flesh tones. But for the fabric intended for inner layers, lips, and inner mouths, and for the various colors of animals, the fabric must be dyed. White nylon is the most convenient to start with.

Because nylon stocking is transparent, it is crucial to use polyester fiberfill for the top layer. The fiberfill should have no large fibers or irregularities that can show under the skin. You can test it by stretching a piece of stocking over it and examining it. If the texture is even, and if it is flexible and resilient, it's okay.

Less stretchy are the silky fabrics, like Spandex, milliskin, and stretch satin (sometimes called disco satin), the matte fabrics, like cotton knit jersey, and the nappier stretch velours and stretch terry. Nylon stocking is so stretchy that it can cover an entire face without needing a seam for the nose, but these medium-stretchy fabrics usually require one.

The next important characteristics to consider are weight and durability. These two qualities, which almost always go together, will determine how easy the material is to work with and how long the finished piece will hold up. Nylon stocking is exceptionally durable for its weight, but it is delicate compared to the thicker fabrics, so sculpture made of it should be kept in display cases. The thicker fabrics are less prone to tearing but can still get dirty; soft sculpture made of them should be stored in cases or clean boxes, as these materials can be a nightmare to clean once a piece is finished.

Last come the aesthetic characteristics: pattern, texture, color, and special effects, like metallic shine or iridescence. Fabric is unmatched in its variety here—no other sculpture material offers the artist such a resplendent, ready-made selection of instant effects. This is particularly useful for fabric collagists and picture quilters, who use fabric as their palette. It really doesn't matter what kind of fabric you use for this type of work, as long as you prepare it so that it doesn't stretch or slip about during the sewing. Thanks to the huge available variety of iron-on backings, stabilizers, and spray- and brush-on products, such as spray starches and glues, this is easy. The important thing is to make the fabric dimensionally stable, and to find a way of attaching it to the background against which it will be appliquéd. If you plan to do some hand embroidery and your fabric is reasonably substantial (muslin or heavier), putting it in an embroidery hoop or fastening it to a simple frame makes it easy to handle. If you want to embroider by machine, mount the fabric in a hoop or frame, remove the presser foot of your machine, and slip the hoop or frame underneath; then reposition the foot, and off you go. It's worth noting, however, that if you do simple embroidery, like cross-stitch, it helps to use a fabric with a visible weave, which will act as a guide for your stitchery. The best for this are Aida and Hardanger cloths, both cotton weaves, which come in several colors and can easily be tinted or dyed. Any good needlework store will carry these.

Organize your fabric so you have easy access to all the fabrics you plan to use. I organize mine by fabric type (chiffons, velvets, cottons, stretch versus nonstretch) and pattern type (small versus large florals, stripes, checks, solid colors); Margaret Cusack adds a third parameter, color (reds in one box, blues in another). I cut off two little pieces of each fabric and make two identical bunches of swatches. I use one bunch to mark the outside of the box each fabric is kept in and hang the other on a nail inside a convenient closet door; this functions as a display rack, so I can see everything I've got. I can also take down appropriate swatches to show art directors what kinds of colors and patterns I'm considering for a job.

## DYES AND FABRIC PAINTS

Using nothing but existing fabric colors is severely limiting to the fiber artist. Sometimes it is impossible to find an sample of the color you want—just try to track down flesh tones in cotton knit, for example. Cases like this require custom dyeing; I have a few boxes containing skin colors appropriate to light- and dark-skinned blacks, Hispanics, Asians, Native Americans, and half a dozen shades of light skin. Dyeing is essential to special effects, like a sky that is dark blue at the top and paler toward the horizon, or asparagus that is green at the tip and cream-white at the base. And I have occasionally used fabric paints or permanent inks to give a subtle blush to a cheek or an apple.

Most fabric illustrators rely on *union dyes*, so named because they combine different dyes appropriate for different fibers. These household dyes, like Rit and Tintex, are widely available and easy to use, and they come in many colors.

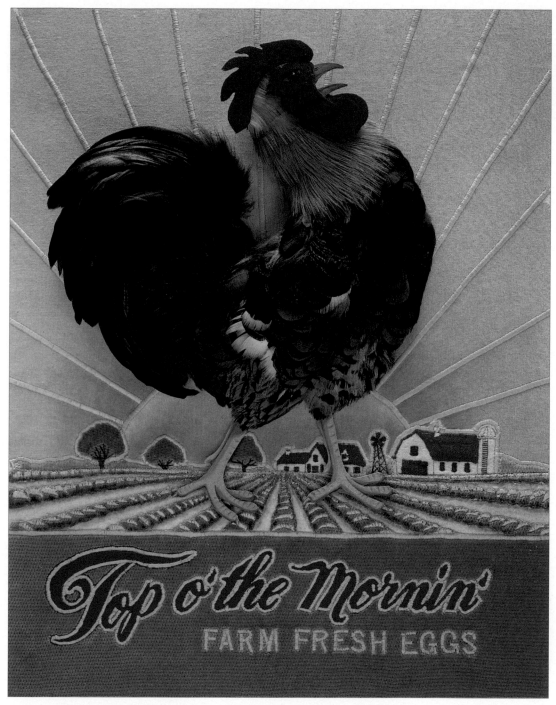

But they are not considered professional dyes, and their wash- and lightfastness fall far short of what can be obtained with professional-grade products.

Dyes in the basic colors can be prepared pretty reliably. These in turn allow the dyer to mix many other hues, and to achieve a broad range of tints (hue plus white), shades (hue plus black), and tones (hue plus gray) with a small, economical inventory of dyes. The procedure for these dyes is relatively simple; an average dyeing takes an hour to an hour and a half.

Although professional dyes are more time-consuming, they resist changing and fading much better than their household counterparts, so fiber artists creating works meant to last almost invariably choose the higher-grade stuff. I confess to using household dyes by the dunk-and-inspect method for temporary effects—I mix a batch of color, dip the fabric in it, and then yank it out when it reaches the desired intensity, with no regard for giving the color sufficient time to develop into the fabric. But I would not do this on a piece that I

expected to keep or to sell to a client.

There are relatively few workhorse dyes that feature the ideal levels of wash- and lightfastness, color range and brightness, mixability, even distribution on the fibers, economy, safety, and ease of application. For relatively simple jobs, where time and convenience are at a premium, the Deka L series is a good choice—the dyes are of good quality and tend to be the most lightfast among the household brands. *Direct-type dyes* (for cotton and rayon) and *acid dyes* (for silk and wool) are good for immersion dyeing and for batik, as are *fiber-reactive dyes*, which can also be used for painting and printing on the fabric if thickeners are added. The most familiar brands here are Procion and Cibacron (also known as Fibacron F). There are many other specialized dyes, but they have too many safety problems or are too difficult to use to be of much utility to the dimensional illustrator.

For the more experimental among you, try fabric paints, which are simple to use and safe—you can paint them on or print with them using any kind of stamping material (including rubber erasers and even carved potatoes). You can even make a monoprint on glass or acrylic plastic for transfer onto the fabric. Some fabric paints can marbleize fabrics; others come in metallic, fluorescent, and iridescent colors. The higher-quality ones are permanent and lightfast, work on nearly any kind of fabric, and can be thickened for silk screen, stencil, and stamps or thinned for a watercolor effect.

Finally, a few caveats: Use a mask or respirator while measuring and mixing powdered dyestuffs, use gloves while working with paints and dyebaths, and don't use your kitchen pots for dyeing. Pregnant and lactating women should

refrain from dyeing altogether. Follow directions to the letter. Use only dye-ready fabrics and fibers; any fabric treated with finishes to make it wash-and-wear, soil-resistant, permanent-press, or flame-retardant is unsuitable. Experiment on scraps first, and keep good records of what you did each dyeing.

## STUFFINGS

There are three materials you can use under the skin of a soft sculpture figure, or as stuffing for raised, or *trapunto*, quilt work: batting (either natural cotton or polyester), polyester fiberfill, and foam. Natural cotton batting is the oldest and most trational, and is usually sold in big rolls used as filling for bed quilts. Polyester batting, also sold in rolls, is non-biodegradable and easier to sculpt. Batting fibers tend to stay compressed and lump up when squeezed together; fiberfills spring back to their original configurations and puff up again, making these materials useful for

different functions. Soft sculpture is, after all, sculpture, and it's important for a form to keep its shape. Cotton and polyester batting do this well, holding small forms like the end of a nose or the bony form of a knuckle solidly under the cloth. Some judicious needle-modeling holds the lumps and bumps in place, and the form is there to stay. Fiberfill performs the opposite function: it smooths and softens contours, making forms rounded and even looking.

There are several artificial stuffing materials on the market. If the soft sculpture is made with an opaque skin, nearly any even-textured, resistant stuffing will do; for sculpture made of nylon stocking or other semitransparent skin, find a stuffing free of large fibers or other peculiarities that might show through and look like scars or skin lesions.

Larger pieces, puppets, and costumes, along with anything that must move, are more stable, easier to handle, and lighter when made with foam. Stuffing tends to slide and lump up inside a moving form. I learned this the hard way when the hands of some puppets I'd made began to look arthritic after a few performaces. I later learned that armatured puppet hands are nearly

ELLEN RIXFORD
The Yeast Beasts
*costumes, for a walking promotion for a medication to combat yeast infections. Reticulated foam (mostly Scotfoam), with some large carved foam pieces for mouths and eyelids, all covered with stretch terrycloth. Mouths can be manipulated by the wearers. Life-sized. Client: Ortho Pharmaceuticals. (Photographer: Ellen Rixford)*

always covered with foam gloves and then covered again with skin-fabric gloves. This keeps the shape of the hand constant, no matter how many positions it assumes.

The best foam for puppets and costumes is polyurethane foam—it's light, strong, and durable. Other foams, like latex, can be used too, but latex is about three times the money and much heavier, and other foams lack the urethane's major advantages. To wit: Urethane can be sewn, glued, dyed, brush- and spray-painted, and dry-cleaned, and is available in many densities (the weight of a cubic foot of foam in pounds) and porosities (the number of pores per linear inch). Densities generally range between a half to 10 pounds per cubic foot, and porosities between 15 to 80 pores per inch (PPI). The lower the number of PPI, the more the foam "breathes."

Polyurethane has two subcategories: polyester and polyether. Polyester foams are strong, easily sewable, and porous, but do not retain their shape after compression as readily as the polyethers. Some polyethers have a more open porosity, which makes them good for filters and for costumes, especially if they must be worn a long time under hot lights. Polyether foams are quite strong (though not as strong as the polyesters), do not rip easily when sewn, and bounce back to their original shape after compression. They come in many thicknesses, from ⅛-inch sheets to blocks 40-inch blocks, and the nonfilter polyether foams come in several colors (most filter varieties come in only white or black, although they can be dyed).

Among filter foams, Scotfoam is a well-known brand and an excellent product. It comes in sheets of white and yellow—the white is a little softer, the yellow a little more crisp and springy—and is commonly sold in ½- to 2-inch thicknesses for costumes. But any good-quality filter foam from a reputable dealer will work. Polyether foams are also excellent for foam carving, either by razor, knife, electric knife, or hot wire. Lisa Lichtenfels uses polyurethane blocks, which she buys from a furniture factory, for the understructure of her soft sculpture figures. Cathy Lazar uses filter foam sheets for her costumes, and I use them for puppets. Foam of any kind should be stored in sealed plastic bags, away from light and air, which slowly cause it to oxidize and deteriorate.

DEIDRE SCHERER
After Light. *Calico, woven cottens, silk fabric, and thread. Dimensions: 7¼ × 6½" (18 × 16 cm). Private collection. (Photography: Gamma One Conversions)*

Although foam is perfect for large, broadly modeled forms, the kind of delicate definition obtainable with polyester fiberfill and batting is difficult to get. More experimenting needs to be done with layering cotton and polyester fiberfill over foam and needle-modeling the combination. Foam sheets are dimensionally stable and can't be bent in more than one curve simultaneously. But you can get nice round curves, points, and other protuberances by cutting the foam in appropriate shapes and gluing it back together again. The most common glues here are brown glue and Barge. Brown glue is nontoxic, strong, and dry-cleanable. If joints are to be covered by something else, like fabric, it's a good choice, but it dries very dark. There are two kinds of Barge: The light-colored flammable version,

which comes in a red and yellow bottle, shows less at the glue joint and can be dyed to match dyed foam; the darker, nonflammable variety, which comes in a yellow and green bottle, is safer

## HAIR AND FUR

There is an infinite number of fibers and furry fabrics to choose from, materials that will give almost any effect. I like synthetic fur better than real, for both environmental and practical reasons—fake fur lasts longer than real, which deteriorates if not refrigerated in summer. Fake fur is now made in so many textures and colors, some of which can be overtinted or dyed, and all of which can be combined or embroidered with other fibers, that you should have no trouble finding the right skin for your beast-in-progress.

Hair fibers are available in even greater variety than fur, and require more careful discussion, because human figures are commissioned more frequently than animals, and clients are quite particular about hair and its relationship to a character's face. The most commonly used materials for hair are wigs, yarns, wool roving, mohair, and crêpe hair. But you can use anything else too, including ribbons, spaghetti, and the wonderful multicolored wire found inside telephone cables. Wigs are the best (or at least the most realistic) for life-sized figures; pieces for particularly fussy clients may even warrant custom-made wigs. For more ordinary illustrations, you can usually find what you need in a wig outlet, where the cheap ones are often at least as good as the pricier models. Try to get one with a thin, soft, flexible net at the scalp, to which the strands of hair are attached. You may not always use a whole wig for one head, and this netting makes it a lot easier to divide a wig into usable sections. It also allows you to change the style and arrangement somewhat, and to use pieces of the wig for other things, like mustaches and beards.

Ordinary yarn tends to make a character look doll-like rather than human. Sanae Awatsuji uses yarn for her big patchwork dolls, and the effect is appropriate and charming. Yarn chosen for a realistic figure, however, should be fuzzed out or otherwise treated to make it consistent. If you want an otherworldly look for a character, some of the specialty yarns, like the metallics or those with unusual textures or colors, can give the perfect finishing touch. Embroidery floss, because it comes in a huge variety of subtle colors, is good for hair that evokes a feeling of wild grasses and flowers.

Unspun yarn, or wool roving, comes in natural gray or a fine-textured bleached and combed white. It makes beautiful character hair—the gray for grizzled hair and beards, the white for platinum blonde. Try to get the gray roving prewashed, or else the lanolin in it will smell like a sheep.

For smaller-scale heads, or when you want to use a fine-textured fiber and control the color and degree of curliness, use mohair or theatrical crêpe hair. Both can be dyed, curled, or straightened with ease. Crêpe hair, available from theatrical makeup firms, comes in lengths varying from a few inches to a few yards, and in several colors that imitate most natural human hair colors. The crêpe comes braided with strings, which you pull out, leaving the hair crimped in a little wave, which can be fuzzed out with the fingers, steamed over the spout of a teakettle to relax the wave, ironed flat, or soaked in water and recurled as you like. You can use real curlers or wrap it around a dowel rod or chopstick. For a more natural color than the monochromatic crêpe braids, you can mix several colors together or selectively dye or stain the hair by painting only certain strands. Crêpe hair tends to dye unevenly—a desirable effect.

Mohair, usually used for doll wigs, has a slightly glossier, silkier look and comes in several colors, but is a bit harder to get. Look in doll-supply catalogs, or for ads in doll magazines, like *Doll Reader*. Many mohair suppliers are small mail-order operations and don't always ship right away—not so convenient if you need a special color for a rush job. If you plan to do a lot of soft sculpture, get a big supply of several colors, or use white and dye it yourself.

## TOOLS
The basic tools of an artist working with fabric are essentially the same as for a seamstress or tailor. Let's start with *needles:* For ordinary hand sewing, there is a range of appropriate needle lengths and thicknesses. I like rather long, thin needles, like No. 7s or even the 9s, although these tend to bow with use and have to be gently straightened out with pliers. For more specialized use, there are several outstanding special needles. For sewing through leather and heavy vinyls, either by machine or by hand, there are leather needles, whose shafts are triangular rather than round, giving a point that penetrates the leather more smoothly. Beading or pearling needles—super-long, thin needles originally designed for stringing beads with tiny holes—are good for sewing the nylon stocking gums around teeth, and for making invisible seams. There are large and curved needles, which are wonderful for needle-modeling thick facial details when you're working on a base of Styrofoam with stuffing over it and can't get to the back of the piece to

CHIKAKO TOMITA
*Left:* Lobster. *Soft sculpture in silver metallic fabric. Approximate length: 2′ (61 cm). Client: Master Eagle Gallery, New York. (Photographer: Akira Matsui)*

SUSAN MOERDER
*Opposite page:* Electronic Turkey. *Fake skin, fishing line, polyester fiberfill, satin, wire, and electronic parts. Approximate dimensions: 20 × 20 × 12″ (51 × 51 × 30 cm). Private collection. (Photograph © Susan Moerder)*

pull the needle out and insert it again. Quilting needles—somewhat heavier than regular sewing needles and very long—are good for needle-modeling when you're sewing through a soft sculpture mask that is too thick for an ordinary needle. There are also embroidery and crewel needles for hand embroidery. Most of these needles are available at notions stores or even in the sewing section at Woolworth's.

A medium-large pair of good *scissors* will do for most ordinary shapes; get a small pair for detail work. Scissors should be super-sharp, or they become a constant aggravation to use. Never use your fabric shears to cut anything but fabric, or they will get dull pronto. If you need to cut a lot of heavy fabrics, get separate pairs for this.

Most *thread* sold nowadays is cotton wrapped with polyester, and works fine for most projects. For a shinier effect on appliqué or satin stitching, extra-fine rayon or silk thread is nice, but harder to find. Any unique or out of the ordinary thread should be checked for colorfastness and ease of use on your sewing machine. If your thread becomes brittle and snaps easily during machine sewing, as can happen when the thread dries out, try moistening it with a damp sponge or holding it under the tap for a few seconds, and then dry it off with a towel.

Your individual needs will determine what demands you place on a *sewing machine*. One artist may get along fine with an old straight-stitch model; another may need an elaborate computer-controlled device. Before buying a machine, consider the following questions:

❏ Is the machine well-designed? Will it be comfortable for you to use for long periods of time? Is it easy to thread? Easy to wind the bobbin? Are the bobbins too small—will you constantly be running out of thread on a long project? Can you decenter the needle? Can you switch the machine to slow speed? If slow speed is pedal-controlled, does the machine run smoothly that way? Is the presser foot easy to change, and is there a good selection of alternate presser feet? Can you regulate the pressure? Is the needle plate even with the rest of the work surface? Can the feed dogs be easily lowered for darning or embroidery?

❏ Is tension reliable and consistent? Can you go in a smooth progression

from one tension to the next, or are there incremental jumps, as in some computer machines, where you can't get between two settings? Will this matter to you?

❏ Is the satin stitch smooth and even? Can you get it to taper evenly from thick to thin and back without much effort? Can you adjust the length and width of the zigzag easily, and are the dials accessible and convenient? What is the widest zigzag available?

❏ Is the machine strong enough to sew through several layers of fabric, or fabric plus stabilizers, batting, and so on? Will it sew vinyl and leather?

❏ What special features does the machine have? Are there a lot of different embroidery stitches, or the capacity to do monograms automatically? Can new stitches be added, or existing ones altered or combined? Can the machine use a double needle?

❏ Is the manual clearly written? Does it explain how to open the machine for cleaning, oiling, and troubleshooting? How long is the guarantee? Does the dealer do more than just sell and repair

machines—for example, does he offer supplies, classes, or updates on new equipment?

If in doubt, a top-of-the-line machine with a solid reputation is best; if you can't afford that, try to find a good used one. And if you depend on a machine to earn your living as an illustrator, it's good to have an extra machine, just in case something goes wrong at a critical time.

Another helpful piece of equipment is an *opaque projector*, which allows you to make large working drawings from small sketches. Some models work vertically—they slide up and down on a pole and project the image downward on a table; others work horizontally—they sit on a flat surface and project the image forward onto a wall. The vertical models offer fairly fine control in enlarging images, and many can also reduce, but the enlargement capacity is limited. Since I like working big, I use the horizontal projector to produce a huge working drawing on a piece of brown wrapping paper or a wide length of vellum.

# WORKING PROCESSES

## SOFT SCULPTURE WITH NONSTRETCH FABRIC

Soft sculpture forms can range from the super-real to the doll-like. The less the fabric stretches, the simpler the configurations tend to be, and the more the figure becomes like a "big doll." Big doll–style sculpture relies almost solely on a good set of patterns for its effectiveness. The patterns, sewn and stuffed, give the figure its form. By contrast, soft sculpture in super-stretch fabrics like nylon stocking rely more on understructures and needle-modeling, rather than patterns.

## SOFT SCULPTURE WITH STRETCH FABRIC

Some sculptures look so real they can fool the unwary. The deeper you go into realism, the more complex the working process becomes. Nonstretch materials and a heavy reliance on sewing patterns are fine for figures with little reliance on anatomical realism like the doll Sanae Awatsuji makes in the demonstration on this spread; but as soon as you try to incorporate musculature and bone structure, it becomes necessary to use a skeletonlike understructure, stuffing that can mimic flesh bulges, and

extensive needle-modeling to define precise forms.

Soft sculpture in nylon stocking entails no patterns, a comprehensive understructure, and lots of needle-modeling. For now, let's look at knit jersey sculpture, which is a bit less extreme—there is an understructure of sorts, and a fair amount of needle-modeling, but patterns are still essential to the figure's final form. After many years and many failures, I have developed a working sequence that produces a fairly realistic face and body in this demanding medium.

Photographs courtesy of Sanae Awatsuji

Awatsuji makes a full-scale drawing of the figure.

Using the drawing as a base, Awatsuji makes patterns and constructs a rough doll in white cloth to test them.

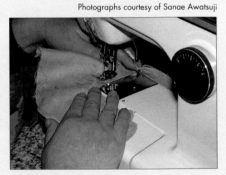

After correcting details of the rough pattern, Awatsuji makes the final patterns, decides which colors to use, and begins to pin together and sew the seams.

The figure is constructed like an intricate bag that will be stuffed tight. All the seams must line up properly and the edges must fit, so Awatsuji alternately pins and sews, taking in a bit here, adjusting a bit there, so that the pieces come together just right. She clips corners and places where the pattern forms sharp curves, and uses fabric glue to strengthen areas that may feel extra stress during stuffing.

Awatsuji's emphasis on simple, rounded forms obviates any need for small muscular details. She stuffs the figure very tight with polyester fiberfill, using a chopstick to push the filling tight and hard into small areas, like fingers. After the figure is completely filled, she closes the last open seam.

Now come the details. If the figure's clothes have really large patterns, like wide stripes or big dots, Awatsuji sews them on; otherwise, she attaches them with glue. She uses linen yarn for straight hair, wool yarn for curls. She makes a sketch of the facial shapes she wants and tries them out on the face before cutting the shapes out of cloth and sewing them on.

All photographs in this sequence: Ellen Rixford

*The Pattern.* Knit jersey is stretchy only across the grain, not with it, so patterns must be drawn with this in mind. All fingers and toes should be pointing in approximately the same direction, and if you want to angle the thumb out, compensate by adding a bit of width and subtracting a bit of length. A little diagonal angling is okay, but for a real right-angle bend—for a bent arm or leg, say—the part at right angles to the grain must be much fatter and wider than it would normally look. For faces, the grain should run from forehead to chin, with the nose jutting out perpendicular to grain. Don't cut a realistic human profile, or the fabric's stretchiness will give you a beak instead of a nose—cut nose patterns small and rounded instead.

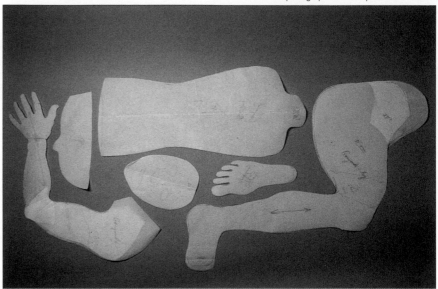

*Patterns for various body parts.*

Sanae Awatsuji's charming and witty "big doll" figures have been shown and published all over the world. Her process of putting together one of her dolls is the most straightforward approach to soft sculpture, and a good place to examine the step-by-step process.

*The completed doll, along with the rest of its family, ready to be photographed for the cover of an automotive safety brochure.*

*The Face.* Most people look at faces more than at the rest of the body, and the face is usually seen as the key to another person's identity, so it is the most important part of an illustration. For this reason, it's the part I do first. In addition, it's encouraging to have that little face looking up at you, an ally and friend for the balance of the creative process.

Start by making a supply of eyeballs. Eyes can be spherical and hemispherical; hemispherical eyes are more easy to glue in than spherical ones, but you will need round balls if your figure has poppy-looking eyes, or if the eyeballs will need to roll around in their sockets. I use wooden beads with fairly small holes; the holes become the pupils. The size of the eyes is an important factor—women and children have proportionally larger eyes than men, and oversized eyes generally look cartoony. For a half-life-sized figure, I usually use ⅝-inch diameter balls; for life-sized pieces, about an inch.

For hemispherical eyes, I cut the beads in half with a coping saw—slower than a jigsaw or a reciprocating saw, but more accurate and less dangerous. If the bead is painted or varnished, I sand it so it will take a second coat of paint, prime it with a fast-drying sandable primer, like white shellac, and then use acrylics to paint the white of the eye, which should be slightly blue-gray, like a real eyeball. I then paint the iris around the pupil, or hole in the bead. A little round template makes this easier—you can make one of acetate, mylar, or stiff paper, or use an architect's template set. Iris colors should not be painted solid—use tiny strokes with thinned-out color radiating from the center.

Now begin sewing the face. Using foam-core or some other soft board, cut an outline of the face shape you want seen from the front. The board should allow a quilting needle to pass through it and should permit you to soften its edge, because when you mount it on the head form, you will not want a hard edge visible through the cloth at the face's edge. In the middle of this face shape, cut a T-shaped hole; this will allow you to do the needle-modeling around the eyes, nose, and mouth.

Cut a pattern for the face's profile, fold your knit in two, wrong side out, lay the pattern along the grain, and faintly trace down the nose seam with a pink or orange (*not* conventional lead) pencil. If you can't tell the wrong side from the right, pull an edge cut at right angles to the grain and see how it curls. The side on which it curls outward should be the outside of the face. This way, when the little cuts at the eyes are made, the edges will curl out, thereby making eyelashes.

Do not cut your fabric close to the seamline before sewing, and allow plenty of extra fabric at the top, bottom, and sides of the face; you will need this later for mounting the face on the head. Using thread as close in color as possible to the fabric and a very fine, tight machine stitch, carefully sew the nose seam with a smooth, accurate line. Don't be afraid to sew very slowly, stop the machine, and turn the fabric by tiny degrees around the curves, especially at the point of and just under the nose (but remember to leave the needle in the fabric when you stop sewing or you will lose your place). This is the most visible and important seam of the whole figure; if there's a slip or a jagged bit in it, discard the piece and try again. Trim the sewn edge to about ⅛ inch from the seam and turn the face right side out.

Now force a little wad of cotton batting tight into the nose bump, stretch your face over the foam-core face shape, and draw lines where you want the eyes and mouth to be. Take the face off the board, cut on these lines, and prepare the eyeballs for setting in. Using a clear, flexible, fabric-friendly glue, make thin lines of glue where the upper and lower lids will rest on the eye. Apply a bit of glue to the inner eyelids and allow it to dry for a moment, so the glue will stick fast but not squish around when you put the eyes in. Then insert the eyes.

*Hemispherical eyes of assorted sizes and colors.*

*At this stage, the face shape has been cut out of foam-core board and the T-shaped hole has been cut into it to allow for needle-modeling around the face.*

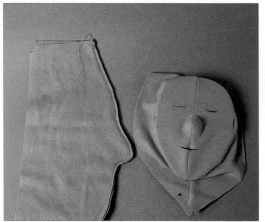

*The facial profile, before and after being stretched over the foam-core face shape.*

*The mouth flaps have been sewn on and pinned under*

Once the eyes have dried a bit, move on to the lips. They are made like a cloth buttonhole: You sew a little rectangle of fabric along the upper and lower edges of the mouth opening with your seam extending just to the corner of the mouth or a few stitches beyond. Your seam should be about ⅛ inch from the edge of the mouth and as parallel to the edge as possible. Fasten your seams at the corners of the mouth and turn the lip flaps under. It helps to put a few pins in there at this stage, to keep the flaps from pulling around. Put a shallow pile of stuffing—I use a fluffed-out mixture of cotton batting and polyester fiberfill—on your face board, make two little wads of cotton batting for nostrils, place them on either side of the big wad in the nose, and lay your cloth face on the board, ready for needle-modeling. Pull the fabric smooth and gently but securely pin it all around the edges of the board, sticking pins horizontally into the foam.

The first needle-modeling I do is generally around the nose. Making sure the wad in the nose is securely in place, choose two points corresponding to the upper edge of the nostrils and two more corresponding to the lower edge, with the lower two slightly indented from the upper. These points should all be spaced a little bit wider than you think you will need them; you will pull them closer to the center later on. Stitch these points back and forth, pushing your needle deep under the stuffing of the face to pull as much stuffing as possible up into the nose. Check that your little wads of stuffing for the nostrils are in place on either side of the nose, and then stitch little half-moons outlining the nostrils. These seams can go all the way around the nostril or can outline part of it, depending on the form you like. Sewing from front to back makes a rather flat nose; going from one side of the nose to the other gives a narrower one. Or you can combine the two.

Unless the mouth is doing something unusual, like blowing a horn, you'll want to take a few stitches at the corners, to pull them in. Pull the stitches straight back, up, and to the outside for a smiling mouth, or down for a frowning one—experiment with various expressions. Stitch in the corners of the eyes; again, you can pull them about a bit if you like. Dimples, crow's feet, and such can be added by stitching where you want indentation and pulling stuffing up where you want a bulge. You can even change the face's outline by adding some stuffing, gluing on a bit of extra board, or cutting some away. Since we're doing a full-round figure, mount the face on a round head shape and proceed to sew it on to the figure's neck.

*The Head.* Using the same pattern you used for the face board, cut out a shape for the front of the head and another for the back, leaving a ¼-inch seam allowance all around. Onto these edges sew a band of knit 1½ to 2½ inches wide, depending on the size of the face. Cut the band with the grain, so it stretches wider. The resulting form should be a thick cylindrical shape. Slash the back and stuff it with a mixture of fluffed-up batting and polyester fiberfill. Don't let the face side of it round out too much, since the face will mount there. Now remove the pins holding the face fabric to the edge of the board and use pliers, a knife, or your fingers to soften the board's edges a little. Pad it out with a little polyester fiberfill. Put the face on the head form and pull the fabric smooth, pinning it in place. Make sure the face fabric covers all areas to be left exposed—the ear area, the neck area, and, if applicable, the bald spot. When you're certain it's right, carefully sew it into place.

If the face bulges out in the center, thread up a long quilting needle with nylon filament, dental floss, or button thread, fasten the thread above where the nape of the neck would be, and push the needle through the head and out the holes in the eye beads (if you haven't used beads, push out at the corners of the eyes). Return the needle to the nape of the neck and pull a little. Do this several times and fasten the thread. We are now ready to turn our attention to the body.

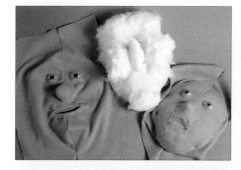

*Putting the stuffing on the backing, and putting on the face.*

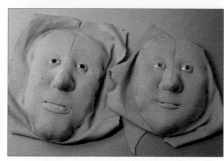

*The nose is finished, and the eyes and mouth are secured to their backing.*

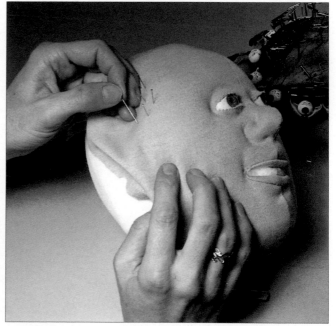

*Attaching the face to the head.*

*The Neck and Torso.* On my jersey sculpture, the head is mounted on the end of the neck and attached by a ring of very fine hand stitching where the cylinder of the neck and the sphere of the head meet. This connection is strengthened by a heavy wire "backbone" inserted up through the neck into the head.

The torso pattern should be laid along the grain of the knit. Sew the fabric with very fine, tight stitches, leaving the bottom part open, and stuff firm and smooth with a mixture of cotton batting (for solidity) and polyester fiberfill (for softness and roundness). If you are making a woman with well-defined breasts, make cloth cones, sew them in, and fill with stuffing. If you plan to show cleavage, make two C-shaped cuts where the lower edge of the breasts would be and add two crescent-shaped pieces of cloth, stuffing the forms full. If your woman is nude, stitch a line under each breast, needle-modeling to define it, and try to stuff the form as full as possible. Using a curved or long, straight needle, sew from front to back, taking care to reinsert the needle *exactly* where it emerged at the back, so that no trace of a stitch appears.

For a belly button, use a real button or a little cotton wad covered with the body fabric, and anchor it in place with a few stitches.

*The Armature.* Unless your figure will be externally supported, it should have some kind of simple armature to make it semirigid and enable it to hold a pose. For a half-life-sized figure, 16-gauge wire is fine; for life-sized work, use 10-gauge. You can also use flexible aluminum armature wire, which can be bent repeatedly without breaking. But unless you plan to bend the limbs back and forth a lot, it isn't worth the expense. In my simple skeleton, the wires of the arms and legs are not attached to anything; they're just pushed into the stuffing of the torso. Bending big U turns into the ends keeps them from slipping out or poking through the skin. Prepare the wire by cutting it to the proper length, putting some white glue along one end of it for a few inches, and wrapping some cloth strips or heavy yarn around it. Proceed down the length of the wire, alternately applying glue and twirling the wire so the wrap is clean and tight. Let the wire dry for an hour or so before using it.

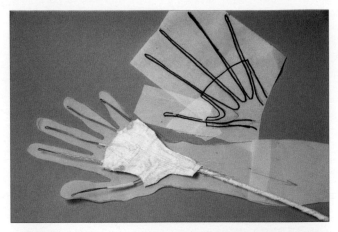

*The pattern and understructure for an armatured hand.*

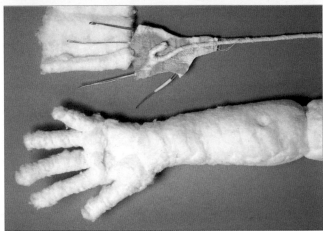

*After the armature is completely wrapped in batting, a fabric "glove" is placed over the hand and arm.*

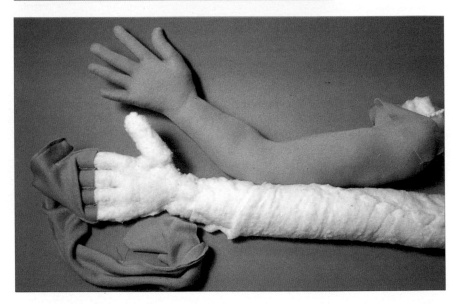

You may want to armature the hands of larger figures, especially if the fingers must bend to hold things. Use 20-gauge wire and sandwich the bottom turns of the finger wires in a palm of thin leather or heavy cloth. Cut two palm pieces for this, and glue them together.

To give the torso a wire backbone, either insert the wire as you stuff, or wait until you are through stuffing and make an opening by burrowing a brush handle, a chopstick, or your fingers into the stuffing. Push the wire into the hole; then cut a tiny hole in the top of the torso at the center of the neck and push the wire out through the hole. Make a cut in the bottom of the head at the center of where the neck will join the head, make an opening for the wire, and shove it in. Now use straight pins to pin the cloth of the neck to the cloth of the head in a neat ring, making sure the shape looks right. Sew this by hand with teensy, precise, invisible stitches.

*Arms and Legs.* Arms and legs are sewn by machine and turned inside out; after sewing, the seams are trimmed to about ⅛ inch. If you armature them, insert your wire first and stuff around it; it's almost impossible to make an opening for wire in a long tubular form after it is stuffed. The hand armatures, if you use them, should be completely padded out with cotton batting for the fingers and palm, with the batting fastened in place by a few stitches. Then the hand glove can be pulled over. If you don't have an armature, just stuff the hand with small wads of cotton batting, using a pushing tool. Little wads give fingers a feeling of boniness and knuckliness. Don't overstuff the palms, or they'll look too puffy; you may want to take a few stitches front to back to help them stay flatter. Insert the armature wire for the arm so that it extends just a little into the hand at the wrist. Stuff around it with the cotton-poly mixture, emphasizing the real form of an arm and using wads for elbows and large muscle groups.

Expressive hands are as difficult to sculpt as faces. If your figure is at least half-life-sized, details like fingernails and skin creases can give hands form and personality. Study the kinds of hands you want to imitate—the gnarled hands of old people, for example, or the plump hands of children. Since modeling in soft sculpture consists of stitching in and stuffing out, look for the places in the hand that crease and bend in, and stitch there. For ease of sewing, combine the indentations and sewn lines so you can push the needle in on one side and have it exit at the other, re-enter where it emerged, and come out again where it started. You can use this back-and-forth motion to sew two lines at once, thereby combining the line defining the bottom of the fingernail and the little palmside crease separating the tip from the middle joint. Beginning at the corner of the fingernail, sew either a straight or slightly curved line until you get to the other corner; you will simultaneously be sewing the crease inside the finger. This done, make the lines on either side of the fingernail, pushing the needle in on one side and pulling it out the other. Use a light touch; if you pull too hard, the fingernails will begin to look like claws.

The ends of the nails are not stitched, except for a large free stitch or two taken from one side to the other, imitating the white end of the nail. If you want long fingernails, cut down a set of artificial nails from the drugstore, paint or polish them, roughen the inner sides with sandpaper, glue them onto your sewn fingernails, and clamp them with padded clothespins.

If the palms are visible, make the other finger creases. Then detail all the creases, puckers, and dimples on the backs of the hands. Sewing back and forth through the finger, sew these creases as you did the first one, but this

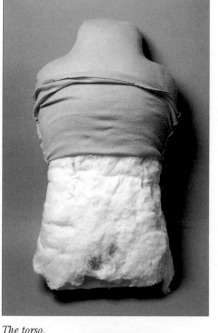

*The torso.*

time your needle will exit at either of two spots on the knuckle to give the indentations. On a young, soft hand, this should be enough. For a pucker, catch up some cloth above and below these indentations, stitch, and pull toward the center. For knobby knuckles, insert beads or batting wads in there and take a stitch or two around them.

The legs, feet, and toes, if they will show, are armatured and stuffed just like the arms and hands. Take care when modeling the knees—more knobby is better than less, since the stuffing tends to relax a bit later—and model the calves and thighs so that the right leg is well differentiated from the left. I keep an anatomy book on hand, just to make sure.

Each foot requires a separate toe piece, which is sewn, stuffed, pulled over the point of the foot like the end of a sock, and sewn neatly in place. If the foot is bare, use invisible stitches. Toenails are done the same as fingernails.

To attach the arms and legs to the torso, start by making room for the armature wires of the limbs in the socket points at the torso. Sew the ends of the arms and legs on. If this joint won't show, the sewing can be rough; if it will, find a line that approximates a natural modeling line or body crease and use that for a very fine seam, stitched as invisibly as possible.

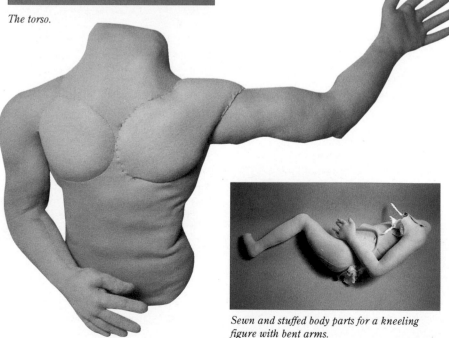

*Sewn and stuffed body parts for a kneeling figure with bent arms.*

ELLEN RIXFORD
Four Happy Athletes, *for an advertisement for*
*athletic shoes. Soft sculpture with real shoes.*
*Approximately life-sized. Although done for*
*Reebok, this photo was shot using different*
*brands of athletic shoes.*
*Client: D.D.B.*
*Needham/Reebok.*
*(Photographer:*
*Ellen Rixford)*

*Hair.* At last, the finishing touch—the hair. If you use a wig, just tack it on firmly at the forehead, back of the head, and ears; if you use loose fibers, like yarn or floss, you have a laborious task ahead of you: Try mounting them in a fringe before sewing them on. Lay them in parallel lines on a thin strip of flesh-colored cloth and brush on a bit of flexible white glue. When this dries, sew the ends down on the cloth with a medium machine stitch. Begin with the lower part of the head, then layer the hair on until you get to the top, tacking it down as you go. When you reach the top area or any of the edges of the hairline, sew it so that the fabric edge of the fringe is turned under, and try using two layers of fringe.

Roving comes in a mass, not loose, so you can fuzz it out with your fingers and just sew it on with small, hidden stitches. Mohair and crêpe hair also come in masses; I sew them directly onto the head.

For curly hair, wind a long strand around the head, fuzzing it out a lot, and allow it to form loops and curls. For long hair, cut the fibers into the appropriate lengths and sew one end of each strip onto the middle and lower areas of the scalp. When you get to the top of the head, cut lengths equal to twice the hair's desired length, drape it over the head, make a fine seam for the part, and

tack the rest down with invisible stitches. If hair will be swept back, hand-stitch a fine seam all around the hairline, letting the hair hang forward; then lift the hair and flip it back over the seam. For a really elaborate Victorian hairdo, or if you want a lot of body in a pompadour or a chignon, insert some stuffing or scrap foam (colored to match the hair, ideally) and tuck the hair around it.

Beards and mustaches are best prepared in advance and glued on. I make mustaches by gluing the hair to a cloth backing, pulling the hair ends at the top around in back, and tucking them in however I can. Sometimes I sew them, sometimes I press them under with an iron and put a touch of glue to keep them from popping up again. Long, luxuriant beards, because there is so much hair, are a lot easier than short, neat beards, which are best done like mustaches, on a cloth backing, with the upper edges turned underneath. A long, curly beard can be sewn onto the face in pretty much the same way curly hair is sewn onto the head, or it can he glued on directly with white glue. For five o'clock shadow and arm and chest hair, using spray glue to attach tiny chopped-up bits of hair works okay for a temporary piece. But the glue will yellow and lose its hold in about a year. A very tiny wipe of white glue is much

more permanent but tricky to control. Forget about hand-sewing hair—you'll be at it for years. I usually go with the white glue, but apply only the tiniest bit, and dust on the hair very slowly and gradually.

*Clothing.* Clothing for realistic soft sculpture figures is made very much like real clothing. Here are some soft sculpture–specific guidelines: First, don't reflexively use children's clothing or shoes for sub-life-sized figures—the proportions are often so different that everything will look awkward. Use fabrics that drape softly and naturally. You can cut corners on some things, like linings and hand hemming (use tiny dabs of white glue instead), but for garments that must appear crisp and fitted, like suit jackets, use interfacing to get a good shape, and attend carefully to details, like sharp edges on lapels and pocket flaps.

Shoes are the hardest and trickiest. Use a soft, somewhat stretchy material to wrap the foot, giving the shoe its shape. Cut the shoe material to resemble the various parts of the upper shoe and sew them together on the machine, like a real shoe's heel seam. Then hand-sew the shoe onto the foot (like side seams), tuck the lower edges in under the foot, and sew or glue them. Cut out a sole—either cardboard with a thicker section for the heel or, even better, wood. Then apply glue all over the sole and glue it to the foot, clamping with lots of rubber bands. Use a very strong permanent glue that will hold wood or cardboard to whatever you're using for the uppers. Clean off any glue residue, so the shoes will not get stained, and let everything dry.

*Details.* The last step is the tinting of the character's face to give the impression of living flesh and the addition of little details, like teeth and eyelashes. If you are unsure of what details to apply or what colors to use, look at the paintings of such wonderful colorists as Frans Hals, Watteau, Fragonard, John Singer Sargent, or Sir Joshua Reynolds. I favor soft coral red for cheeks and lips, gray-blues and -greens for eyelids and razor-stubbly cheeks, and lavender for under eyes, but specific choices depend on the job and on my feelings about the character.

I use only dry pastels, with no oil content, as oil tends to deteriorate fabric. Sometimes I use brushes, rubbing them on the pastel stick; sometimes I rub the pastel on a bit of paper and pick up the color with my finger, smudging it a little first so the color won't be too strong. If you overdo it, you can tone things down with a fresh, clean kneaded eraser, picking up about half the color.

For eyebrows, use the edge of the pastel applied directly, or a colored pencil. Same goes for eyelashes—just draw around the edge of the upper lid. If you want to add false eyelashes, use a light pair from the drugstore; the stickum on the edge of the lash will hold it down pretty well, and you can reinforce the corners with a little extra stickum (included in the package) or a tiny drop of white glue.

If the mouth of your figure is open and stuffing shows behind the lips, take a small piece of cotton jersey and paint or color it darkish pink, like the color of a tongue; I keep a small, "tongue-dyed" piece of jersey for just this purpose. Cut it in a shape like the mouth, only a ¼ inch wider all around; then open the lips and slip it in, settling it in place with tweezers.

Using two- or three-ply bristol board, cut an oval-shaped set of teeth to fit the mouth. Don't forget to attend to details, like cutting indentations between the teeth, spacing the teeth naturally, and coloring in the gums. You can even make the teeth a little crooked if it makes the mouth look more realistic. Finally, slip in the teeth with a pair of tweezers and put in a touch of glue to hold them and the tongue material firmly in place.

Finished!

ELLEN RIXFORD
Happy Hands. *Ten hands dressed in different outfits made of various fabrics treated by Pat-Chem fabric-finishing chemicals. Slightly larger than life-sized. Client: Pat-Chem Co. (Photographer: Ellen Rixford)*

## SOFT SCULPTURE WITH NYLON STOCKING

Although this is the most difficult and time-consuming soft sculpture method, it is also the most interesting, because it captures so completely the look of a real body. Nylon stocking soft sculpture provides precise development of body forms, because the sculptor actually builds them from the "bones" out—the nylon "skin" stretched over the batting "muscles" is just the final, flexible covering to a body that has already been perfectly built up.

Putting such figures together is an exacting, complicated task that few artists have adopted as their specialty. Two exceptions are the late Judith Jampel and Lisa Lichtenfels. Nobody knows exactly how Jampel built her figures—she was reticent about her methods and refused to discuss them in much depth. Lichtenfels, having seen only pictures of Jampel's finished work, created her own technique, adding many improvements along the way. Fortunately, she does not guard her secrets, as Jampel did; here is the sequence she uses to build a human body.

*The Armature and Body.* The first step is building a wire skeleton, which will act as a framework for the body and help to define the form and gesture of the finished figure. Aluminum armature wire is best, as it is strong, light, and easy to bend. Depending on the figure's size and the position of its body, Lichtenfels uses thicknesses varying from ⅜ inch, for the arms, legs, and spinal column of life-sized figures, to ¹⁄₁₆ inch for fingers. For smaller figures, usually 30 to 36 inches tall, she uses ¼-inch wire for the legs and spine, ⅛-inch for arms, and ¹⁄₁₆-inch for fingers.

Arms and legs are stiffened by the inclusion of another wire, which ensure that they bend only at the proper joints. For joining the wires together, Lichtenfels eschews solder in favor of wrapping the connections with thin wires. The armature wires have small retaining loops bent into the ends, so they cannot slip after wrapping.

The skeleton wires are wrapped in yarn, so that the layers of foam and batting "muscle" can be sewn to it (or at least fit snugly without slipping). Foam serves as "flesh" for the deeper layers of life-sized bodies; polyester batting is used for the outer layers of large bodies and for the entire innards of smaller

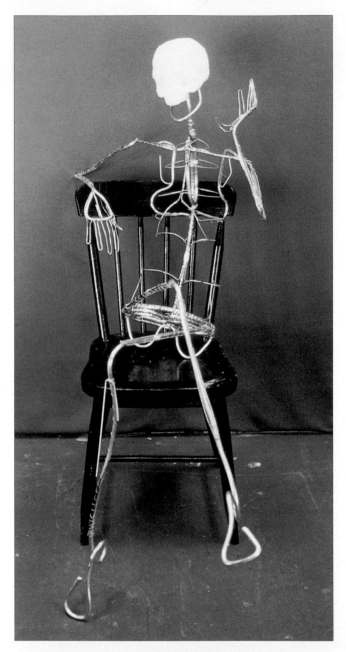

*The aluminum armature, with the Styrofoam skull attached. Note the wire for the lower jaw on the skull.*

*Below: Pinning and sewing the "flesh" to the armature. The inner foam layer is covered with polyester batting, with polyester fiberfill added in spots to soften contours.*

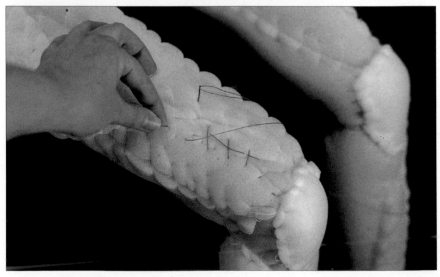

*The basic body structure on the armature.*

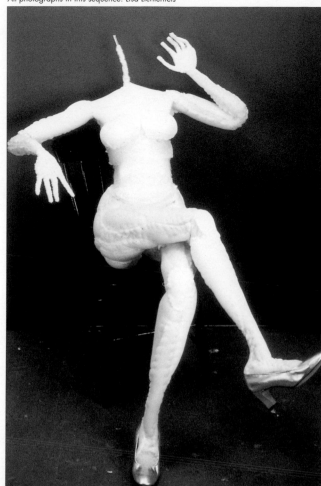

*Below: Fleshy details like breasts are layered and contoured out of additional foam.*

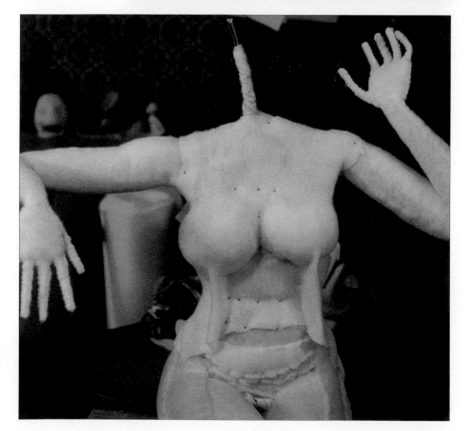

ones. If the piece is meant to last, be sure the foam is durable. Lichtenfels uses upholstery foam, covering it completely with batting sewn on at least ½ inch thick, to protect it from air and light and keep it from showing (any exposed foam eventually turns brownish). For torsos, she sometimes uses armrest foam, as in Bette Midler's body here. You can shave it down to the proper form using any sharp blade; electric carving knives are particularly convenient. Legs, breasts, and buttocks are 2-inch foam layered over and contoured with 1-inch; arms are 1-inch. The general pattern goes like this: thick, heavy foam on the bottom, to fill out the basic body masses; thinner foam for general contours; batting for musculature; and polyester fiberfill to soften muscle contours, conceal the rough texture of the batting and the stitching in it, and give the covering skin—the nylon stocking—a look of evenness, softness, and transparency. The formative layers—foam and batting—are cut, pinned, and sewn, using a curved needle (often called an upholstery needle).

*The Head.* The skull is of Styrofoam, carved generally in the shape of a human skull. It has no nose (this will be made later), but features eye sockets and a heavy wire lower jaw, which is wrapped in yarn, like the armature. The ends of the jaw wire connect to the skull at a joint, which allows the jaw to open and close.

Attaching the jaw to the head and the head to the spinal column is tricky—Styrofoam is crumbly, and just sticking the jaw or spinal column wire into it would result in a weak, wobbly connection. So Lichtenfels hollows out a space where the connection will be and pours in water-based wood putty (oil-based can dissolve Styrofoam). The wire is then shoved into the putty-filled hole, straight pins are pushed around the hole and into the putty while it's wet, and the whole thing is left to harden. After it's hard, the wire is given a quick, hard twist to dislodge it; then it is pulled out, leaving a fitted hole. In the case of the spine, this hole is a temporary connection. The final fitting of head to body takes place after the head is completely finished and ready for permanent attachment, since it's much easier to work on the head when it's separated from the neck.

The head will be built up with polyester batting, just like the body, but first it's useful to make and insert teeth and eyes, as they lend reference points and a sense of scale to the face. Lichtenfels uses materials that mimic these features' wet, shiny look. For eyes, she favors marbles (big "shooters" for life-sized faces, smaller ones for half-life-sized), painted off-white where the white of the eye should be; she models teeth from Sculpey. Both are dipped in polyurethane varnish for a wet look. When they are ready, the upper jaw is carved back to allow room for the teeth to be set in; as the upper teeth are put in place, silicone glue—a jellylike glue that dries to the consistency of rubber—is applied around them.

This silicone glue, available in white and clear, can be modeled and smoothed around the teeth to look like gums. If a tooth breaks after the glue has dried, yank it out and Krazy-Glue a new one into the hole. To make a place for the attachment of the lower teeth, Lichtenfels crisscrosses the whole lower part of the lower jaw with yarn, creating a bed to suspend the teeth as she glues them into place. Gum material (pink nylon) is folded double, folded at the gum line to avoid raw edges, and stitched around the teeth with a beading or pearling needle—a long, thin needle designed for stringing beads. It will slip between the cracks in the teeth. The excess gum material is spread out at the sides to make the inner mouth.

Making the teeth the right size, shape, and proportion and setting them into the jaws in a lifelike pattern are among the most important steps in the creation of the face. Because the teeth must be done first, it is possible that they may not look just right after the head is built. At this point, you have no choice but to rip the face off, right down to the teeth, and start over. Sound awful? It is.

After completion of teeth and gums, two layers of lip material—one pink, one flesh-colored—are sewn on with rough but strong seams, one over the upper teeth, the other under the lower teeth. The pink layer, visible on top as it's sewn on, will later appear underneath the flesh-colored one, as the lip material emerges out of the mouth. It will eventually be sewn to the facial skin around the edge of the lips; for now, push the lip material between the teeth and out of the way, and close the jaws.

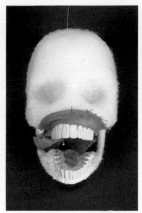

*The Styrofoam skull, covered with a soft layer of polyester batting and housing the completed teeth.*

*Stitching the gum material into the mouth.*

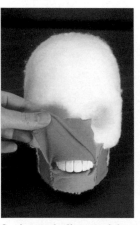

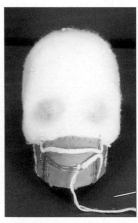

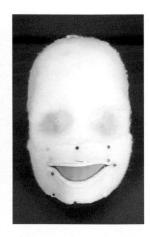

*Sewing on the lip material. Note the two distinct colors for the two lips.*

*Defining the lips.*

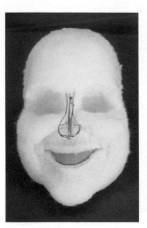

*The nose support.*

*The right eye is set in its socket and wire has been added to define the lids; the actual eyelid material—white nylon for the lower lid and three nylon layers for the upper—has already been added to the left eye.*

*Wire is used to define the eyebrows.*

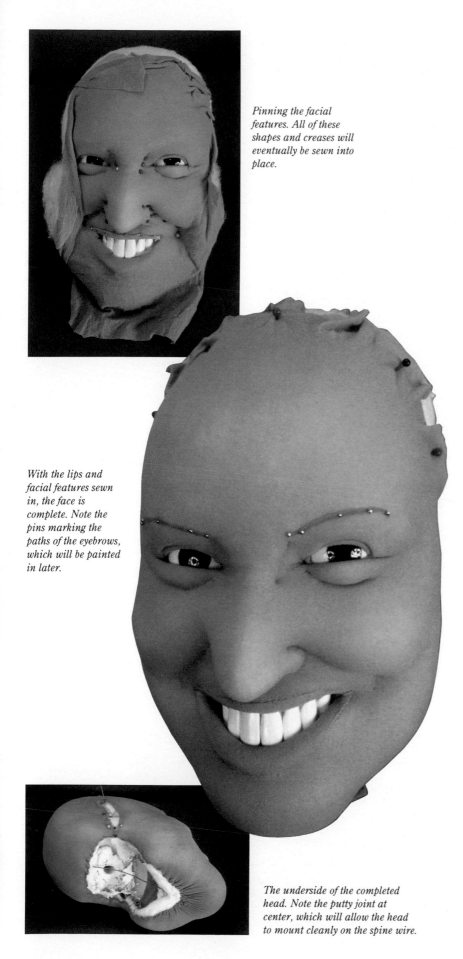

*Pinning the facial features. All of these shapes and creases will eventually be sewn into place.*

*With the lips and facial features sewn in, the face is complete. Note the pins marking the paths of the eyebrows, which will be painted in later.*

*The underside of the completed head. Note the putty joint at center, which will allow the head to mount cleanly on the spine wire.*

For the lips to have their own shape, falling over the teeth, their edges are supported and defined by wires. Lichtenfels prefers copper wire, because it is soft, easily formed, and pink. The ends of the upper lip wire are pushed into the Styrofoam at the lower part of the zygomatic arch; the ends of the lower lip wire are attached to the jaw by wraps of thin wire, just like the connections between the armature wires. The lip supports are wrapped in yarn; then white nylon is stretched over them, pinned, and sewn in place, covering the lip and gum material. Now begins the modeling of the features.

Lichtenfels uses wire for exact or prominent forms, batting for softer, more easily manipulated forms, and polyester fiberfill, which offers no real support or control but covers the wire and batting with a soft, uniform layer. This layer can be needle-modeled together with the nylon skin, giving definition and detail to the large masses.

Jaws, cheeks, chin, and forehead are built up with batting, pinned, and sewn in place until the face takes on the desired contours. Then a support for the nose is made from three wires: The first defines the nostrils; the second, the bulbous tip; and the third, the bridge. Like all the other wires, these are wrapped in yarn and finished with batting, to resemble a well-modeled cotton nose. The ends of the support are then pushed firmly into the skull.

The eyes are set into the sockets, and then wire supports for the eyelids are set into the skull over them. A thin, white layer of nylon is stretched over the lower lid, and three layers—white, pink, and flesh color—are stretched over the upper. Some batting is added around the eyes to contour them.

Next, eyebrow wires are set into the skull. They are unattached at the center, next to the nose, but pierce the skull at their outer corners, where they make a right-angle bend and go right through the Styrofoam until they emerge at the back of the skull. Lichtenfels makes a channel for these wires with a very long quilting needle, and then pushes the wires through from the outer corners of the eyebrows to the back. Here she cuts a small hollow into the Styrofoam, twists the ends of the wires into loops, and secures them in the hollow. The lower jaw is similarly wired, with the wires attached to both sides of the jaw to open and close it.

When the face is complete and all wires and batting structures are in place, it is time to lay on the skin of the outer face. This is done in multiple layers—here there are two, colored pink and tan, but Lichtenfels sometimes uses more—to give an extremely realistic transparent glow to the skin.

The modeling of the eyes begins with a slit cut from one side of the eyeball to the other. Then the nylon is pushed into the flesh around the eye. Contours are pinned and then sewn with very fine clear thread and a curved needle. When the other facial features, including the mouth, have been similarly pinned, the mouth is opened. The lip material anchored inside the mouth is now pulled out, pinned into place, and sewn with the tiniest possible stitches along the lip lines. These same delicate stitches are then used to secure the rest of the features into place, the pins come out, and the face is complete. Eyebrows are simulated and pinned on; they will be painted on later, when makeup is added to the rest of the face. Excess facial skin material is gathered together at the underside of the head, where it will be concealed by the neck.

Now the head is mounted on the neck by inserting the wire of spine into the special joint made for it in the skull. Oil-based putty is put into the hole just prior to insertion, and the excess is smoothed around the joint. When dry, this joint is extremely solid but can be slightly cracked, thereby allowing the head to turn. The neck is built up to join the head.

*The Skin.* The last stage of construction, and arguably the most painstaking, is sewing the nylon stocking skin onto the body. Seam lines are placed where they will be inconspicuous or hidden; usually they follow the natural folds of the body—where the jaw joins the neck, on the underside of the arms, in between fingers, and so on. But the edges are joined by the tiniest, most even stitching possible, and since multiple layers are used, each one must be stitched individually. If a seam is truly hidden from view, it is possible to stitch all the layers together, but the seam looks ragged this way.

*Details.* Ears are shaped with copper wire, like the nose, eyelids and lips were, and similarly wrapped in yarn, covered with layers of nylon (three, in

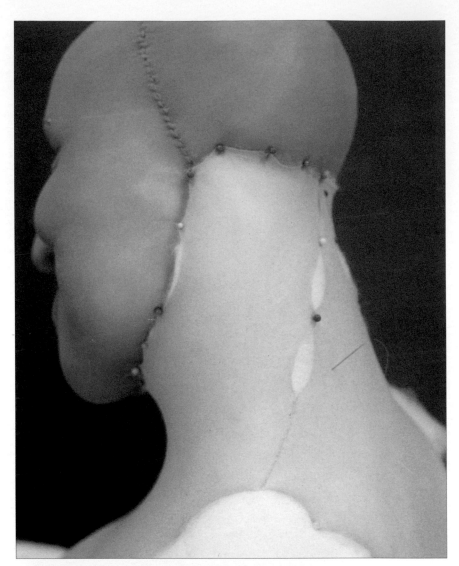

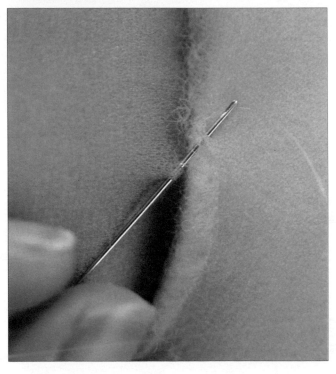

*Above: With the head mounted on the body, the first skin layer is applied.*

*Left: Seams in the skin must be stitched as finely as possible.*

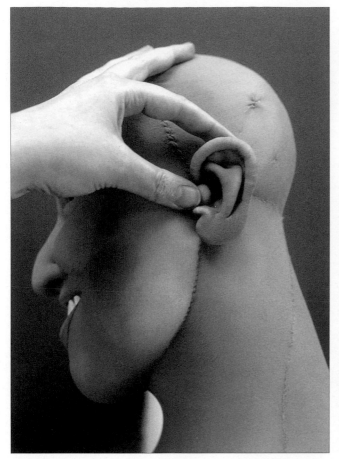

this case), and needle-modeled. Hidden stitches behind the ears attach them to the head, and the connection is hidden by hair. The hair—strands from a wig, or sometimes other fibers, like fine yarn—is either sewn or glued onto the head, depending on how the figure will be handled. If the hair will be pulled, such as if the figure's hairstyle will be changed or manipulated, small bunches of it are silicone-glued onto the head in layers, beginning at the bottom and working toward the top. Long pins are used to push the hair into the puttylike glue to help set the bond. The pins come out after the glue dries, which takes 24 hours. Since each layer is a separate gluing operation, a whole wig done by this method can take several days. If the hairstyle will remain constant, the hair can simply be sewn on, or a complete wig can be silicone-glued to the head at the edges. This takes only an hour or two.

Acrylic paint, applied as dry as possible, is used to color the lips and eyebrows. Dry pastels also work well, but test them for oil content first—oil eventually breaks down nylon, so avoid all oil-based paints and makeup.

*Top left: Adding the ears.*

*Above: Gluing on the hair.*

*Left: After the addition of makeup and hair, the face is complete.*

*The completed figure.*

Lisa Lichtenfels's Bette Midler figure conveniently wears gloves, obviating the need to cover the hands with skin, but not all projects will allow you to skip this task. While the basic method for finishing the hands follows the general principles of covering the rest of the body—place seams where they will be least visible, follow the contours of the anatomy, and so on—the work entails enough detail to merit a closer look.

*All photographs: Lisa Lichtenfels*

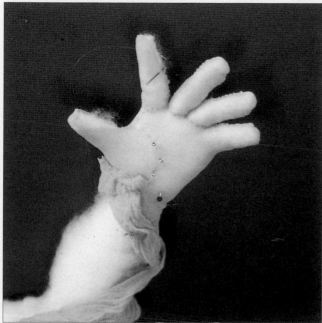

The hand is built of cotton batting and polyester fiberfill over the armature. The first nylon layer—pink—is pinned around the hand; its edges are cut to follow the lines of the palm, the division between palm and fingers, and lines between fingers. This layer is sewn in place with clear thread and tiny seams, and continued down the length of the arm.

A new layer is added and the whole procedure is repeated.

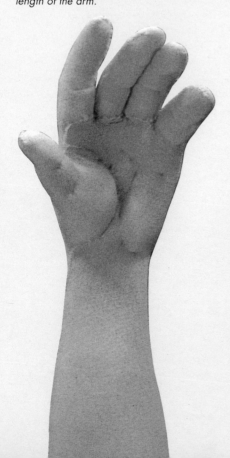

*Lichtenfels frequently leaves the hands without fingernails, as they can sometimes be a visual distraction. If they are important, she either uses fake nails from the drugstore or makes her own by cutting up plastic report binders, sanding the pieces smooth, and curving them with pliers. Then she glues them on, paints them with acrylics, and finishes them with matte or satin varnish.*

This sequence follows the steps taken by costume designer Cathy Lazar in making a series of large, wearable letters for the cable network The Comedy Channel.

Photographs by Cathy Lazar, except as noted.

 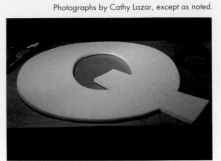

Lazar begins most projects with careful drawings, which are checked by the client. When these are approved, she builds a foam prototype, without any fabric or other covering, to test for proper size, proportion, and fit. If the prototype is satisfactory to her and the client, she proceeds with the final piece, covering it with fabric if appropriate.

Lazar uses brown wrapping paper for patterns, and the usual assortment of drawing tools—ruler, T square, triangle, and extra-large extendable-leg compasses. Laying the pattern on the foam, she draws its outline with a marker, then cuts out the shape with an extendable blade snap knife. Lazar is using 1- to 1¼-inch foam—sufficiently thick to hold the shapes but thin enough to give them a soft sculpture look.

A capital Q has an open bowl, or center; if left open, this would reveal the wearer's body and weaken the letter, so Lazar design, cuts, and mounts in a recessed white shape—essentially the negative-space version of the letter—to fill the gap.

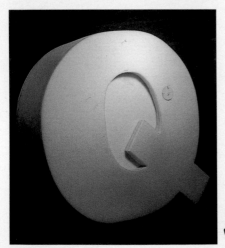 

The sides of the letter are cut deep enough to accommodate the width of its wearer's body. When all the elements have been cut, they are carefully fitted together and glued up with the appropriate contact glue. Holes for the arms, legs, and head are added last.

The finished letters. Note that the P, unlike the Q, is truly open at the bowl, with the wearer's body encased in the letter's stem. (Photographer: Yuri Marder)

## SOFT SCULPTURE WITH FOAM

Foam holds one great advantage over the other materials that can be used for the interior of a soft sculpture: It can be made hollow. You can put almost anything inside a form constructed of this light, flexible material, from a jointed movable puppet armature to a human being. The foam has enough body to hold the form, but it can flex and bend realistically and easily. Foam can be dyed, painted, and covered with any kind of fabric, leather, vinyl, fake fur, or other flexible material; foam puppets are frequently covered with stretch terry or velour, resulting in a slightly furry, cuddly-looking skin. But since velour and other coverings don't necessarily behave like foam does, often a whole new set of patterns must be drafted in order to give the skin a smooth fit.

Since foam is a flat, nonstretch material, it must be cleverly contoured to imitate bodily bulges and indentations. If necessary, foam pieces can be roughly basted together at the edges prior to gluing, to see if they fit properly. Once the glue joint sets, it is extremely permanent, and grows even stronger as time goes by.

All photographs: Brad Williams

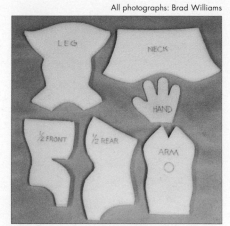

Brad Williams's Mr. Nevo puppet, designed for the National Technical Institute for the Deaf, offers a good contrast to Cathy Lazar's wearable letters, because here the foam shapes must be cut to imitate the form of a human body—a trickier proposition.

The puppet is conceived as a character sketch shown to the client. A full-scale working drawing helps plan out the body proportions and dimensions of the hinged wood-and-leather skeleton under the foam body. The skeleton is made of pine, the joints of leather; grommet joints at the shoulders and elbows allow more range of movement. The ankles have metal bracket joints, and the waist has a metal hinge. The puppet's lower arms are plastic PVC tubes; control rods are simply run through the elbows and fitted into them. A similar set of control rods handles the legs. Using these rods, the puppeteers can control Mr. Nevo's motions. The body is covered with stretch velour, and the head—cast in Celastic from a plasticene mold—is attached, painted, and fitted with eyes.

*Scotfoam body pieces cut from patterns based on earlier test pieces of foam.*

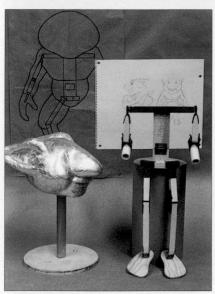

*The foil-covered plasticene head mold, working drawings, and the wooden body skeleton. The drawing in the background is drawn to size and shows the planned skeletal assembly; the one in the foreground is a character sketch that was shown to the client for approval.*

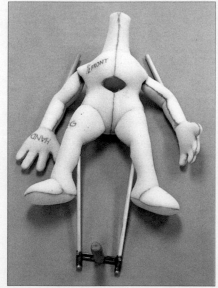

*Foam on the skeleton, with arm and leg control rods attached.*

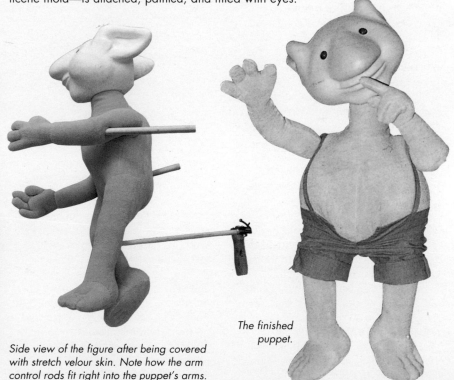

*Side view of the figure after being covered with stretch velour skin. Note how the arm control rods fit right into the puppet's arms.*

*The finished puppet.*

## PICTURES IN FABRIC

Approaches to making pictures in fabric vary by artist. Some illustrators plan their pictures ahead of time and stick to a client-approved layout; others use no drawings, adding pieces of cloth as a painter adds areas of color, and using thread for shading, nuance, and even pattern. As a rule, most clients want a large degree of control and are intolerant of surprises, even beautiful ones, so would-be fabric illustrators should learn to do good, accurate comps, and stick to them.

Sometimes it helps to do several comps showing a variety of potential solutions. Prepare several small sketches for the client to see; when one is chosen by the client, use an opaque projector to enlarge it by 150 to 200 percent (or higher, if you plan to work very large, or if the situation otherwise warrants). This will be your full-scale working drawing.

Sometimes the scale of your chosen fabrics or patterns necessitates working at a larger size. In my *Adam and Eve*, for example, the size of the chintz flowers I wanted to use for the frame fairly mandated a large format; and for my *Peaceable Kingdom* quilt, I planned to use fake fur that wouldn't have looked as good at a small scale. But a large scale means proportionally smaller stitchery in the final reproduction, which can diminish the piece's textural qualities and make it look too much like a painting. And in any event, tight deadlines make large works a rare indulgence.

The working drawing, whatever its size, should give you an accurate pattern to follow as you put together the final. I make one working drawing to use as an all-over pattern for placement of all the elements, and another that I cut up and use as patterns for individual pieces of cloth.

Be careful when choosing the fabric—the color and pattern have an enormous effect on the composition. A slight change in color, pattern scale, or even texture can substantially change the balance of the picture. Sometimes I end up dyeing some cloth to get what I want, or painting sections of the finished composition.

Embroidered lettering is an integral

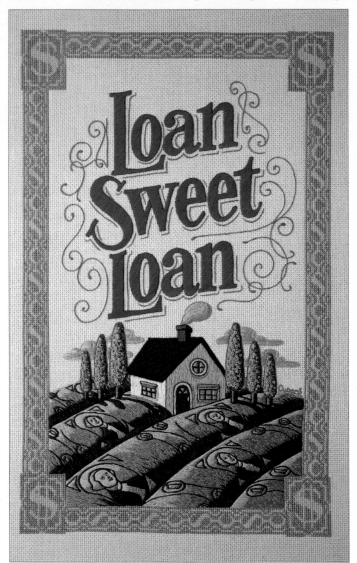

MARGARET CUSACK
Loan Sweet Loan *advertising poster.*
*Embroidery and cross-stitch. Dimensions:*
*24 × 18" (61 × 46 cm). Client: Freddie Mac.*

part of many fabric collage jobs—sometimes simple cross-stitch or satin stitch (the most consistently useful stitch for illustrators), sometimes fancy stitches, like those found in crewel work. These are carefully planned in advance; often the client will even choose a typeface, specify its size, and determine how much space the letters will occupy. Embroidery is a time-consuming and demanding task, especially on highly decorative or very small letters. Traditionally, freehand machine embroidery is done by mounting the fabric in a hoop or frame to hold it taut (flimsy fabrics should be stabilized first with some kind of backing), lowering or covering the feed dogs, setting the stitch length at 0, and using the darning foot or darning spring to keep the fabric pressed close to the plate, so the stitches will catch. You may use no foot at all, but you run the risk of puncturing your fingers. (The most adept machine letterers, Margaret Cusack and Kathy Lengyel, set the stitch length to give a good satin stitch—not at 0—and don't lower or cover the feed dogs or use a hoop. They vary the stitch width to conform to the varying letter widths, and can actually change the direction of the stitching to make the right angles of serifs.)

It is usually easiest to embroider a section before incorporating it into the rest of the piece. After the letters to be embroidered are designed and drawn out on paper, use a lightbox to trace them onto your cloth; if the cloth is opaque, use an opaque projector. You can just outline the letters, or paint them in with the appropriate colors, which fills in any gaps in the stitching. Deka fabric paint is good for this, but it is very permanent, so wash it out right away if you make a mistake. I have used acrylics successfully, too.

For hand embroidering small, slender letters, you can stitch from one side of a stroke to the other. But avoid this if the letter is large or the strokes are wide, or you'll pull the cloth together into a tube shape. Stagger your stitches in the middle while lining them up neatly at the edges of the strokes, and the fabric will stay flat and the satin-stitched area will have a nice, even texture. For traditional sampler stitching—the little x's found on so many Early American embroideries—use a fabric with a pronounced weave to guide you in lining up your stitches. Plain linen, heavier weights of cotton, and Aida and Hardanger cloths work well.

When the pieces are cut out and embroidered, you must fasten them down temporarily. Margaret Cusack stiffens her pieces with spray starch and an industrial fabric treatment before cutting out the final shapes and spray-gluing them together; other artists, like Anne Cook and myself, use iron-on backing, like Pellon, to stiffen flimsy or stretchy fabrics. Because pieces are appliqué-stitched together, leave some allowance at the edge to accommodate the seam; ⅛ inch is sufficient for overlapping edges, but sometimes, for stability, it is good to allow a margin of extra fabric *under* a neighboring piece. If such underlaps involve heavy or thick fabric, pink or fuzz the edges to avoid a visible line. It helps to cut out the larger background pieces first, and then layer the smaller detail pieces on top of them. Some artists use *only* spray glue, which is temporary, and therefore rely on the appliqué stitching to hold the work together. If your pieces are big or will be folded for storage, stay away from glues and from too much stiffening. I baste pieces down or pin them; Deidre Scherer just pins.

When doing the appliqué work, fill your bobbins with the colors you will need—satin stitching uses a lot of thread. You can use the same color as the piece you are stitching on, or vary the colors to create expressive outlines. By varying the thickness of the stitch, you can edge a form with a line, which will give it definition, solidity, or a sense of light playing along its contours. And you can use a satin stitch to draw in details—the weave of a basket, the folds of a dress, the features of a face, and so on.

Your machine will accommodate a small piece, allowing you to stitch pretty much anywhere on it as a unit. If you work very large, do the piece in, say, thirds, finishing one third at a time and then sewing them together. When you're done, add the border, if there is one; it can be a piece of trimming, a hand- or machine-embroidered border, or just a plain binding. Because my fabric pictures are more quilts than anything else, I either bind the edges in a print that complements the whole or do a special border, like the frame of appliquéd flowers for *Adam and Eve* or the embroidered Biblical quote around the edges of *Peaceable Kingdom*.

ELLEN RIXFORD
*Above:* Adam and Eve *appliqué quilt, for magazine sewing project, with pattern and instructions included for readers. Border is cutout flowers from floral patterns; snake is silver lamé. Entirely machine-sewn. Dimensions: 6 × 8′ (1.8 × 2.4 m). Client:* Good Housekeeping *magazine. (Photographer: Ellen Rixford)*

ELLEN RIXFORD
Peaceable Kingdom *appliqué quilt, for magazine sewing project, with pattern and instructions included for readers. Border is embroidered with Biblical quote; animals are mostly fake fur. Entirely machine-sewn. Dimensions: 6 × 7′ (1.8 × 2.1 m). Client:* Good Housekeeping *magazine. (Photographer: Ellen Rixford)*

## STITCHERY FOR TYPE

Kathy Lengyel's embroidery technique is a fine example of machine-stitched letters.

Lengyel begins with a line drawing of the layout, with the type sketched in.

Using a lightbox, Lengyel paces her fabric over the layout and sketches the type onto the fabric with a fabric marker.

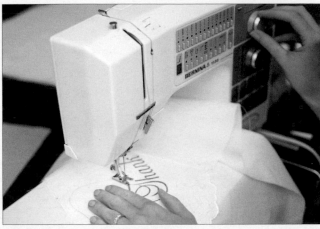

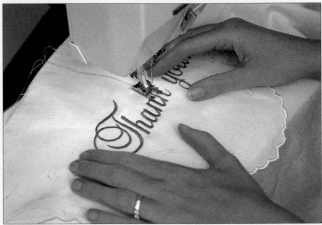

Lengyel begins to stitch in the letters over the marked area. She uses a Bernina 1130 sewing machine, which features adjustable stitch widths and a knee pedal that allows her to make smooth curves without manually raising the foot control.

Lengyel continues stitching, adjusting zigzag widths as she goes. She keeps her original drawing close by to refer to as a guide. When she finishes, she clips all loose threads.

The finished piece, with all elements in place.

Fabric collagist Anne Cook offers an instructive look at appliqué work as she creates this self-promotion piece.

Cook starts with two preliminary drawings—one in color, one in black and white.

Choosing fabrics.

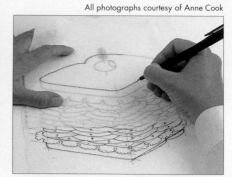

Cook transfers a drawing for each individual piece of fabric to the adhesive side of a Stacy Shape backing sheet.

When the backing is ironed onto the fabric, the design is transferred from one to the other.

After the fabric pieces are cut, Cook gives them a light coating of spray glue.

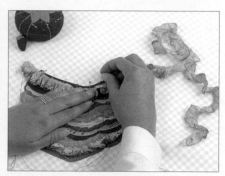

Some pieces must be done by hand. Appliqué stitch colors are changed to fit the color of each piece.

Others are handled on the machine. To make the bread look puffy, a little polyester fiberfill is inserted between the bread-slice fabric and the base fabric.

The finished piece is mounted on Gator board, to keep it flat and smooth.

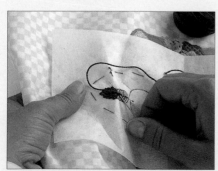

Hand details are drawn on tearaway craft Pellon and attached.

# 6 | METALWORK

For certain effects and certain kinds of jobs, nothing rivals metal. It suggests hardness, weight, and, frequently, value. It is an elegant medium capable of producing beautiful shining surfaces and of reproducing any kind of form, and because of its long history as a sculpture and jewelry material, it suggests wealth. This is particularly true of gold, silver, and bronze, of course; other metals connote other qualities. Iron brings to mind images of weight and strength; rusted iron, age and decay; aluminum, lightness.

Only a few illustrators specialize in metal sculpture, in part because metals are not as "forgiving" as other media—if you make a mistake in a piece of metalwork, you may end up doing it over again. Moreover, the space and tools required are not easy to come by for the average illustrator: Many procedures require a flameproof space; working with relatively thin sheets of metal is possible on a tabletop, but cutting thick, heavy pieces, or machining them into dimensional forms, requires large, heavy, expensive tools; transferring designs or sculptures formed of other materials into metals, by either casting or plating, calls for a professional-quality foundry or plating facility. And in contrast to these large demands the medium places on the illustrator, there is not enough work out there to justify the investment. The best solution is to set up a working relationship with a professional facility that can handle the big technical jobs and advise you on how to prepare for them.

Because the use of metal in dimensional illustration is fairly limited, my purpose here is to offer only a basic understanding of the most important techniques, and to emphasize those used most frequently by illustrators. For more information, metalwork is covered extremely well in many readily available books and publications.

The first use of metals in dimensional illustration was a series of sculpture portraits done for the *London Daily Telegraph* in 1972 by George Giusti, an eminent Swiss-born and Bauhaus-trained designer-sculptor who had pursued metal sculpture casually until

the *Telegraph* series. Giusti soon received several editorial and advertising commissions for metal sculpture in aluminum, brass, and stainless steel, and executed others, mostly in stainless steel, for private collections. Giusti was adequately equipped for small work in light-gauge metal, but he relied on a professional metal shop for fabricating and welding his larger and heavier pieces.

Giusti relied on construction and fabrication for his metal sculptures. Plating made its dimensional illustration debut in 1975, when Stanley Glaubach produced a chrome-plated portrait of Attorney General John Mitchell for a *Time* magazine cover. Glaubach, who had generally worked in paper, wood, and assemblage, constructed a life-sized balsa wood portrait of his subject, adding plastic wood for details and finish, and gave it a real pipe. The piece was then professionally plated to prepare it for the final photo.

The most technically proficient and active dimensional illustrator in metal is Bonnie Rasmussen, who regularly works in ferrous and nonferrous metals. Her repertoire includes fabrication, welding, plasma cutting, casting, plating, repoussé, tooling, and engraving. On the more experimental side of the medium is Takashi Fujita, a designer who has invented a new way of illustrating and designing in metal by embossing lines and shapes onto sheets of aluminum 0.3 to 0.4 millimeters thick to make pictures and letterforms. These aluminum board pieces can also reflect, like distortion mirrors, allowing Fujita to introduce color and pattern into his works.

GEORGE GIUSTI
*Left: Art Directors Club Annual poster. Steel, brass, and clock faces. Height: 14" (36 cm). Client: Art Directors Club of New York. (Photographer: George Giusti)*

JERRY PAVEY
*Above: The Protocol's Bug illustration. Different sizes of nails on leather. Pavey often uses small nails as decorative details in this manner. This illustration shows a ferocious medieval bug devouring the Star of David and excreting anti-Semitic literature. Dimensions: 18 × 24" (46 × 61 cm). Original client: Liberty magazine; later used for a calendar by S&S Graphics. (Photographer: Tom Radcliffe)*

# MATERIALS

Gold is the most expensive and precious metal, but unless you find a client with a whopper of a budget, you won't be using it for fabrication or tooling. It is very good for these, though—extremely malleable and ductile, and its crystalline structure does not change and get harder as the metal is hammered and worked (a phenomenon known as *work hardening*). Gold is yellow in its pure 24-karat state, but can be alloyed with other metals to produce various colors, save money, and add strength—indeed, pure gold is too soft to stand up to much wear. For the illustrator, gold is most likely to be used either as a plating material over a base metal or in its leaf form, where it is adhered to another

material, like paper or carved wood, with a *size* (a sticky varnish). Gold is usually available only through jewelry supply places, but gold leaf is sold at craft suppliers and frequently at sign painter's supply stores as well.

*Silver*, a precious white metal, is not as expensive as gold. It is considerably harder and stronger than gold but is malleable and ductile; it does work harden, however, and will tarnish and oxidize, so it requires polishing and sealing with varnish or wax. Silver can be machined, tooled, cast, and plated, and is commonly joined with silver "solder." It is very commonly used in jewelry, as well as in flatware and expensive eating and drinking vessels,

usually as *sterling silver*, which is 92 percent pure (the remaining percentage is usually copper). The illustrator is most likely to use silver as a plating material, or as silver leaf, which, unlike its gold counterpart, must be varnished after application to protect against tarnishing. Like gold, silver is bought at jeweler's supply stores, and silver leaf is a craft or signpainter's supply item.

*Copper* is a base metal, pink to reddish brown and quite malleable and ductile. It work hardens, oxidizes, and tarnishes to many different colors—purplish, bluish, reddish, and brown—and can weather to a nice green patina (which can also be chemically induced). It can be machined, tooled, forged, cast, and plated, and is commonly joined with soft lead- and tin-based solder, silver braise, or copper-phosphorous braise. Copper sheets in various thicknesses are readily available in small quantities at scrap metal dealers, who are likely to have copper wire, rod, and tubing as well. Plumbing and electrical supply sections in large hardware stores have ready-made copper parts, which are nice for assemblages. Avoid copper rivets and nails from hardware stores—they're usually plated. Instead, go to a marine supply place, which should stock the solid copper varieties.

*Aluminum*, a silver-white base metal, is extremely lightweight, and ductile in its pure form. Aluminum can be joined by welding, and is used in many different alloys with sharply differing properties—some can be machined, cast, spun, or hand-worked, while others cannot. Aluminum does not tarnish or oxidize readily, and is very difficult to plate, but it can be *anodized*—a process of forming a very hard and durable aluminum oxide coating that can be dyed various colors. This method is used in making nameplates, signs, and jewelry. Scrap dealers have aluminum in sheets of various thicknesses, as well as in rod, tube, and wire form; some craft

FIFTY CENTS MAY 21, 1973

TIME

THE INQUEST BEGINS

John Mitchell

STANLEY GLAUBACH
John Mitchell: The Inquest Begins, *for a magazine cover story on Mitchell's part in the Watergate scandal. Chrome-plated balsa and plastic wood. Life-sized. Client:* Time *magazine. Copyright © 1973 Time Inc., reprinted by permission.*

stores carry various diameters of aluminum tubing. Large regular metal supply stores also carry aluminum (as well as all base metals), but they usually have minimum-purchase requirements that are unworkable for illustrators. Several thicknesses of dead soft aluminum wire are sold at sculpture suppliers as armature wire. And of course, aluminum can also be found at the grocery store, as soft drink cans and as foil, which can be cut with strong scissors or tinsnips. Large hardware stores often sell aluminum nails and sheet aluminum, although there isn't much variety, and the sheets are too thick to tool easily.

*Tin* is an inexpensive silvery-white base metal. It has a low melting temperature, and is frequently used in alloys and plating. One of the more important of these alloys is pewter, which is about 91 percent tin, 7 percent lead, and 3 percent copper. "Tin" cans are really steel cans plated with tin, which prevents rust or oxidation on the steel. Tin is very soft, malleable, and ductile, and can be worked with the same tools used on copper and the softer grades of aluminum. It is not easily available, however, so you'll probably find it easier to choose other metals.

Pure *iron* is silver-white, malleable, and ductile, but is rare to find it in this form. It most often appears as an alloy, frequently with carbon. Among the most common ferro-alloys, *mild steel* has a low carbon content and can therefore be easily worked and welded. It does not heat-treat and harden, and therefore can be worked a long time without becoming brittle. It is used most often for blacksmithing (the iron is called "black" metal because of the black oxide coating that forms when it is heated). *Corten steel*, another ferro-alloy, forms a smooth, pecan-colored protective rust coating upon exposure to air, and is used by some sculptors. Sculptors and illustrators often work with *stainless steel*, especially the "food-grade" or "300 series" type, which has a bright silver color, works more easily than other kinds of stainless, and has a high corrosion resistance. Unlike other base metals and alloys, stainless steel cannot be cut with an oxyacetylene torch, but, like all ferro-alloys, yields easily to a plasma torch. It can be joined by welding, and can be plated with other metals. It is available at scrap metal dealers and metal supply shops.

*Brass* is an alloy of copper and zinc. The proportion, which can vary, is typically 70 percent copper to 30 percent zinc, but yellow brass is 65–35, and red brass is 85–15. Brass is durable, ductile, and malleable, and varies in color from lemon yellow to amber to reddish yellow. Yellow brass is the most commonly used alloy. Brass is stronger and harder than copper, and can be cast, welded, braised, and plated with other metals. Other metals can be plated with brass, too. Brass is available through regular metal suppliers, at scrap metal dealers (which tend to stock sheet metal, wire, and sometimes tubing), and in some hobby stores (which sell tubing in round, square, and rectangular varieties).

*Bronze* is an alloy of copper and tin, and sometimes includes zinc. Again, alloy proportions vary, but the most common is about 88 percent copper, 10 percent tin, and 2 percent zinc. *Commercial bronze* is 90 percent copper and 10 percent zinc. Bronze is extremely durable and casts beautifully, making it the premier metal for statuary and commemorative plaques. It is fairly hard, making it somewhat difficult to work by hand. Bronze can be plated both with and onto other metals. It is available from scrap metal places and metal suppliers.

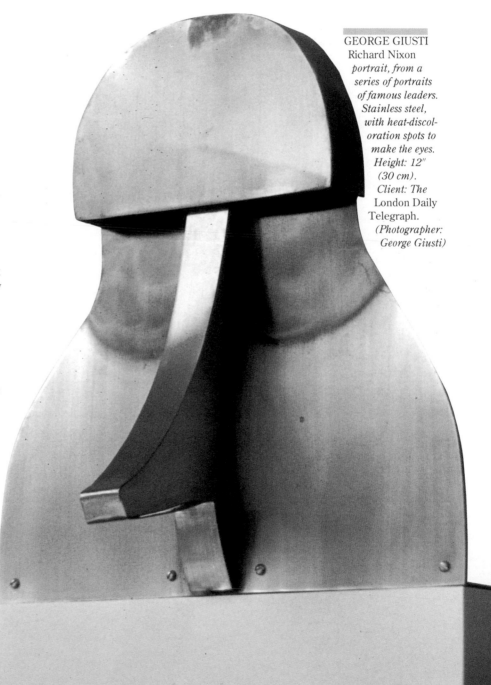

GEORGE GIUSTI
Richard Nixon
*portrait, from a series of portraits of famous leaders. Stainless steel, with heat-discoloration spots to make the eyes. Height: 12"
(30 cm).
Client: The* London Daily Telegraph.
*(Photographer: George Giusti)*

# TOOLS AND TECHNIQUES

Metalworking techniques are widely varied and tend to require their own special tools, so we'll discuss tools and equipment as we examine each working technique.

### METAL LEAF
This ancient craft is relatively simple to perform. The biggest problem involves learning to handle the super-thin sheets without them crumbling or blowing away. Gold leaf is usually available at art and craft stores, or at signpainter's supply places. Besides the standard 23-karat gold leaf, which never tarnishes, there is 12-karat, which is white and looks like silver, and several grades in between. The much cheaper imitation gold leaf, a mixture of brass and zinc, will tarnish, but can be okay if varnished

for protection. There is also patent leaf, which is lightly adhered to a tissue backing for easier handling, glass leaf, for use on glass surfaces, and double leaf, which is about 50 percent thicker than the others. Gold and silver leaf are the most common varieties, but leaf is also made in copper, bronze, and aluminum.

Metal leaf work is fairly easy to do on a tabletop with the following equipment: size, or adhesive, a varnishlike substance that is painted on the surface to be gilded and comes in both slow- and fast-dry varieties; a gilder's tip or a flat camel's hair static brush, for applying the leaf; and some soft cotton swabs to burnish on the leaf. Any surface can be gilded if it is clean, dust- and grease-free, and either nonporous or sealed.

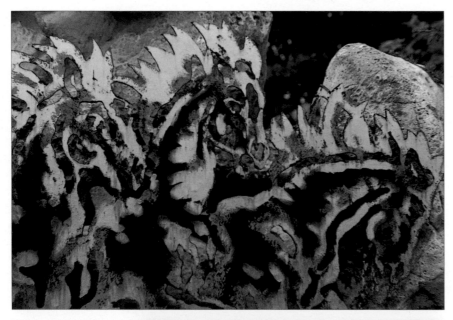

Start by preparing your surface. Apply the size; when it is ready, give your brush a little static holding power by rubbing it on a sweater or your hair, and then pick up a piece of leaf with it and hold it against your sized area, pushing it into any depressions. If it tears, you can add bits to fill the gaps; if it wrinkles, smooth out the area with your cotton, which will flatten irregularities and shine up the metal. Gold and aluminum leaf need no further protection, but you may want to varnish leaf in other metals to keep them from tarnishing. Or, if you like, you can let them tarnish just a bit, for an antique look, and then varnish them.

### PLATING
This really should be called *electroplating*, because it is done using an electric current traveling through a water-based solution of metal salts from an anode (a positive terminal, made of the metal you want to apply) to a cathode (a negative terminal, made of the object you want to apply it to). Almost any metal except aluminum can be plated. To plate an object with an alloy, such as brass, the chemical bath should include compounds of both metals—copper and zinc—and often there will be separate anodes for each metal. In some cases, as in bronze plating, the anode is just copper, because bronze anodes don't dissolve well at high currents. The tin is supplied by tin salts dissolved in the plating bath —otherwise, you are plating copper, not bronze. It is also possible to plate nonmetal objects (bronzed baby shoes are the classic example), although demand for this type of work has decreased.

The object to be plated is first sealed with a spray coat of varnish or lacquer. Then a coat of conductive paint is applied, so that when the object is hooked up to the cathode in the electroplating bath, it will attract ions of the plating metal.

One commonly misunderstood plating process is *chrome plating*. The really shiny finish of, say, a "chrome" bumper is not actually chrome, but bright nickel, a compound of nickel and carbon-based brighteners. Plating

BONNIE RASMUSSEN
Wildhorse Spring Farm
*sign, for a housing development near St. Louis. Plasma-cut mild steel, finished with gold leaf and paint. Thickness: ¼" (6 mm); width: 8' (2.4 m); height: 4' (1.2 m). Client: The Larimore family. (Photographer: Daniel T. Magidson)*
*Above: Detail of the sign shown at right. (Photographer: Bonnie Rasmussen)*

suppliers carry a wide variety of these materials, which smooth out irregularities on the plated object by selectively laying down metal deposits in surface depressions, rather than on the high spots. The result is a nice, polished effect.

## BRIGHT DIPS
These chemical baths work like an acid etch on the metal, selectively removing metal from high points and bringing the surface down to a smooth, shiny finish. Some platers do bright dipping, or you can buy your own solutions at plating supply places.

Plating and dipping require chemical baths, tanks, and sometimes racks, which must be covered in nonreactive plastic so they won't be affected by the baths. Plating requires electrical current as well. Plating in particular takes a fair amount of space, so if you have access to a professional plating facility, you may prefer to use it.

## ANODIZING
Aluminum is next to impossible to plate, but it can be coated with a thin, tough oxide layer that can be dyed. This is done by attaching the aluminum piece to the anode (rather than to the cathode, as would be the case with plating) in an aqueous electrolytic bath. The most common solution is sulfuric acid, which produces porous, durable coatings, and is the basis for most of the decorative coloring on anodized aluminum.

To dye the oxide film, use a nonreactive tank to make a dyebath of between 0.025 and 1 percent ordinary dyestuff in 150° F water. Immerse the piece for about 10 minutes, and then seal it in a hot water bath. The temperature during the dyeing should be constant, and the bath should be agitated constantly. Since some dyes won't work in the presence of the sulfate ions in the anodizing bath, either rinse the anodized aluminum before dyeing it, or bathe it in a neutralizing solution of sodium bicarbonate.

## PATINATION
Patinas build up on metal naturally as a result of chemical reactions, but many artists want to control a patina's color and location. Patinas can be applied by dipping, swabbing, painting, or spraying on various chemicals; numerous references offer patination recipes. One traditional chemical for gold, silver, and

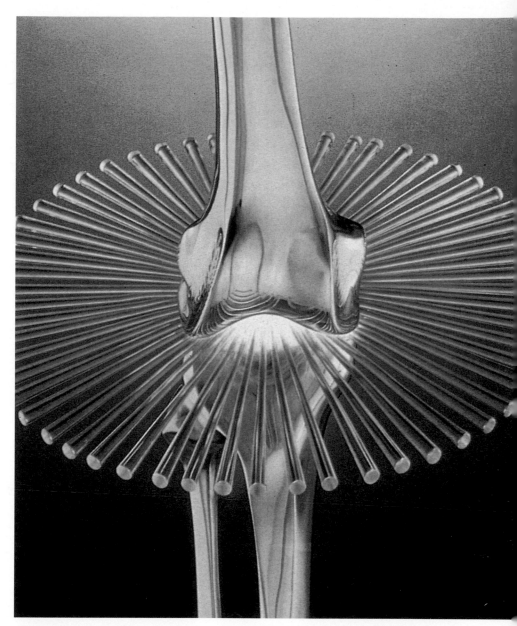

LOU BORY
The Aura of Arthritic Pain, *for a medical advertisement. Cast and polished bronze bone with rolled-glass rods. Dimensions: 20 × 20 × 20″ (51 × 51 × 51 cm). Client: Wyeth Laboratories. (Photographer: Chris Collins)*

copper is liver of sulfur; the oxygen and sulfur create oxides and sulfides on the metal's surface, which produces the coloring. Another fast, effective chemical is a tellurium compound—an oxidizer for silver that works well on copper and its alloys.

Heat can induce lovely patinas as well—this is how George Giusti did the eyes for his *Richard Nixon*. Under intense heat applied by a torch, steel can color up to yellow bronze tones, purples, or blues; copper will turn yellow, red, violet, and then brown. The effects can be unpredictable, so always experiment on scrap until you are sure of how to get the effect you're after.

## METAL CASTING
Foundry casting has been in use for many centuries all over the world, and is clearly described and illustrated in several books oriented to the gallery and museum artist. An excellent reference is *Sculpture Casting*, by Dennis Kowal and Dona Meilach (Crown, 1972). Since illustrators will probably not find themselves casting their own pieces, a description of how to prepare a piece to send to a foundry for casting will be sufficient for our purposes.

**GEORGE GIUSTI**
*Right:* Mick Jagger *portrait, from a series of portraits of famous leaders. Painted brass. Height: 12" (30 cm). Client:* The London Daily Telegraph. *(Photographer: George Giusti)*

**McCONNELL & BOROW**
*Opposite page:* Absolut Intelligence *print advertisement. Electron microscope photo of a computer chip blown up and altered. The artwork was brass-etched, plated, and assembled. Bottle size: 18" (46 cm). Client: TBWA Advertising and Carillon Importers. (Photographer: Steve Bronstein)*

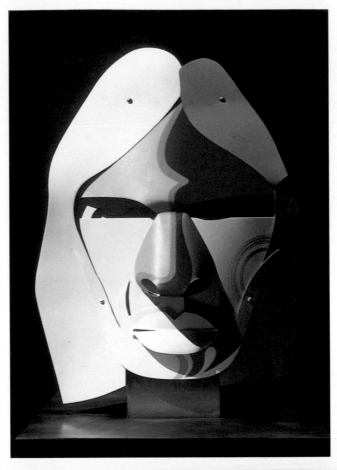

**GEORGE GIUSTI**
Arts in USA *poster illustration. Discolored steel and brass. Height: 14" (36 cm). Client: The United States government. (Photographer: George Giusti)*

Choose a good, reliable foundry—perhaps a local art school—and ask for permission to watch the process. The final piece will be in wax, since "lost wax" casting is done by making a hard mold around a wax model, then burning the wax completely out of the cavity, and then filling the cavity with molten metal (partially for a hollow cast, or completely for a solid cast). But the illustrator can often provide the foundry or client who is arranging the cast with no more than a good clean model in any medium. The foundry will often make its own wax cast of your model and go from there. I know of illustrators who produced models in plasticene and in Hydrocal, had them cast in wax and then in metal, and came out with excellent results.

**TOOLED METAL RELIEF**
*Repoussé* is relief done in metal by hammering on the metal's reverse side. It is second cousin to *chasing*, which is ornamenting by engraving or embossing, and the two are often used in conjunction with each other. These techniques are used in making decorative eating and drinking vessels, armor, lamps, wall plaques, and architectural decoration, and can be done in gold, silver, copper, aluminum, brass, and steel. The thickness of the metal can vary from $\frac{1}{120}$ to $\frac{1}{16}$ inch, with some preparatory annealing required for the harder metals. As the metals (except gold) are hammered, they will work harden, and will thus be able to withstand daily wear and tear. Because metal decorated by these methods is usually fairly substantial, it is tooled with special metalworking equipment: ball peen and planishing hammers, anvils, stakes, and engraving and stamping tools. The demonstration of Japanese designer Takashi Fujita's method on page 136, however, shows that for very thin metal, a simple approach can work just as well.

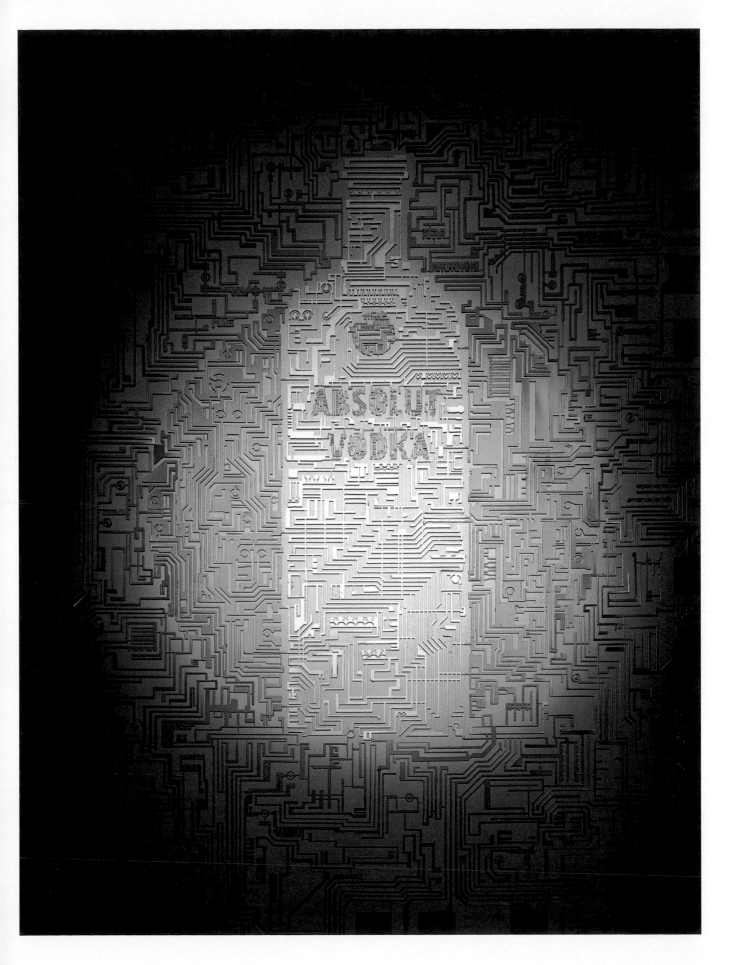

## REPOUSSÉ

Takashi Fujita's repoussé method requires none of the special tools usually associated with repoussé. You need a steady table, a layer of newspapers about half an inch thick, any appropriate household objects to make lines and/or depressions when pushed into the metal (Fujita uses various sizes of pens), and such graphic design aids as rulers, compasses, triangles, and a T square. The best metals for this operation are 0.03-millimeter-thick aluminum for delicate detail, and 0.04 for heavier shapes or simple strong lines.

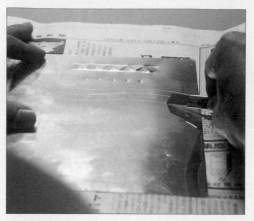

Placing his sheet of aluminum on a newspaper cushion, Fujita traces and lays out the first elements of the design with an out-of-ink ballpoint pen. Next, he uses a knife to make thin scoring lines, which are later bent up to form curves.

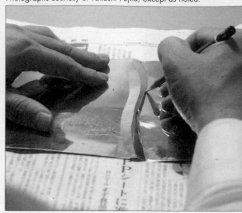

Here Fujita creates a convex area by pressing up from the back. A concave area could be made by pressing from the front.

TAKASHI FUJITA
Bee and Beetle *peace poster. Aluminum board. Dimensions: 29 × 40" (73 cm × 1 m). Depending on the lighting angle, insects can look peaceful, as they do here, or violent, so proper lighting is crucial to the piece. Client: JAGDA. (Art director and designer: Takashi Fujita; photographer: Katsumasa Saito.)*

TAKASHI FUJITA
Chitose Ame *peace poster. Aluminum board. This is an expansion of the traditional paper bag containing "1,000-year candy," which is traditionally given to Japanese children on their third, fifth, and seventh birthdays. The children take the candy to a temple, where they pray for a happy future and a long and prosperous life. The various animals and vegetation symbolize these goals. Dimensions: 31 × 40" (78 cm × 1 m). Client: JAGDA. (Art director and designer: Takashi Fujita; photographer: Katsumasa Saito)*

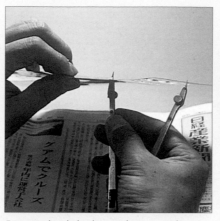

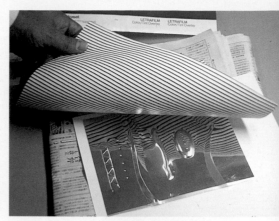

Using a pencil to emphasize form. After using the round end of a fat pen to make the oval shape at center, Fujita outlines it on the reverse side with a ballpoint pen tip, which puffs up the line a bit.

Fujita makes little dots and points with a compass tip. There is always the risk that the point will scratch or puncture the metal, so this work must be done delicately.

Aluminum relief showing reflections of pattern and color, used to take photographs of designs.

TAKASHI FUJITA
*Above:* Metal Man *book cover design. Aluminum board. Dimensions: 31 × 40"* (78 cm × 1 m). *(Art director and designer: Takashi Fujita; photographer: Katsumasa Saito)*

TAKASHI FUJITA
*Rex Gallery poster. Aluminum board with reflected grid pattern. This piece shows another fine example of Fujita's style. Dimensions: 31 × 40" (78 cm × 1 m). Client: Rex Gallery. (Art director and designer: Takashi Fujita; photographer: Tomosada Ukegawa)*

## FABRICATION

Fabrication refers to a variety of metal operations, the first of which is *cutting*. Very thin sheets of metal, called foils, can be cut with ordinary scissors or X-Acto knives; for harder or thicker metals, metal cutting tools are necessary. Some sheet metals, like copper and aluminum, are fairly easy to cut; but the same thickness of stainless steel, for example, is not. Thin metal sheets thicker than foil but thinner than the heavy stocks that require saws, can be cut with tin snips. Regular straight snips are okay, but can leave a bent edge on metal, so snips are also made in right- and left-angled curves for greater cutting ease and a finer edge.

Thin sheets of metals can be softened, or *annealed*, by playing a torch over their surface, or even by holding them over a stove-top flame. Nonferrous metals can be annealed by heating them just to the point at which their color begins to change, and then letting them oxidize, tarnish, and cool down. Cooling can either be natural or by quenching in water.

Steel can be annealed, but it should not be overheated—just play a torch on it until it dulls and changes color. You can polish it up again or bright-dip it later. Do not cool steel in water, as this tends to harden it. Not all grades of stainless behave the same way when annealed, so fool around with some scraps first to determine how your metal responds to this treatment.

*Tempering* is a process in which a metal, usually steel, is heated and quenched in cold water until it is extremely hard and brittle, then softened by annealing it to exactly the desired flexibility. Blue tempered steel, used for watch and clock springs, is treated this way—after reaching extreme hardness, it is heated until it turns blue, making it just flexible enough to be curved into a spring.

Thicker or harder metals require a saw, sometimes in combination with a milling machine. The harder the metal, the cleaner it cuts on the saw blade; for softer metals, the blade is beeswaxed for smoother cutting. Different metals are cut at different speeds. An 18-foot (5.5-meter) bandsaw blade, for instance, might cut brass at 600 feet (183 meters) per minute, and aluminum at 1,000 feet (305 meters) per minute. Steel, although it is hard, can be cut at up to 4,000 feet (1,219 meters) per minute by *friction cutting*, in which an old, dull blade is

JERRY PAVEY
Promise *illustration, for 1990 self-promotional calendar, additionally sponsored by S. D. Warren Paper Co. and S&S Graphics, Inc. Brass, copper, and tin sheets. Dimensions: 18 × 18" (46 × 46 cm).*
*(Photographer: Tom Radcliffe)*

used to carry tiny bits of air into the cut, oxidizing and consuming the metal. Another tactic for hard metals is using an abrasive saw, which grinds its way through the metal.

*Milling machines* give precise edges to shapes that have already been cut. Their speeds can be adjusted to the metal, and their cutters are usually made to handle anything from soft metals up to hardened steel.

Metal is also cut with and *oxy-acetylene torch*, which is a combined jet of oxygen and acetylene gases, giving a much hotter flame than a simple propane torch. Depending on the torch's size, it will be able to cut through very thick plate—several inches for the really big industrial models. Torches don't give as clean a cut as a blade, but are very useful in the following situations:

❑ When a shape is very intricate and involves a lot of cutting

❑ When a shape is too big to get onto a bandsaw or maneuver with a reciprocating saw

❑ When a piece needs to be done in place, and can't be moved to a saw

❑ When a piece has a lot of L-, T-, or E-shaped angle cuts

The newer and more expensive *plasma torch* is even better. It throws an arc, like a tiny lightning bolt, between the end of the torch and the metal. This, combined with pressurized air, melts and oxidizes the cutting surface. A plasma torch is faster, cleaner, easier to control, and hotter than other torches, and leaves a cleaner edge to boot.

Most sheet metals can be *mechanically joined*, or *cold-joined*, by bolts, screws, and nails, and can be bent at angles so one edge of the sheet overlaps and grips another. Pieces that don't need much joint strength can even be epoxied.

*Hot joining* is done when you don't want to mar the surface with screw or bolt heads, or when you must join a flat piece with something else—a rod, say—that doesn't have enough room for a screw or bolt hole. One such method is *soft soldering*, which can be done with an ordinary soldering iron (or, for more heat, a torch) and works like a glue bond—the solder, after being melted, flows into the joints between two pieces of metal and seals them together. It works fine on copper, brass, and steel, but not on aluminum, which builds up a solder-repellent coating when heated.

Soft soldering requires flux, which

ELLEN RIXFORD
Tree of Life Menorah *magazine illustration, for readers to build at home. Sheet copper, wood, beads, wire, and other materials. Copper leaves were braised onto copper wire stems with an oxy-propane torch; their colors were achieved by controlled heat "tarnishing." Height: 18″ (46 cm). Client:* McCall's *magazine. (Photographer: Ellen Rixford)*

helps the solder flow. There are two kinds: rosin and zinc chloride. The zinc chloride works better, and is necessary to get a good bond with steel, but it is very corrosive and tends to rust all the iron in a workspace. Rosin is okay for copper and brass, and is usually used for wiring connections, because it won't corrode the wires.

Soft solder works at temperatures ranging from 450 to 600° F. Above this temperature, silver or *hard solder* works between 1,145 and 1,650° F. Technically, anything done above 800° F is considered to be *braising*. Silver soldering, or, more accurately, silver braising, works on silver, copper, brass, bronze, and

steel. Again, there are two kinds of flux: fluoride (more corrosive) and borax (less effective, but safer).

The best way to get a strong joint with either soldering or braising is to have as much surface-to-surface connection as possible, and to make sure the surfaces fit together very closely. Consult handbooks to learn more about the specifics of each operation. A good metal supplier or welding supplier should have what you need.

Cast iron and steel are usually joined by *welding*, an electric process that involves melting the two pieces to be joined. The major types of welding are as follows:

❑ *Spot welding* heats up spots on a joint by putting a strong electrical current through them. The current runs through two tongs, which can be positioned on either side of the proper spot.

❑ *Arc welding*, the cheapest and most common kind, uses a flux-coated rod on the weld area. The flux coating melts more slowly than the metal rod inside, leaving a little hollow at the end of the rod that directs the metal into the weld.

❏ *Tungsten inert gas welding* uses a tungsten electrode and a variety of inert gases (argon and helium are typical). The gas flows over the weld spot and prevents oxides from forming. Weld rod, if desired, is fed into the weld by hand.

❏ *Metal inert gas welding* also pipes inert gas over the weld, but has an automatic wire-weld feed through the nozzle. It is the most expensive unit, but is easy to use and produces beautiful, clean welds.

Welding can be used on any metal, but it is not usually done on highly conductive metals, like copper or its alloys, because the electricity gets conducted away from the weld spot before it can heat up properly. Welding is ideal for iron and steel; stainless steel spot-welds beautifully, and gives very clean welds with both of the inert gas methods.

All hot joining equipment can be purchased through welding suppliers, who can give helpful advice about what to buy and use. They also carry safety equipment, which is very important when executing any of these operations. In addition to the obvious possibility of severe burns and fires, welding torches emit ultraviolet radiation, and the more corrosive flux materials are hard on the lungs. In addition, never wear contact lenses when welding, as the radiation can literally glue them to your eyes. Because of these and other dangers, seek out someone with plenty of experience before trying any of these techniques on your own.

While many metalworking tasks can be done in an ordinary studio, jobs involving kilns, furnaces, and torches require fireproofing; the bigger and hotter the rig, the more fireproof the space should be. Small, hand-held torches can be used in the home or studio, providing you enclose your work area with a flameproof material, like firebrick. In no case allow *any* flammable material—including paint thinners, acetone, or any solvents—anywhere near the work space. These should be kept in solid metal cabinets far away from the job, or in another room. Even papers can suddenly catch fire, as can clothing and hair, so keep hair pulled back or wear a hat, and don't wear clothing with loose ends or flaps that can fall into the work. Have fire extinguishers handy, and keep a first aid kit.

## FABRICATION

Here we follow Bonnie Rasmussen through a logo sign job that entails various processes with several commonly used nonferrous metals. The job gives us a look into the sort of well-equipped metalworking shop you might expect to find if you cooperated on a metalworking project. In this case, Rasmussen used the facilities of the Wm. Plumpe Engineering Co. The client was The Tin Man Press, of Starwood, Washington. They wanted a business sign for permanent exterior use.

The horizontal design for the sign is adapted from an original vertical design. The shiny "face," its "hat," and the letters are placed on a dark background. The basic drawing is enlarged on a copy machine, and then a finished working drawing is laid out in preparation for fabrication.

The pieces of the sign are prepared for cutting. Basic shapes and letters are cut out of paper and hot-waxed to stick to the copper, with black paint applied to the edges as a stencil to show the outlines clearly. Rasmussen intends to tin-plate the shapes later, so she chooses ⅛-inch copper, because it is relatively easy to machine and to plate.

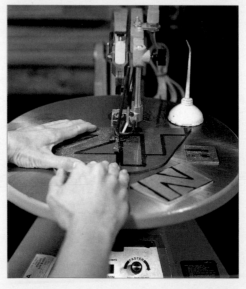

First the basic shapes are cut out, leaving some allowance around the edges, on a Delta 18-inch scroll saw with a metal cutting blade (shown). A hand-held Bosch sabre saw, also fitted with a metal cutting blade, is used as well. Oil is used to lubricate the cut. Since copper, a relatively soft metal, tends to gum up in the blade, beeswax is used on the blade to keep it from clogging.

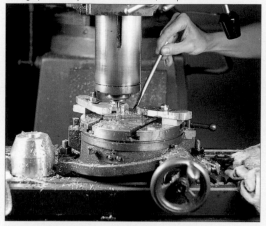

The blanks are put on a milling machine for very precise cutting. A small rotary table is bolted to the bed of the machine, allowing easy access to the angles of the letters. The mill bed moves vertically and in four horizontal directions, all with great precision—settings are measured in thousandths of an inch. The cutter is held in a chuck in the spindle, and is lowered onto the work by a hand lever.

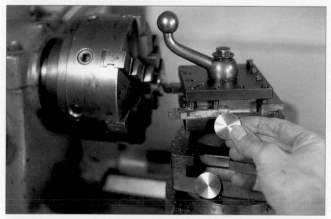

The "eyes" for the Tin Man are made on a Southbend lathe, which trims down brass bar stock to a 1⅛-inch diameter and a ⅛-inch thickness. The radial pattern marks are left on the discs because they make the eyes appear to flash and rotate. Brass is used because it is available, is compatible with copper, and can be gold-plated. The very sharp milled edges of the letters and sign parts are filed. To ready them for plating, the parts are cleaned in a vapor degreaser vat, since metal must be chemically clean to assure an even plating layer. Letters with tricky curves—P, R, and S—had to be formed by hand on a grinder/sander and then hand-filed to shape.

Lapping, or surface polishing, the letters on a Delta belt sander using a 400 grit belt. Rasmussen clamps an extra flat plate on the sander so the letters won't slip down between the belt and the table. The letters are then pressed flat on the sanding belt. Because they get hot fast, it's necessary to cool them periodically in water. Some additional lapping is done by hand on a hard, flat surface.

After the sign parts and letters are glued together with rubber cement and register marks are added to guide in the drilling of rivet holes, Rasmussen chooses three graduated sizes of rivets, all to be tin-plated, to assemble the sign. Here, the mill is used for drilling the rivet holes. Note the final S, which has already been plated as a test. Four hidden mounting holes—under the face corners and under the large N and S—are drilled and tapped in the large backing piece of the sign. The rubber cement is cut with oil and trichlorethane, the pieces are disassembled, and the rivet holes are deburred. Then the pieces are cleaned.

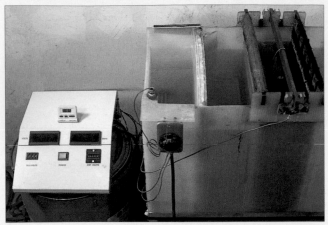

In order to texturally distinguish the face and hat from the letters, Rasmussen subjects the face and hat to a sand-blasted barrage of glass beads, a process known as peening. Here, the sandblasting cabinet door has been left open to show the metal object being placed inside.

Plating the letters and shapes. From left to right are the timer and electric control panel; a tank section with caustic hot cleaner and a control dial; a tank section containing water; the tin-plating solution; and, extending out of the shot, the first of four water washes.

Flathead copper machine screws are silver-soldered to the rear side of the eye discs for invisible mounting to the face. The eye discs are held on an aluminum centering pocket turned on the lathe, ensuring that their centers will align. An oxy-acetylene torch is used to melt the solder, and fluoride flux is used to help it flow.

After making the mouth part, Rasmussen again silver-solders flathead machine screws, this time with the aid of a bridge assembly, to the rear of the mouth so it can be mounted on the face. The mouth piece is held in a vise for this operation, so that the torch can be used freely without the force of the flame moving anything around. The eyes and mouth are then cleaned, degreased, and gold-plated.

The background part of the sign is treated with an "antique black" conversion finish. This patina, which works fast and is extremely durable, is applied with a sprayer. The piece is then rinsed and quick-dried with compressed air.

The mahogany backboard shape is cut, textured, and sealed with a clear finish. Shallow clearance holes are drilled into the wood to clear the rivet backs on the rear of the metal sign. The rivets are snipped about ³/₁₆ inch from the back of the sign and hammered down. The back of the sign is shown here in front of the wooden backboard, with the hammered rivets and mounting holes clearly visible.

The finished parts, ready to be assembled. The metal sign is mounted onto the backboard by four Allen screws; the holes for them, as described earlier, are under the face, the N, and the S.

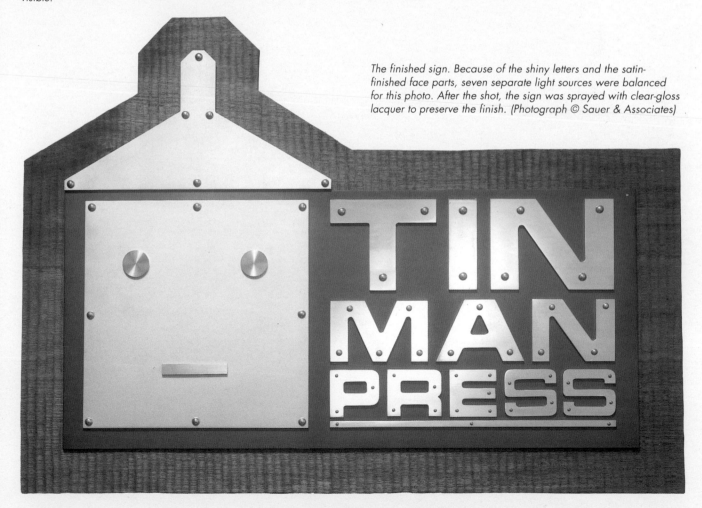

The finished sign. Because of the shiny letters and the satin-finished face parts, seven separate light sources were balanced for this photo. After the shot, the sign was sprayed with clear-gloss lacquer to preserve the finish. (Photograph © Sauer & Associates)

# 7 | FOOD SCULPTURE

**E**dible sculpture is one of the most charming and delightful areas of dimensional illustration. It is an impermanent medium—few food sculptures last much beyond the photo stage—but no less expressive than all the others. Feasting is a holiday experience, and holidays are the occasion for most edible dimensional illustrations. For the most part they are based on fantasy and folktales, and the best of them are witty and magical.

Except for the very occasional assemblage of fruits and vegetables, or perhaps a produce shot illustrating a nutrition article, food sculpture is primarily a matter of baked goods: gingerbread architecture, cakes that look like baskets of flowers, and the like all have long traditions, especially around Christmas. It is out of this tradition that the current market for these pieces comes. Every November and December, women's magazines, particularly *Good Housekeeping*, publish pictures with how-to-do-it directions for gingerbread projects: cathedrals, palaces, dream mansions, crèches. And celebrants planning the party of a lifetime commission cakes that their partygoers are guaranteed never to forget.

The queen of gingerbread architecture and mise-en-scène is Olive Alpert, who began a long business relationship with *Good Housekeeping* in 1980, when the magazine's art director saw one of her pieces and asked her to do a cover in gingerbread. This was the *Covered Bridge*, published in the December 1980 issue.

Rosemary Cheris Littman began as a designer and printmaker. Her cake business began when neighbors noticed the beautiful cakes she made for her children and asked if she could make some for sale. Applying her knowledge of letterforms and art training to her cake projects, she became more ambitious and imaginative, and her client list now reads like a who's who of

society: Paul Newman, Elizabeth Taylor, Muhammad Ali, Andy Warhol, Phil Donahue, and Donald Trump, to name just a few.

While bread dough sculpture is not, strictly speaking, something you'd want to eat, and while its composition makes it more long-lived than gingerbread cookies and cake, it is much more in the tradition of baked dough than anything else. Its childlike, innocent look makes it suitable for fantasy and holiday subjects, as well as for illustrations aimed toward the children's market.

For Brenda Pepper, a children's fashion illustrator whose clients included nearly all the large department stores in New York City, bread dough began as a hobby. Making intricate Christmas decorations with it gave her so much pleasure that she began to wonder if it could find a market as illustration. This was in the 1970s, when dimensional illustration was making many new inroads, so Pepper felt encouraged to build a bread dough portfolio and try her luck. It was a success, and she soon added several publishers to her client list.

Robert Crowther works primarily as a designer and paper engineer of pop-up books. But he has also designed and made several edible biscuit illustrations, which attracted national attention because of their scope, size, and attention to detail. Depictions of Buckingham Palace and the Houses of Parliament are among his standout works.

ELLEN RIXFORD
*Left:* Edible Fairy Castle and Landscape *do-it-yourself Christmas gingerbread project. Honeycake, cookies, pink icing, etc. Approximate width: 30" (76 cm). Client:* Good Housekeeping *magazine. (Photographer: Charles Gold)*

ELLEN RIXFORD
*Above:* Vegetable Man *illustration, for an article on healthful eating. Plastic vegetables and fruits, real beans. Height: 45" (1.1 m). Client:* Quest *magazine. (Photographer: Ellen Rixford)*

# MATERIALS AND TOOLS

The materials list for food sculpture is mostly short and sweet. Almost all of it should already be in your kitchen, and anything that isn't there will probably be in the local supermarket and housewares store. Better still, there is only one piece of equipment: a pastry bag.

## BAKING SUPPLIES
The baking supplies listed on the next page are easy to find. The candies seem to get more plentiful after mid-October, thanks to Halloween and Christmas.

This timing is less than ideal for the gingerbread architect, as most magazines' production schedules require that food sculptures be finished by mid-summer. If you will be doing projects involving a lot of candy, stock up when the stores are full and store the candy in tin boxes, where it won't attract mice or bugs. Or you can go to a candy specialty store, where they will have lots of colors and shapes (this is about visual appeal, remember, not taste).

For cakes, you may want to use a shiny glaze to give a translucent appearance. Jams and jellies work all right for this, but a stiffer, more controllable substance is piping gel. Precolored tubes are available in many supermarkets, and cake decorating stores stock a clear version, so you can mix your own color.

## BAKING TOOLS
Baking tools can be divided into three categories, related to the following three project stages: preparing the doughs and icing, baking the pieces, and

ROSEMARY CHERIS LITTMAN
Bottle of Wine. *Cake icing, piping gel for shiny surface, reinforced with wooden dowels. Height: 30" (76 cm); diameter: 7" (18 cm). Private collection. (Photographer: Rosemary Cheris Littman)*

decorating. The depth of the equipment you'll need will vary widely according to your specialty. If you do more gingerbread work than decorated cakes, for example, you may need fewer icing tips for your pastry bags and more cookie sheets, and cake decorators will need a greater variety of cake pan shapes than gingerbread bakers will. But the basic equipment list is generally the same. Most of these tools are easily obtainable from housewares stores or even your local supermarket; the items in the cake decorating supplies list are available through cake decorating suppliers and specialty restaurant supply stores.

ROSEMARY CHERIS LITTMAN
Chair *illustration, for furniture showroom brochure. Cake, icing. Width: 12" (30 cm). (Photographer: Rosemary Cheris Littman)*

OLIVE ALPERT
Cottage on the Moors *magazine illustration, for do-it-yourself baking project. Gingerbread, icing, shredded-wheat thatched roof. Dimensions: 10 × 6 × 16" (25 × 15 × 41 cm). Client:* Good Housekeeping *magazine. (Photographer: Victor Scocozza)*

## BAKING SUPPLIES

Sugar—plain granulated cane sugar for baking, confectioner's or powdered for icing and frostings
Flour—bleached white has the greatest tensile and compressive strength and best ductile properties
Butter
Hydrogenated vegetable shortening, like Crisco
Cream cheese
Sour cream
Baking soda
Baking powder
Cream of tartar
Spices for gingerbread—powdered ginger, cinnamon, cloves, allspice
Salt
Molasses
Honey
Vanilla extract
Chocolate morsels
Nuts of any kind
Candies of any and every shape, color, and size, such as peppermint sticks and drops, gumdrops, chicken corn, licorice sticks and shoelaces, gold and silver dragées (tiny shiny balls), cinnamon red-hots, nut brittles, Jordan almonds, and colored sprinkles

## BAKING TOOLS

Mixing bowls—a few large ones and a few small ones
Plastic bowls with covers
Small plastic containers
A wide, flat (no sides) cookie sheet—14 by 17 inches
Cake pans—round, square, and rectangular
Measuring spoons
A Pyrex measuring cup—the 2-cup size is best
Wooden mixing spoons
A rubber spatula
An artist's palette knife
Aluminum foil
Wax paper
Any heavy paper, like oaktag, for making gingerbread patterns
A rolling pin
Wooden dowels, for rolling out gingerbread dough and curling patterns
Sandpaper and/or a wood rasp, for shaping and smoothing gingerbread
A small hand mixer (or, if you do a fair amount of food sculpture, an electric mixer)

## CAKE DECORATING TOOLS

A candy thermometer
Food color pastes—for rich, intense colors unachievable with supermarket colors
Pastry bags
Couplers—small plastic nozzles that fit into the pointed end of the bag and hold the tips
Tips—Rosemary Cheris Littman recommends the following:
- Plain round tip Nos. 2, 3, and 4, for writing, squiggly lines, curly hair and little round dots
- Petal tip Nos. 121 and 122, for primrose-like flowers
- Rose tip No. 127 for smaller roses, and No. 127D for larger ones
- Leaf tip Nos. 112 and 113, for little flowers and leaves
- Small star tip No. 65, for borders, stars, and basketweaving
- Smile tip No. 80, so named because of its flattened U shape, for flowers
- Drop flower tip Nos. 224 and 225, for flowers
- Basketweave tip Nos. 47 and 48, for textural basketweaving
- Shell tip Nos. 17 and 98, similar to the basketweave tip

OLIVE ALPERT
Snow Goose *magazine illustration, for Christmas baking project. Shaped gingerbread, royal icing, candies. Dimensions: 9 × 9 × 9" (23 × 23 × 23 cm). Client:* Good Housekeeping *magazine. (Photographer: Victor Scocozza)*

# WORKING PROCESSES

## GINGERBREAD SCULPTURE

You are more likely to have baked gingerbread before than to have, say, worked with molds and casts, so you may have your own experience to fall back on. Here are some general tips, however: Since you are primarily interested in structural strength, not taste, go with a hard, dense gingerbread that will bake into nice, flat slabs. The dough should be refrigerated for about two hours before use, so it won't get too soft and sticky. For largish pieces, or pieces that must fit together, roll the dough directly on the cookie sheet and cut the patterns right on the sheet. Gingerbread should be baked until it is golden brown and springs back against a light touch.

While most gingerbread designs are built with flat pieces baked on a cookie sheet, gingerbread can also be baked on a form. Any three-dimensional form is possible—hemispheres, cylinders, curves, double curves—as long as it is supported in some way when baking. When it comes out of the oven, it will hold the form. Flat pieces should cool a bit on the cookie sheet and then be transferred to a wire rack; formed pieces should cool completely on the mold.

Before starting, figure out which pieces should be decorated with icing before being "glued" together with icing. Royal icing works well as a glue, but only if applied very thick; put it on thick where it won't show, like on the inner seams, and then use a damp cloth to clean off any excess showing on the outer seams. If you need to support something as it dries, use anything solid and heavy—cans, jars, books—and then reinforce it with more icing. Of course, projects that won't be eaten can be additionally reinforced with cardboard interior supports and a dollop of hot glue, which can help a lot if you must transport the piece a fair distance to a photo studio.

Royal icing is strong enough to make filigree or latticework structures all by itself. Make a drawing of what you want with clear black lines, and cover it with a sheet of wax paper. The drawing, which should show through the wax paper, can be laid flat or over a curved form, as long as the icing is supported enough so that it won't slip off. Following the pattern of the drawing, pipe icing over the wax paper. After giving it a full 48 hours to dry, slide the wax paper off any supporting form (or carefully lift it off the table, if you're working flat), remove the drawing, and peel the wax paper off the back of the hardened icing. Pipe more icing on the back, both for reinforcement and for appearance, and let dry again. Then position the icing structure wherever you want it on your sculpture.

## GINGERBREAD SCULPTURE

Here are the recipes, step-by-step directions, and drawings for the construction of Olive Alpert's *Snow Goose*, a sculptured gingerbread project that originally appeared in the December 1984 issue of *Good Housekeeping* magazine.

### ROYAL ICING

| | |
|---|---|
| 1½ | pounds confectioner's sugar |
| 4–5 | egg whites at room temperature |
| ¾ | teaspoon cream of tartar |
| ¾ | teaspoon vanilla extract (only if the gingerbread sculpture will be eaten) |

Put all ingredients in a bowl. Beat with an electric mixer, beginning at slow speed and gradually increasing speed over the course of 5 minutes while scraping down the sides of the bowl with a spatula. Beat at high speed for about 8 minutes, or until stiff peaks have formed. Color the icing with food color pastes, adding only a few drops at a time until the desired color is achieved. Cover with a damp cloth or transfer to covered plastic containers. Yield: about 4½ cups.

### GINGERBREAD DOUGH

| | |
|---|---|
| 6 | cups all-purpose flour |
| 1¾ | cups sugar |
| ⅔ | cup solid vegetable shortening, such as Crisco |
| 1 | tablespoon ground cinnamon |
| 1 | tablespoon ground ginger |
| 2 | teaspoons double-acting baking powder |
| 1¼ | teaspoons salt |
| 1 | teaspoon baking soda |
| 1 | teaspoon vanilla extract |
| 18 | ounces sour cream |
| 2 | eggs |

Put 3½ cups flour and all other ingredients in a large mixing bowl. Mix well with an electric mixer at low speed, and then knead in the remaining flour to make a soft dough. Refrigerate for 2 hours. Use about half a batch at a time for rolling out gingerbread shapes.

*For making the wings and tail:* Enlarge the wing and tail patterns (see next page), trace them onto oaktag or heavy paper, and cut them out. Cut two extra sets of paper wings and one extra set of paper tail pieces—these will be used to make molds to shape the gingerbread. Make molds for the right and left wings by curling the wings with your fingers, curving in where the wings point to at front and out at back. The feathers at the wing tips should curve out. Check to make sure the upper and lower wing pieces fit together—there should be no big gaps between them. The tail pieces curve a little too. The large tail will fit on the outside of the body; the small tailpiece will attach to the inside of the body and to the large tail piece. Make molds for tails.

Cover all these shapes with aluminum foil, and then grease and flour the foil. Roll out the gingerbread dough to a ⅛-inch thickness on a floured pastry board or cutting board, putting ⅛-inch dowels at either side of the dough to keep the thickness even. Using the patterns as your guide, cut out the dough shapes for the wing and tail pieces and place them on their molds, putting wads of crumpled aluminum foil under the areas that must be curled or lifted up to support them while the dough is baking. Bake at 350°F for

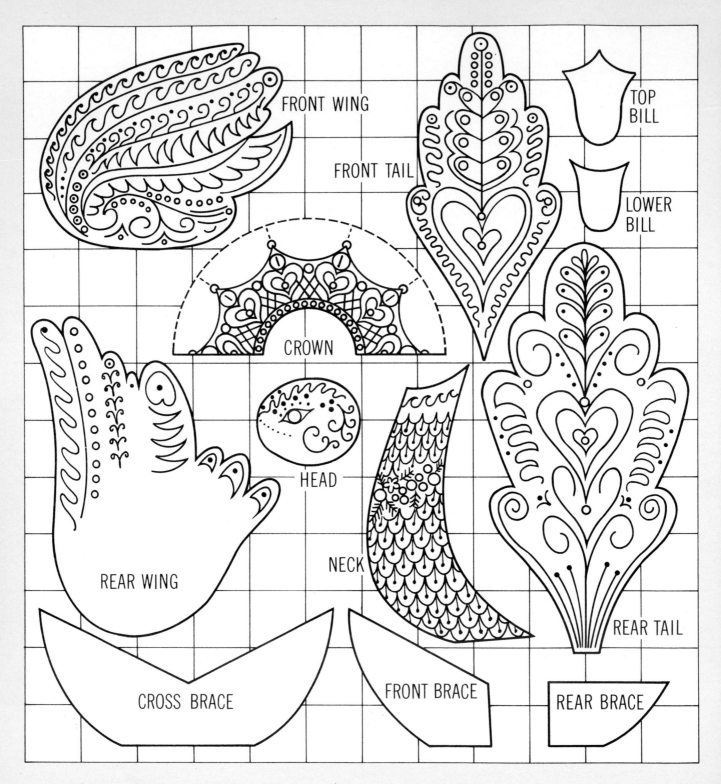

FRONT WING

FRONT TAIL

TOP BILL

LOWER BILL

CROWN

HEAD

REAR WING

NECK

REAR TAIL

CROSS BRACE

FRONT BRACE

REAR BRACE

*Patterns for making the Snow Goose. Scale: one square = 1 inch.*

15 to 18 minutes, or until very firm to the touch and light brown. Cool supported by the foil.

*For making the body:* The dough must be ³/₁₆ inch thick, so roll it between two ³/₁₆-inch dowels. Use the body pattern to cut the dough for the body shape—a circle big enough to fit over a 5-inch stainless steel bowl. Grease and flour the bowl, and drape the dough over it without stretching. You can cut the excess—it will be a sort of triangular notch—out of the front and back, since these will be covered by the tail and the neck. Seal the edges very well as you cut away the excess. Bake at 350°F for 18 to 20 minutes, or until firm and light brown. Cool partially—about 15 minutes—loosen the gingerbread from the bowl, and let it cool completely. Then free it from the bowl, but don't take the bowl out of the "body" form until you are ready to assemble the whole goose. It is fragile.

*For making the head and neck:* The dough must be half an inch thick, so use two ½-inch dowels when rolling it on a greased and floured cookie sheet. Lay the head and neck patterns (dusted with flour) on the dough and cut out the right and left sides (flop the patterns for opposite sides). Leave at least ½ inch between pieces, as they may spread while baking. Pat the edges of the head shapes to make a half-egg shape, and pat the upper and outside-front edges of the neck to make a smooth half-round shape. Leave the bottom-rear edge of the neck alone—it will match to body. Bake these at 350°F for 20 to 23 minutes, or until firm, and cool.

*For making the body braces and the bill:* Roll the dough to ⅛ inch thick, using the ⅛-inch dowels, on a greased and floured cookie sheet, and cut out the appropriate shapes. The braces will be baked flat, but the bill pieces will need a mold: For the top and bottom bill pieces, fold the pattern down the middle and flatten the front edge. Cover with foil, grease and flour, and drape the dough over the molds. Pinch the dough of the upper bill a little to look like a real duck bill, and slip a little wad of crumpled aluminum foil under the raised areas of the bill shapes. Bake the bill shapes and braces at 350°F for 15 to 18 minutes.

*Assembly:* For the head and wings, spread icing thickly on the insides of the neck and head pieces and sandwich them together. Clean up the seam with a damp cloth and let dry overnight. Then sand or rasp any bumps, and shape a bit so the head is a smooth egg and the neck is a graceful curve.

For the wings, sand or rasp the forward half of the lower wing piece so that it fits close to the body, with the outer section standing away from the body a little. Shave away a little of the outer forward edge too, so the upper wing piece will fit closer to the lower piece. Shave the inside of the upper wing to fit the lower wing. The upper piece attaches about 1 inch in front of the lower wing on the body. Follow the picture of the finished piece (see page 148) for positioning.

The outer tail attaches to the outside of the body; the inner tail fits inside the body. Rasp down or sand any rough spots for a close fit.

For the braces, first check for fit; then, using a pastry bag and a No. 3 tip, ice the bottom edge of the large brace and place it firmly inside the body, so that it bisects the inner body area and runs straight across the middle. Let it dry. Then ice the forward and rear braces and place them perpendicular to the middle brace. Let dry, and then reinforce all seams with piped icing on both sides of the braces.

*Decorating the pieces:* For the wing and tail pieces, use a No. 2 tip to pipe a line of icing all around the edges. Do the fronts and backs, letting each dry well. Using a parchment paper cone or a brush, "paint" the wings and tails with thinned-out icing to make a flat even color. For the back of the wings, you need only do the half of the wing that stands out from the body—the half closest to the wing tip. Don't ice any area that will be "glued" to something else. Let both sides of all pieces dry well. Paint the outside and inside of the body, the braces, and all edges, and let dry. Attach the head to the neck with thick icing, clean the seam, and support firmly until set. Let dry.

Ice the head and neck with thinned icing, except for where the back of the neck meets the body. Let dry. Check the fit of the neck to the body. If you like, you can cut a little notch in the neck, so

it will hook onto the body. Ice the seam thickly, press into place, clean the seam, and support while drying. Ice the two halves of bill together, and then attach the bill to head; support while drying. Paint the bill with pink icing.

Use a No. 1 tip to decorate the wings and tails with decorative lines, following the pattern diagrams and the photo of the finished piece. Again, do not decorate where pieces will be glued together. Beginning ½ inch down from the neck seam, pipe "feathers" onto the neck, using a No. 2 tip for the scallop shapes and a No. 1 for the line and dot inside. Use the No. 2 tip to reinforce the neck/head seam with a piped line of icing, and pipe decorative scrolls on the head and neck. Use cinnamon red-hots for eyes.

The tail procedure is similar to the neck sequence: First attach the outer tail (which fits outside the body), then the inner tail (which fits inside the body), sandwiching them together.

Make a decorative border around the edge of the body with a small to medium shell or star tip.

For the wings, first attach the under-wings (follow photo for position), then the upper wings, which should be about 1 inch forward of the under-wings. Pipe reinforcing seams as necessary.

For the "necklace" garland, use ¼ cup of green icing and pipe leaf forms, set with dragées, cinnamon red-hots, and small candies. Or you can mix additional colors and pipe little flowers. As always, let dry.

The crown will be a pure icing structure made around a funnel. Trace the pattern on white paper with dark pen or pencil, and cut it out. Check the fit around a 4½-inch-long metal or plastic funnel with a 4⅛-inch diameter; adjust fit as needed. Tape with clear tape, and tape wax paper over this. Mix ¼ cup of yellow icing and use a No. 1 tip for the lattice design; switch to a No. 3 tip for the outside edge. Use a pair of tweezers to set gold dragées in the wet icing. Let dry at least 48 hours—the icing must be bone dry to be strong enough to hold its shape. Carefully remove the papers and icing from the funnel and peel off wax paper. Use a No. 3 tip to reinforce the design on the inside of the crown. When dry, set it on the head with dots of icing. *Voilà!*

## DECORATED CAKE SCULPTURE

For this type of sculpture, the cake itself is the basic sculptural form. It should be sufficiently dense and heavy to support the icing, particularly for tall or elaborate forms. Rosemary Cheris Littman normally makes her cakes in three sheetcake layers, separates them with foil or plastic, and chills them until it's time to decorate, which keeps them fresh and makes them easier to handle without breaking. When they are ready to ice up, Littman makes a pattern of the final shape on cardboard, glues or staples the cardboard to a wood base, and arranges the layers on that. She applies icing with a large spatula or a large-tipped pastry bag, and shapes it with an artist's palette knife or her hands. Particularly demanding sculptures may require additional reinforcement, such as wooden dowels inserted into the cake or cardboard slipped between the cake layers.

For unusually shaped cakes, Littman bakes the sheetcakes in pans approximating the final form as closely as possible, chills them, and then carves or shapes them. When the cake properly formed and the basic layer of frosting has been applied, Littman adds the details with the pastry bag and a variety of frosting colors and decorative tips.

Buttercream frosting, Littman's chosen medium, has a satiny, opaque finish. For a shiny, translucent look, such as for depicting fruits, vegetables, or glass, Littman uses strained preserves or baker's or piping gel, smoothed on. The buttercream and gel stay soft at room temperature, but they are also repairable—if a section gets squashed, it can be lifted out and resculpted.

## DEMONSTRATION: SPAGHETTI CAKE

Here are the step-by-step directions for the Spaghetti and Meatballs Cake, one of Rosemary Cheris Littman's favorites. Originally created for a friend whose favorite dish was spaghetti and meatballs, it is a combination of strawberry jam "tomato sauce," chocolate and nut "meatballs," and banana cake (although any cake will do), with a French buttercream frosting squeezed through a No. 4 pastry tip to resemble spaghetti. If you have no pastry bag or tip, try a zip-lock plastic bag with a tiny slit in one corner. The slit will probably give you something closer to linguine than spaghetti, but who cares?

### BUTTERCREAM FROSTING

1⅓  cups sifted confectioner's sugar
⅔  cup water
10  egg yolks
2  cups unsalted butter, at room temperature
1  teaspoon vanilla extract

Combine sugar and water in a saucepan. Put in a candy thermometer, and stir over low heat until sugar is dissolved. Raise the heat and boil syrup until thermometer reads 238°F, about 10 minutes. While syrup is cooking, beat egg yolks until fluffy. When syrup reaches its designated temperature, remove it from the stove, take out the thermometer, and pour about ¼ cup of the boiling syrup into the egg yolks, avoiding the beaters. Beat immediately at high speed for 10 seconds. Stop the mixer, pour in a little more syrup, and beat for another 10 seconds. Keep this up until all the syrup is in with the egg yolks. Beat for 8–10 minutes more and, if necessary, set aside until the mixture cools to room temperature. Beat in the softened butter and vanilla extract. Use at room temperature and refrigerate any excess for up to several weeks in a covered container. Yield: about 4 cups.

### CHOCOLATE MEATBALLS

6  ounces semi-sweet chocolate morsels
4  ounces cream cheese, at room temperature
¼–½  teaspoon vanilla extract
 dash of salt
2  cups sifted confectioner's sugar
1  cup finely chopped nuts

Put the chocolate in the top of a double boiler over warm water at moderate heat, stirring constantly until melted. Remove the top of the double boiler and set aside to cool. Mix cream cheese in electric mixer until smooth. Add vanilla and salt, mixing well. Gradually beat in the confectioner's sugar. Add the chocolate and beat until smooth. Mix in the nuts, and form into 1¾" meatballs. Store in freezer or refrigerator until needed. Yield: 25 meatballs.

### AUNT HENNY'S BANANA CAKE

1½  cups sour milk or buttermilk
5  teaspoons distilled white vinegar
6  ounces butter
1⅔  cups granulated sugar
3  eggs
1½  teaspoons baking soda
3  ripe mashed bananas
3  cups all-purpose flour
1½  teaspoons baking powder
1½  teaspoons salt
2  cups finely chopped walnuts

Preheat oven to 350°F and bring all ingredients to room temperature. To sour milk, put vinegar in a 2-cup measure and add milk to measure 1½ cups. Using an electric mixer, beat butter and sugar in a large bowl at high speed until light and fluffy. Add eggs one at a time, beating well after each one. In a 2-cup or larger vessel, dissolve baking soda in sour milk. Add to butter-sugar-egg mixture. Beat in mashed bananas. Sift flour, baking powder, and salt together and mix in at low speed until just blended. Fold in chopped nuts. Pour mixture into a generously greased and floured 9 x 13" roasting pan and bake for about 45 minutes or until a toothpick comes out clean when inserted in the middle. Set aside to cool for at least 30 minutes. Put a large oval platter on the top of the cake, invert, and remove the pan. Chill cake several hours or overnight.

### THE TOMATO SAUCE

1½–2  jars Smucker's Low-Sugar Strawberry Spread

Put the spread in a shallow saucepan and stir over very low heat until smooth, about 2 minutes. Do not overheat, or spread will liquefy.

*Assembly:* Either prepare all components in advance or prepare the cake first and make the sauce, meatballs, and frosting while the cake is chilling. When all the elements are ready, trim off all edges and corners from the chilled cake to make an oval mound, adding cutoff pieces to the ends to elongate the oval. Freeze the cake for several hours so it will be very cold when you put the buttercream on it. then take the cake out of the freezer and dust any crumbs off the platter. Cover the cake completely with a thin coat of buttercream, which will firm up in minutes because of the cold cake. It's okay if this undercoat is a little rough, as it will be covered with "spaghetti" later.

If the buttercream has been sitting around for a bit, whip or stir it just before using it to half-fill a 14-inch pastry bag fitted with a No. 4 tip. Beginning where lower edge of the cake meets the platter, apply frosting back and forth over a 4-inch area, and then continue around the cake in small sections. Don't worry about a slip—it adds to the spaghetti feeling. Circle upward, stopping at the top of mound and leaving a plateau there for the tomato sauce and meatballs; surround the plateau with a spaghetti wall, creating a shallow depression that will be filled with sauce. Return the cake to the freezer for 15 minutes to firm up the icing.

After removing the cake from the freezer again, pour most of the sauce into the well. Spread it around the plateau and up against the spaghetti wall with the back of a wooden spoon, pushing some strawberry lumps over the wall, but not so far that they slip down. Put the meatballs in the sauce, swirling them around in it, and pour the remaining sauce over the meatballs. Serve at room temperature on a red-and-white checked tablecloth.

All photographs: Rosemary Cheris Littman

Pouring syrup into the buttercream mix.

Chocolate meatballs, finished and ready for freezing.

Chilled cake after being carved into an oval shape.

Applying the preliminary icing layer.

Applying the spaghetti icing.

Pouring on the sauce.

With the meatballs added on top, the cake is finished.

## BREAD DOUGH SCULPTURE

This is the simplest type of food sculpture. It involves making a simple but inedible dough of water, salt, and flour, kneading it up to a workable consistency, sculpting forms from it, and baking them. You can make a sculpture all in one piece or, more conveniently, make several components and glue them together with white glue, hot glue, or wood glue.

BRENDA PEPPER
Christmas Tree, *for cover of a Christmas catalog. Bread dough, dyes. Dimensions: 16 × 24" (41 × 61 cm). Client: L. S. Ayres Department Store. (Photographer: Peter Nicholas)*

## BREAD DOUGH SCULPTURE

This is the classic recipe for dough sculpture. It takes very little time or effort, and is a great deal of fun.

### BREAD DOUGH

- 4 cups white flour, bleached or unbleached
- 1 cup salt
- 1½ cups water, or enough to make a smooth, not-too-dry dough

Combine all ingredients in a bowl and knead for 10 minutes, or until desired consistency is achieved.

The texture of the dough is important: too dry, and it will crack; too wet, and it will lose its shape. For coloring, you can add Dr. Martin's dyes to the dough while kneading it, paint the dyes on later, or both. The dye seeps in and gives a nice translucent quality to the surface. Other transparent colors, like watercolors, work well, and the finished sculpture can even be painted with acrylics.

Sculpt the dough on ungreased aluminum foil on a cookie sheet, using your fingers and any little modeling tools you have handy. Small elements and details can be made separately and pushed on or into the main pieces. Part of the charm of bread dough sculpture is its childlike, slightly primitive, feeling, so don't worry about it looking too perfect. When you finish sculpting, bake the forms at 300 to 325°F for about an hour.

Check on the dough periodically as it bakes—occasionally it will puff up a bit while baking. Little mounds and such can be pushed down again, and add to the piece's generally unstudied and insouciant quality, so don't worry about them.

If the sculpture attracts bugs, you can add a quarter-teaspoon of powdered cloves to the dough, but this makes little brown specks. A good varnishing afterward can work just as well, and will enhance the sculpture's aesthetic qualities to boot.

## IMITATION FOOD SCULPTURE

Although food sculptures usually deteriorate or end up as dessert, it is possible to make imitation food sculptures that will last forever. Plastic fruits and vegetables can look exceedingly realistic; iced cakes can be made of cakelike three-dimensional forms made of wood, Masonite, cardboard, or Styrofoam, and iced with Durham's Rock Hard Water Putty (which squeezes though pastry tips quite nicely when mixed to the proper consistency). Perhaps this is cheating. But if you have a client who would rather put the piece in a display case than eat it, what's the harm?

**ELLEN RIXFORD**

Happy Bicentennial, New York, *for a television advertisement for bicentennial programs in New York. Imitation cake made on a base of wood and Masonite, frosted with Durham's Rock Hard Water Putty squeezed through a pastry bag with various decorative tips. The effect is just like real frosting, but longer-lasting. Miniature city is made of wood. Height: 24" (61 cm). Client: New York Bicentennial. (Photographer: Ellen Rixford)*

**ROBERT CROWTHER**
*Above:* Buckingham Palace, *to mark the Queen's 25th anniversary on the throne. Cookie/ biscuit and icing relief sculpture. Dimensions: 48 × 29" (123 × 74 cm). Client: Victoria and Albert Museum. (Photographer: Arthur Titherington, Titherington Photography Witney)*

# 8 PHOTOGRAPHING DIMENSIONAL ILLUSTRATION

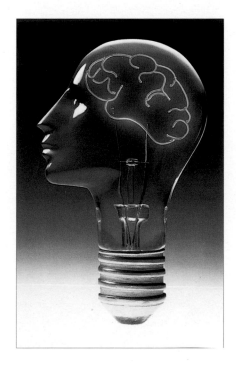

**ELLEN RIXFORD**
*Left:* Merry
Christmas *seasonal
promotion, for*
People *magazine;
also featured in*
Step-by-Step
Graphics. *Soft
sculpture plus other
media. The set was
lit from front and
from above with
warm light. Cold
blue lights shone
from the sides to
accent difference
between indoors
and outdoors.
Dimensions: 3 × 4'
(91 × 121 cm).
Client:* People
*magazine.
(Photographer:
Ellen Rixford)*

**NICK ARISTOVULOS**
*Above:* Light Bulb
Head *poster illustra-
tion. Polyester resin,
Speedstone, Plexiglas,
wire, stencil. This
picture is the result of a
double exposure—the
light bulb head was
first photographed
without the brain. The
glowing brain outline
is actually a stencil,
cut out and backlit to
produce the glowing
effect. The film was re-
exposed for the brain
image and then
developed. Dimensions:
8 × 14 × 2" (20 × 36 ×
5 cm). Client: Council
for the Advancement of
Scholarship and
Education.
(Photographer:
Shig Ikeda)*

**T**he photograph is the culmination of the dimensional illustration process. It will be what the client will use and what most of the illustrator's audience will see. So the illustrator's reputation, earning power, and survival rest upon the quality of the shot.

Quite often the beauty of the original piece will carry the picture without much special help from the photographer. But dimensional illustrations sometimes require artful and inspired use of lighting, color, and special environments created in the photo studio to bring the construction to life. Conversely, a poor photo can drain the vitality out of an otherwise excellent piece.

Most dimensional illustrators do not photograph their own work, primarily because they feel their own studio photography skills are no match for those of a professional. Tight deadlines are another factor—when you've been working feverishly for days or weeks to get a piece ready, responsibility for the photo often feels like the last straw. Also, studio photography requires a sizable amount of space and some expensive equipment. And many illustrators find the prospect of mastering the necessary photographic skills rather daunting.

I do take my own pictures, though, having learned how on the job, little by little. A fairly simple, straightforward course in general photography taught me the basics of composition and lighting. I bought an inexpensive used 4 × 5 camera and fooled around with it, getting useful advice from the people at the color lab that developed my film— things like how to use color filters, and how to use colored gels with my lights to get additional color into white-on-white shots. On those occasions when I did work with professional photographers, I would stay at the studio during the shoot and learn whatever I could— how the pros used lighting, created environments, used colored seamless paper

backgrounds in combination with clever shadow effects, or even imitated clouds on a blue-paper sky with medicated spray for athlete's foot. I soon began handling the simpler shots myself, and used pros only for the more difficult ones; after many years, I made the break completely—a source of immense satisfaction. While my way certainly isn't for everyone, it does have many advantages, and is easier to achieve than you might think. And if you feel most comfortable leaving the photo to someone else, the pictures in this chapter show some excellent partnerships between photographers and illustrators.

One advantage of self-reliant photography is a de facto extended deadline. Since clients routinely allow an extra day or two for taking the shot, the illustrator-photographer's deadline for completing the finished piece is effectively longer. If I am very pressed for time, I sometimes set up the shot when the piece is nearly finished, take all my test exposures, and finish up the details while waiting for the lab to develop the tests. Usually this means I can work on the piece while looking at it as it is set up for the shot— another big advantage, because what looks nearly perfect to the naked eye may have evident flaws when observed through the camera lens. And things can improve when viewed in a photographic context as well. Experience makes it easier to match the look of the piece with the viewpoint of the camera.

Space can be a problem. I don't really have a separate space for photography. I set up small to midsized pieces— anything up to 3 feet—on my dining room table, and big pieces in the living room.

As for equipment, the additional fees you earn (as well as those you save) will probably pay back your costs within a year. And you don't really need anywhere near the amount of stuff most photo studios have.

## ARTISTIC CONTROL

Being your own photographer gives you greater artistic control, because it allows the creative process to continue right up to the last exposure. Sometimes a happy accident or an eleventh-hour inspiration can alter the way you look at a subject, transforming a straightforward normal-environment shot into a picture where the subject inhabits a world of its own. Once I was asked to make a figure of a woman whose skeletal remains had been found in the Olduvai Gorge (see page 39). The art director requested that I make some sort of modest setting—nothing too involved. But after setting up, it seemed to me that the figure really needed a full environment, so we arranged a tree, some rocks, and a selection of mosses, grasses, and small-leaved plants to make a real jungle-by-the-riverbank scene. An image that would have been merely satisfactory thus became memorable.

This scenario repeated itself in the case of a large soft-sculpture vegetable garden I had originally created for a craft magazine (see page 92 ). The magazine's chosen photographer took the vegetables out to the country and shot them sitting on the grass. Unfortunately, this made them look like simple objects, rather than a living garden. Although the magazine did run this photo, I was not content to let this be the final image. I constructed a mock garden, using an atmosphere of blue seamless paper as "sky" and imitation grass sprinkled with sawdust, gravel, and artificial flowers. The background was composed of various potted plants, baskets, and more flowers. Building this garden took a great amount of time, effort, and space, but it was worth it—the resulting photo ultimately became one of the strongest pieces in my portfolio, and later appeared as a magazine cover and a jigsaw puzzle, and the whole assemblage became an exhibition centerpiece. If you spend a lot of time on creating a piece, it's usually worthwhile to have the responsibility for the final image as well.

ELLEN RIXFORD
Three-Headed
Dragon *puppet, with moving eyes, mouths, and fiery tongues. Dragon made of Celastic, wood, fabric, and laminated paper; cave made of foam and crumpled newspaper sprayed gray, black, and white; vines are green lace. Dragon is lit from above and front. Sky is colored with gels placed over spotlights. Dragon length: 5' (1.5 m). (Photographer: Ellen Rixford)*

## LEGAL CONTROL

When I began gathering the pictures for this book, I discovered that the copyrights to the images are controlled by their respective photographers. This means dimensional illustrators cannot use or profit from photos of their work without their photographers' permission. But I also found that since the photo of a given piece is *derived* from the original piece itself, the illustrator has some rights as well. In trying to sort this out, I spoke with copyright attorneys, photographers, and a staff member of the American Society of Magazine Photographers, as well as the President of the Graphic Artists' Guild. They cited several legal precedents, notably *Reid vs. Creative Community for Non-Violence*, in which it was judged that an artist's

work cannot be used without the permission of the artist, who retains the copyrights to his work and rights to other works derived from it; and *Rogers vs. Koons*, which held that works done in one medium that imitate or represent works done in another can be held to be derivative works, and that the author of a derived work has legal obligations to the author of the work from which it was derived.

Most illustrators and photographers negotiate settlements among themselves regarding fees for various uses of dimensional illustration photos. But until there is a uniform set of standards, there will always be the danger that the image on which you labored long and hard will be controlled by someone who may refuse to allow you to use it, except under the most punitive conditions. While most photographers work out fair arrangements with illustrators, I have heard several horror stories of photographers who refused to be reasonable. So if you're not taking your own photos, be sure to find a photographer who will give you a fair deal on the picture's reproduction rights. And, most importantly, get those rights spelled out *in writing*, before the photo is taken. Of course, the concept of a "fair deal" may vary from person to person—some illustrators stipulate that all rights belong to them, while others divide reproduction rights according to the amount of time spent on the job by each participant.

## FINANCIAL CONSIDERATIONS

Photographers usually get paid a lot more per diem than illustrators. While the typical photographer may have high overhead expenses (space, equipment, assistants), the same could be said of the typical dimensional illustrator, who also tends to spend much more time making a piece (sometimes a week or two) than the photographer spends shooting it (usually a day or two). But the photo budget is often 25 to 50 percent of the whole job, which often prices dimensional illustration beyond the reach of clients who would like to try it but cannot afford both fees. By learning to shoot the simpler jobs yourself, you can give such clients an affordable package and increase the number of people you can work for. And if you progress to the point where you can do complex, demanding shots, you can command higher fees than if you were just doing illustration alone.

There is one last good reason for being your own photographer: You can take as many extra shots as you wish. This will leave you with plenty of extra transparencies for additional portfolios, or for sending around to magazines who might want to do a story on your work. This is far from insignificant. Printed proofs tend not to look as good as the original transparency. In my own case, fully a third of my best work either never made it into print at all or looked much worse in print than it had originally looked in the chrome. Frequently I do jobs that are never meant for print— puppets for theatrical performance, or little sets for television—work that might otherwise go undocumented and therefore be unrepresented in my portfolio.

In fact, I have three portfolios, and keep several extra transparencies of each piece. And I have a selection of loose transparencies filed in the studio for sending out as print promotion samples, to publications that might be featuring dimensional illustration, and for clients who might want to purchase secondary rights to an image. Before I began taking my own photographs, I had to beg photographers for extra shots, and rarely got more than one or two; this meant I had to have them duped by a film lab, to the tune of hundreds of dollars for a few images. Now I just shoot as much as I need, and the only extra expense is the additional film and processing.

## TEAMING UP WITH A PHOTOGRAPHER

There is a happy medium between learning to be a photographer and giving up all control of your work: Try to establish a good working relationship with a photographer who appreciates dimensional illustration, whose prices are not wildly out of line with your budgets, who will be willing to make solid written agreements regarding shared rights, and who will take lots of extra shots for you. If you can find such a person, both of you will profit over the course of your careers. I have had a few such a relationships with photographers myself. The problem was that my clients were not always willing to work with my photographers. So if you have a team or a partnership, make it clear to your clients that the two of you come as a package deal, and that you don't want to work with anyone else.

# PHOTOGRAPHIC PRINCIPLES, MATERIALS, AND TOOLS

Even if you are not going to take your own pictures, it is useful to know about the basic equipment of the photo studio, and how it is used. The more you know, the better you can plan your shots, and the better suggestions you can make to the photographer as you work out the individual problems of each image together.

## CAMERAS

If your shooting is confined to your own work, your needs will be much simpler than those of a professional photographer. The *35mm single-lens-reflex camera (SLR)* is small and portable, and its small format allows you to take a roll of 24 or 36 pictures of a subject, varying exposure, lighting, and viewpoint for a moderate price. SLRs come with a vast array of interchangeable lenses, which enable you to shoot wide-angle views or to home in for close-up shots. But the photographs from these 35mm cameras cannot be significantly enlarged without a loss of image sharpness and an increase in grain, so you must use slow-speed films.

The *2¼ × 2¼ SLRs* have bigger film and produce shots that can be enlarged more, and they have a good selection of replacement lenses, too. Like the 35mm models, they use roll film, which is more economical than the sheet film used by most studio cameras and allows you to shoot a series of pictures more quickly and effortlessly.

*View cameras*, though they are big and cumbersome and don't have the variety of spare lenses offered by the smaller cameras, are the tool of choice of most studio photographers. Their large film size allows greater enlargement and gives an image that is easy to scan for details and possible errors. The smallest view camera is the 4 × 5, which is sufficient for most illustration assignments. It uses relatively inexpensive film, which allows you to shoot extra pictures for spare portfolios and insurance against loss and damage.

The 4 × 5 size has one limitation—it is too small for *color retouching*, a process of painting on or bleaching out flawed or unwanted areas in a transparency. In order for the retoucher to have enough

room to work, the film must be at least 8 × 10. This kind of problem arises very rarely—too rarely to justify the investment in a large camera early on in your photography career. If necessary, you can rent one, or just let a studio photographer do the job for you.

View cameras have another substantial advantage over small-format cameras: They can alter the subject's perspective and either create or correct apparent distortion in the image, which is a mighty handy thing when photographing objects that must be photographed from below but must appear as if they were shot head-on, like buildings. You can also impose or exaggerate perspective in any other situation. I use my view camera to photograph miniature cityscapes, buildings, or rooms in which I want the ground or floor to be visible, so I can't shoot directly from the front midpoint. I shoot from above, but adjust the camera to "straighten out" the walls.

Also, the camera's large ground glass makes it easy to check right angles and make sure opposite sides are the same length and distance apart—essential for photographing fabric illustrations, or pieces built inside frames or boxes.

As the view camera is big and heavy, you should have a good *tripod*. There is nothing worse than a rickety tripod that sends your camera sliding into the wrong position every time you touch it; if in doubt, get the heaviest and mostly solid you can afford. A good tripod will allow you to position your camera close to the floor or 6 feet high. If you need to shoot looking down on a subject, most good tripods can be fitted with a sidearm—a pipelike attachment that clamps onto the body of the tripod and substitutes for the regular tripod mounting piece. Since the tripod will no longer be balanced when the camera is mounted on the sidearm, be sure to counterweight the tripod to compensate for the weight of the camera.

## FILM

Film is available in many levels of light sensitivity, or *speed*. The faster the film, the greater its light sensitivity, and the less light (and, therefore, exposure

time) is needed to produce an image on the film. A shot of an image taken at a small aperture on a cloudy day with slow film might require a 1/25-second exposure; the same shot taken with fast film might call for 1/250 , 1/500 , or even 1/1000 of a second. Film speeds are expressed as either ISO or ASA numbers: 100 to 125 is considered medium speed; 25 to 64 is slow; 160 to 200, medium fast; and 200 to 400, fast. Film can also be *pushed*, a technique in which the film's effective speed is doubled, so that you need not be too limited by the rated speed of whatever film you have on hand.

Fast film allows you to photograph in low-light situations, or to use very small exposure times to "freeze" moving objects. But there is a tradeoff: The faster the film, or the more slow film is pushed, the more *grain* it has. In this context, grain refers to the light-responsive particles in the film that form the image, which are distributed in finer granules, or grains, on slower films than on fast ones. As a fast-film image is enlarged for printing, the actual grains become visible and give a sort of sandy appearance, rather than smooth light-to-dark transitions. Your dimensional illustrations will not be moving when you photograph them, and your studio should have sufficient light, so fairly low-speed films are the way to go.

Black-and-white film is generally sold as negative film, to be printed later, after developing. But for color, slide film or transparencies, or *chromes*, as they are called, give the best print-reproduction quality. If you do commercial color photography, you will probably be asked to use *color reversal film*, which is made specifically for daylight or for incandescent or tungsten light, and must be used accordingly—shots taken with daylight films under incandescent light come out yellow, and shots taken with tungsten-light film taken in daylight come out blue. Filters can compensate for these problems, but you're better off using the right film with the right kind of light in the first place.

Color films tend to change their color balance during their shelf life, and react with the atmosphere and to heat, so it's

a good practice to store film in the refrigerator if you're not planning to use it right away. Nonprofessional films sometimes have slight color imbalances when used fresh off the shelf, but as they sit in storage, the balance normalizes; professional films are stored or "aged" somewhat and refrigerated prior to sale, so that their color balances are just right when you buy them, but will deteriorate from that peak if stored unrefrigerated for too long.

Even if you always use the same brand and type of film, the color and speed can vary. Film is manufactured in batches, which are numerically marked on each film box. Try to buy enough of one batch to last for a few months, store it in the refrigerator, and then run some tests to determine the actual speed and color balance before you take final shots of anything.

Even if you work with a reputable lab, film developed at different times can look slightly different, even if the equipment settings and environments were identical. Film development is very delicate, and tiny differences in developer concentration, timing, or temperature can cause small but percep-

**PAT ALLEN**
Europe, *for a travel brochure. Colored paper from Italy, France, Germany, Japan, and the United States, with some airbrushed greens. Two lights were used—a spotlight, lighting the background from above, and a diffused light for the foreground. Dimensions: 10 × 12" (25 × 30 cm). Client: Creative Leisure International. (Photographer: Laurence Bartone)*

tible changes in your results. Results can also differ from lab to lab. This can cause problems if, for example, a client wants a series of pictures of different subjects against the same color background—warn the client that no matter how tightly you control the photographic parameters, the backgrounds may not develop identically.

Sheet film, which is used for view cameras, is perfectly flat, and is preferable to roll film because less distortion can occur at the corners. Even though roll film is held fairly flat by pressure plates inside the camera, the corners of the image will never be quite as sharp as the center. And sometimes straight lines at the outer edges of the picture can become distorted too. Usually this doesn't matter, as the subject is

normally placed at the center. But it can adversely affect pictures with square or rectangular borders, which can register as curves instead of as straight lines. A good way to test your camera in this respect is to hang a page from your newspaper's classified section on a wall and take a picture of it. Use a tripod, to make sure your camera is directly parallel to the surface of the paper. Enlarge the photos and see if you can read the fine print at the corners as well as the middle, and check the edges for distortion.

Film for view cameras, sold in boxes of 10 and 50 sheets, is loaded into *film holders*—flat, lightproof containers with slides on each side, so that each holder contains two films. The film holders are inserted into the back of the camera, just in front of the ground glass, where the focused image falls. If you work with a view camera you will need at least five film holders during a shoot. If you have a darkroom to load your film in, wonderful; if not (and it's worth mentioning here that a darkroom really isn't necessary for a dimensional illustrator), use a *changing bag*, which functions like a tiny portable darkroom.

It has a lightproof center section, where film unloading and loading is done, and two sleeves with elasticized cuffs leading into it. After shooting, you can use the changing bag to safely remove the film from the holders and put it into a film package box for taking to the lab.

Most studio cameras 2¼ × 2¼ or larger can take a *Polaroid back attachment*, which will give you a Polaroid print instead of an exposed film. Taking preliminary Polaroids on a studio shot is an important step—you can take as many test shots as you need, immediately see the results, and adjust your lighting arrangements as needed. A Polaroid will also reveal hidden flaws in lighting and composition, or even in the construction of your sculpture, that might not be apparent through the viewfinder, and will give you and your client an accurate idea of how the shot will look. And it will give the art director a working image to use in preparing the page layout while waiting for your final shot to be delivered. Polaroid film is available in both black-and-white and color; the black-and-white, which is much cheaper, is usually fine.

## LIGHT METERS

Given all the light-related variables affecting camera settings and film, you will need a good light meter. Most good SLRs have built-in light meters; for large-format studio cameras, you must buy a separate hand-held meter, which you can point at different areas of the subject to determine light levels. The built-in meters measure only the light coming into the camera lens; hand-held meters, in addition to measuring levels at brightly lit and shaded areas, can also measure incident light (the level of light falling on the subject) and reflected light (light bounced back off the surface of the subject). This can be quite useful when light levels vary widely, or when some parts of the subject—a black velvet dress, for example—absorb light much more than others.

## LIGHTING EQUIPMENT

In my studio I have three ordinary light stands, which take a light reflector clamped onto the shaft or the top, and a big light stand with a boom, counter-weighted at the bottom. Unlike the ordinary light stand, the boom can easily be maneuvered to position light directly over the subject, rather than just to one side of it. The boom gives you the

freedom to position your light exactly where you want it.

Photo light bulbs are powerful—ordinarily sold in 250 and 500 watts—so don't even think about putting them in ordinary sockets. Get good reflectors with strong housings and sockets, and well-made, reliable switches. Most of the time you can get by with two reflectors, but occasionally a large or complex setup requires four. Reflectors come in various sizes, but I use 12-inch ones for almost everything.

Sometimes you may want to light a subject indirectly, to give a softer shadow and less contrast between light and dark. The best way to do this is to bounce the light off a nearby surface, such as a wall or ceiling (preferably a white one, unless you don't mind if the surface's color affects the color of the reflected light). Or you can use a white silk photo umbrella, or a big piece of white foam-core or illustration board as a bounce screen. The umbrellas can be clamped to your light stand, and the white boards to an adjacent stand.

Bounce screens (also called bounce cards) can also be placed on the opposite side of the photo setup from the main light source, to reflect light back into the setup. This is useful when the light source is positioned far off to one side. Otherwise, your shot may suffer from *light fall-off*—the composition will appear bright on one side and dark on the other. But they can do a lot more: A colored bounce screen can throw a blush or tint into a white-on-white shot, making it more lively and interesting; a mirrored or shiny bounce screen can throw glints of soft light into the composition, especially if it has an irregular surface.

Additionally, you can make a lot of small tools and equipment to help achieve exactly the effect you want. To block out light from one small spot in a setup, for example, you can use a *gobo* (short for *go-between*), a piece of cardboard taped onto a wire or rod and held in front of the light. To narrow down a light source to simulate a spotlight effect, you can make a *snoot* or cone out of a piece of sheet metal painted black on the inside, and wire it to the front of your reflector. I have even used a string of Christmas lights hidden behind a sculpture to give a little glow to the background that I couldn't get any other way. To hold your bounce screens, auxiliary lights, gobos, and

whatnot in place, get about 10 strong clamps with rubber teeth.

Personally, I don't use *strobes*, though they are found in nearly every photo studio. They are excellent if you are taking several pictures every day, but they are large and expensive, and sometimes need repair. Besides, strobes can limit your creative choices. For example, I often like to move the light a little when taking the shot—it softens shadows and makes it easier to get shadows with no particular outline. But you need a long exposure to do this, and the strobe gives only an instantaneous brilliant flash.

## BACKGROUND MATERIAL

Finally, you will need background material. Some photo studios have a sort of permanent background structure—a vertical wall that curves out gently to make a horizontal floor, which can be painted the exact background color a client wants. The gentle curve eliminates "horizon lines," or lines between the wall and floor. *Seamless background paper*, sold in a variety of colors at shops supplying set materials for photographers, does the same thing. It comes in 9- and 12-foot rolls, although shops will often sell you a small or partial roll if you're short on space.

To use seamless paper, you first need a stand for it—two poles to hold up the ends of the roll, and a third pole to run through the center of the roll and attach to the side poles at the ends. The poles are all made so they can be shortened and lengthened to accommodate the size of the paper. Unless you work very large, you can use a table or a piece of plywood on sawhorses to hold up your illustration. Mounting the paper so it unrolls to expose the inside, pull down enough to cover your table, anchor the ends in place with tape or weights, set up your piece, and go to work.

Seamless paper is not cheap, and there is no reason to buy a lot of colors unless you are asked for them by a client. The colors I use most often are the blues—a pale atmospheric blue plus a deeper sky-blue and cerulean blue—a warm gray, a cool gray, and white. If you want to add interest to a background—a cloud effect, or an impressionistic series of color tints to evoke the feeling of a foggy landscape or a sunset—you can paint abstract soft-focus backgrounds on artist's canvas, either with ordinary paints and brushes or with spray paint or a large airbrush, and keep them ready for appropriate assignments.

Set shops also stock materials that imitate natural environments—large rugs of fake grass, artificial snow in spray cans, Styrofoam rocks—although dimensional illustrators are probably as well-equipped as anyone to make their own materials of this type. The shops even rent out rainbow projectors, which will give you a rainbow on your seamless paper sky.

Other possibilities to keep in mind: If you are shooting a landscape piece, you can make nice clouds using antifungal foot spray powder, like Desenex (but watch out—it smells very strong and gets a lot of white dust in the room if you use too much). Since my pieces are too big for this, I use talcum powder and a powder puff on blue background paper, or smudge in my clouds with soft-white pastels. And if you have a lot of spare time to experiment, you can get any background you want by projecting it onto a translucent screen behind your image with a slide projector.

Transparent or translucent backgrounds are rarely used in photographing dimensional illustration, but they can give wonderful effects, especially if you want the background to appear to glow. Dan Lenore, the photographer who photographed my *Fish* (see page 169), set up the picture by clamping a huge piece of flexible translucent plastic to vertical and horizontal supports, so that part of the plastic functioned as a shelf for the fish to rest on, and the back part curved up to form a backdrop. He shone lights fitted with blue gels behind the plastic, for an effect of shining water. Then he lit the fish and we took the shot. A second shot of the fish was done by simply suspending it from above—a good example of how one dimensional illustration can yield two or more very different images.

*Photo setup for David Csicsko's* Lady for Step-by-Step. *The photographer uses a combination of strobe a light reflected off a white silk umbrella at upper left, a small spotlight plus a red gel at center left to throw a red glow onto the background behind the sculpture, lights on the right pointing directly at the sculpture, and a white bounce card. Such combinations of different kinds of lighting are common to more complex dimensional illustration jobs. (Photographer: Tony Kiesman)*

DAVID CSICSKO Lady for Step-by-Step *paper sculpture. Colored foam-core board, wrapping papers, Japanese paper, novelty stickers, wallpaper, some scoring. Height: 4' (1.2 m). Client: Step-by-Step* Graphics *magazine. (Photographer: Tony Kiesman)*

# WORKING PROCESSES

Here we'll examine some basic setups and situations you might find yourself dealing with as you begin photographing your own work, or as you participate in a shoot with a photographer. Taking a good picture is ultimately a matter of playing around with your camera angle, your lighting, and the environment you create for your piece until you like what you see in the viewfinder. Keep a notebook with records of exposure times and aperture openings used, sketches of your lighting setups, records on what filters you needed to get good color balance, and so on. When you are working with a professional studio photographer, watch what goes on, and make sure you understand the process. Don't be afraid to ask questions of the photographer.

## CONTROLLING LIGHT

Most amateur snapshots are taken with sunlight, a camera flash, or a combination of both. Natural light is plentiful and free, but it can't be controlled and varies from one hour to the next. If you want control over your photographic environment, you have no choice but to use artificial light. But artificial light sources are small and relatively weak, which can

## CONTROLLING LIGHT

Here are some of the basic ways of controlling artificial light in the studio.

Diagrams: Lenor Robinson

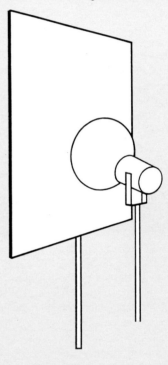

Bouncing light off a white card or board. For small bounce lights, the board can be silvered or mirrored material.

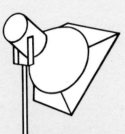

Direct lighting through a diffusion screen. The screen can be paper, fiberglass, plastic, or any translucent material.

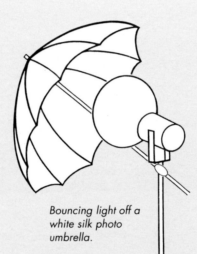

Bouncing light off a white silk photo umbrella.

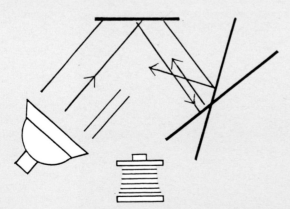

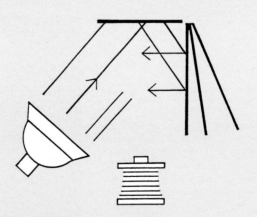

Varying positions for bounce screens. The setup on the left throws light back onto the entire subject area, softening shadows, while the setup at right throws less light back over the subject area but greatly minimizes light fall-off at the edges.

cause problems. When a subject is lit from one side, as many are, to dramatize the sculpture's three-dimensional qualities, artificial light rapidly falls off in intensity from one side to the other. This is because the extra distance to the farther side of the object—a few feet, say—is a significant amount of additional space when the light source itself is only a few feet away to begin with. (The sun, on the other hand, is 93 million miles away from everything.) To correct for this, you can reflect light back into the composition with a bounce screen, which balances the lighting and reflects light into shadowed areas, improving detail.

You could also correct this situation by shining another light into the composition from the other side. But this creates another problem: *ghost shadows*, double shadows falling on both sides of an object, or at different angles to it. One way to defeat ghosts is to blur them by moving the lights during a long exposure. A better way, though, is *diffusion*, or softening the effect of a harsh light source. A naked photo bulb, for instance, is too contrasty for most shots, but it can be diffused by hanging any translucent material in front of it— tracing paper, vellum, thin fabric, or thin fiberglass cloth. If your diffusion material is flammable or can scorch, be sure to set it up several inches from the bulb.

Another option is *bouncing* the light off walls, ceilings, white photo umbrellas, or carefully angled white cards or boards. Shadows cast from light bounced off a surface at the opposite side of the composition from the light source have no outlines (or such vague ones as to be nearly invisible)—this solves the ghost problem.

Direct lighting with a bounce screen at right to minimize light fall-off. The board is positioned so as not to reflect much light back on the subject.

Direct lighting with a bounce screen positioned to reflect as much light as possible back on the subject area.

A balanced lighting setup designed to give even lighting to a flat subject. The disadvantage to this arrangement is that it will greatly reduce any feeling of dimension or texture.

Direct lighting on the figure, plus additional lighting to lighten the background.

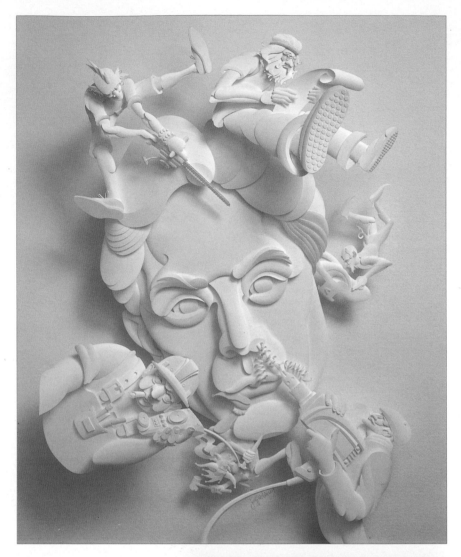

## SETTING UP THE SHOT

There are five general categories of photo setup for dimensional illustration: simple bas-relief, like a bas-relief paper sculpture; fabric collage, embroidery, picture quilts, or other fairly flat pieces that demand even, all-over lighting; small to midsized fully three-dimensional sculptures, or a small group; large fully three-dimensional compositions covering 4 feet or more of space; and special situations, effects, and lab techniques. The ordinary dimensional illustrator can master the first four; the last category requires a lot of time, knowledge, money, and the help of a professional photographer to act as a backup should something go wrong.

*Bas Relief.* The most common kinds of bas-relief are paper sculpture and clay. These are usually lit from the ten o'clock or two o'clock positions—the light source positioned a little up and to the side, to imitate the position of natural light source, emphasize dimension, and give some depth. The light is usually diffused or bounced, with an additional bounce screen positioned opposite the light source, and sometimes above and below as well, to even up the lighting. Unless you want long, pronounced shadows, the light source should not be placed too close to the edge of the bas-relief, but out at about a 45- to 60-degree angle. The closer the light source is to the piece, the darker and more dramatic the shadows and the greater the contrast between light and dark; pulling the light back fairly far from your piece evens everything up. (All of this, of course, applies to low-relief and fully three-dimensional subject situations as well.)

Because a bas-relief is usually glued together before the start of the shoot, it's difficult to rearrange things once the shoot is in progress. Gluing paper sculpture together with temporary adhesives, like rubber cement and foam tape, isn't a bad idea if you're not sure the client will accept the shot without changes. But there's a danger of the piece coming unglued later, which would be particularly disastrous if the client is purchasing your piece as part of the deal. Usually I killer-glue everything I'm certain won't need to be changed, and reserve the temporary gluing for the elements that are still in doubt. If you have a sidearm on your tripod, you can lay out a bas-relief flat on a table or the

### JEFF NISHINAKA
Self-Portrait. *Stonehenge paper. This piece was lit by a main light source coming from lower right, and two "sublights"—one covered with a red gel and coming from right, and the other covered with a blue gel, on the left. Dimensions: 30 × 40" (76 × 101 cm). Client: The Workbook (California). (Photographer: Eddie Ikuta)*

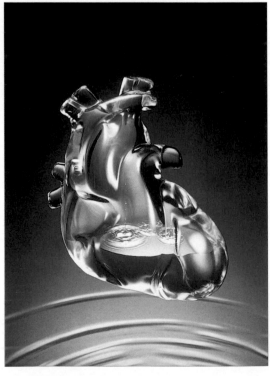

### LOU BORY
Edema, *for a medical advertisement. Cast polyester resin. The shot was taken in three parts—first the background with the water rings, then the heart, then the water dripping inside—which were taken to a lab and photocomposed. Dimensions: 10 × 15 × 4" (25 × 38 × 10 cm). Client: Roche Laboratories.*

**HIDEHARU NAITOH**
How to Become a Businessman As Strong As a Lion *illustration, for a magazine cover. A strobe light and bounce screens were used for this shot. For the background, a large, pinholed sheet of dark paper was hung behind the sculpture. Lights directed from behind the paper shone through the pinholes, simulating stars in the background sky. Client: AD Circle Co., ltd. (Photographer: Shigeru Tanaka; diagram: Lenor Robinson)*

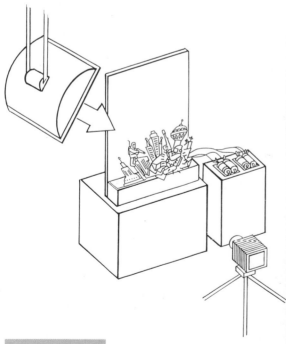

**HIDEHARU NAITOH**
Exoaii Warroid *paper sculpture, for a package design. This shot was made using a small bulb in the body of the warroid and a star filter, which creates starlike rays around the light. Client: ASCII (Photographer: Shigeru Tanaka; diagram: Lenor Robinson)*

ROBERT VOWLES
Quagmire of Self-Medication, *one of three illustrations for an advertising and direct-mail campaign for Entex LA, a decongestant. Figure made of sculpted latex on wire armature, landscape of miniature landscape elements, bottles, twigs, dirt, etc. A bounce card was used to avoid light fall-off. Approximate height of figure: 9" (23 cm). Client: Norwich Eaton Pharmaceuticals. Agency: Lindley Billinghurst Johnson Advertising Limited. (Photographer: Ron Elmy)*

floor, leaving at least the main elements free to move around. But any small details that could fall off and get lost should be attached.

A change in lighting perspective can radically alter the way a piece looks. So when constructing a bas-relief in the first place, light it from the same position you intend to use during the shot. This is especially important for portraits, where the interrelationships between features are so delicate, and for paper sculptures of a nude body, where muscle groupings must meld together to simulate real anatomy.

*Fabric Collage, Embroidery, and the Like.* If you want to emphasize dimension in this type of subject, light it from an angle and use bounce screens to even up the lighting on both sides. If you want a flat, even look, especially for something large, like a quilt, draw your light source back from the subject and align it as close to the subject's center as you can without getting in the camera's way. Meanwhile, place right-angled bounce screens at the sides, bottom, and top, to reflect light back onto the piece. Another approach here would be to put lights reflecting off large bounce screens on opposite sides of the piece, with bounce screens placed on the two remaining sides.

*Small Three-Dimensional Pieces.* Here you want to emphasize the dimensionality of the subject. Normally this can be done with a light source placed somewhat in front of, somewhat above, and a little to one side or the other of the subject. A bounce screen, if needed, will reflect light back into shadowed areas, open up detail, and correct light fall-off. So far, this is pretty much like a bas-relief. But here, the piece is separate from the background—what kind of background will you choose? A neutral, flat surface, like a wall or a roll of seamless background paper, is simplest.

ELLEN RIXFORD
Mourning Flea, *for a flea collar advertisement. Soft sculpture. The flea, which is mourning for deceased friends and family wiped out by the super-strong flea collar, was lit from above and slightly to the left in something resembling a spotlight effect. The background, placed far from the subject, is in shadow, accenting the flea's isolation and loneliness. Height: 20" (51 cm). Client: Schering. (Photographer: Ellen Rixford)*

ELLEN RIXFORD
Fish. *Fish is made of silver lamé (skin), laminated paper (skeleton), and soft sculpture (structure); fins are chiffon, glue-laminated with opaque fishline; background is a large translucent plastic sheet, colored with blue gels. Snapping at a mayfly, the fish is swimming in a plastic wave. Length: 30" (76 cm). Client: Outdoor Life magazine. (Photographer: Dan Lenore)*

**ELLEN RIXFORD**
Zeus and Ganymede *illustration, for an article on the best and worst annual reports of 1989. Soft sculpture in a mixed-media environment. To maintain even lighting, this set was lit from above, in front, and on both sides. Length: 10' (3 m). Client:* Chief Executive *magazine. (Photographer: Ellen Rixford; diagram: Lenor Robinson)*

But some pieces demand an environment—grass, trees, flowers, rocks, water—which you have to buy and/or construct and then compose with your subject in mind. I use plastic (and occasionally real) flowers for larger sets, and mosses and grasses for small ones. Once I even faked a small river in front of the picture, using mirror Mylar, paint, and a large plastic bag.

Once your environment is set, decide what kinds of shadows your subject should cast on the background. If you light the subject from the front and an opaque background is fairly close, your picture will contain a distinct shadow—undesirable if the background is supposed to be a sky. Using a translucent or transparent background avoids this; otherwise, maneuver the subject far enough away from the "sky" so that the camera cannot see the shadow. Maneuvering the light, the camera, or the subject so that the shadow falls harmlessly behind the subject and is invisible to the camera works well if you need your light source toward the front of the subject and picture. Placing the light source above the subject makes the shadow shorter, so it won't fall on the background.

Next, consider how light or dark the background should be relative to the subject. Placing the subject well in front of the background and lighting it from above will leave the whole background somewhat in shadow. If the background is supposed to be a sky, it may look too dark, and need some supplementary light bounced on it with a secondary light source or big bounce screen.

Grouped objects can block light from each other. If this happens, shine a tiny spot of light into the shadowed area by using a 100-watt bulb in a small housing—a small reflector, or an ordinary lamp socket. Rig up a little baffle or a snoot to concentrate the bulb into a single beam, and shine it onto the shadowed area.

Conversely, a composition may have an overly bright area where you don't want one. To solve this, make a gobo and position it between the light and the "hot spot." Unless the gobo is pretty close to the subject, its shadow will be diffused and imperceptible—except that the hot spot will disappear.

*Large Three-Dimensional Pieces.* The environment considerations and lighting problems here are similar to those for a

LENOR ROBINSON
Merrill Lynch Bull *illustration, for a brochure cover. Bull shape jigsawed out of a 4-inch-thick block of wood, sanded, smooth-surfaced, and sprayed metallic gold. The piece was first photographed straight; a red flare was added in the darkroom. Dimensions: 6 × 6 × 4″ (15 × 15 × 10 cm). Client: Merrill Lynch. (Photographer: Jim Stranges)*

small set, except that because of the sheer size of the set and the limitations of ceiling height, light from the primary light source may need to be supplemented by secondary sources. In my *Zeus and Ganymede*, the central light source was a diffused light about 3 feet above and 2 feet in front of Zeus's head. The "sky" on either edge of the picture suffered severe light fall-off and had to be supplemented—on the left by a small diffused light hidden behind the "rocks," and on the right by a larger diffused light shining on the landscape from about 4 feet away. Two other diffused lights evened out the illumination—one small one shining on the lower part of Ganymede's body, the other shining on the right foreground. You might think that having so many lights would give a spotty illumination, but careful arrange-

ment and rearrangement resulted in a fairly realistic and natural landscape.

*Special Effects.* Most dimensional illustration does not involve special effects or unusual situations, but there are a few exceptions. One interesting one is photography of a piece that is lit from within. The photographer must balance the two light sources exactly, so that their relationship will harmonize without one dominating the other. Putting one source or the other on a dimmer, and taking several Polaroids to measure relative brightness is a good approach.

Another specialized technique is *photocomposition*—combining two photos to look like one by masking out parts of each, and projecting the unmasked parts so that they fit together on one piece of film like pieces of a puzzle. I was once asked to do a birthday cake with a model of New York City on it for a television special on the New York bicentennial. I wanted a good photo of it for my portfolio, and a shot against a plain blue "sky" background didn't seem very interesting. A friend lent me a slide of a sky full of beautiful puffy summer clouds, and I had the cake photocomposed together with it.

# RESOURCES

Many of the tools, materials, and assorted products mentioned in this book can be difficult to track down, especially if you're not living in or near a large city. The following listing and accompanying notes should make things a bit easier.

Activa Products
P.O. Box 1296
Marshall, TX 75670-0023
*The source for Celluclay, a cellulose-based modeling clay.*

Airtex Industries
Cokato, MN 55321
*Makes the kind of polyester fiberfill favored by Lisa Lichtenfels for her soft sculpture.*

Alcone
5-49 49th Avenue
Long Island City, NY 11101
(718) 361-8373
*This outlet carries various material useful to the display industry: thermoforming sheets by Unnatural Resources, casting foams, RTV rubber for molds, alginate, safety equipment, etc. Call for information on what you need—the staff is courteous and helpful.*

Aldaster
60 Broadway
Brooklyn, NY 11211
(718) 782-3622
*Makes and sells a super-stretchy material much like nylon stocking, but a lot stronger. It is sold in tubes (like stocking), comes in several colors, and is useful for Lisa Lichtenfels—type soft sculpture, especially if you want to use it for figures that will get a lot of wear, like puppets.*

Aljo Mfg. Co. Inc.
81-83 Franklin Street
New York, NY 10013
(212) 226-2878
*A good source for dyes, including direct, disperse, acid, basic, and fiber-reactive varieties, as well as special dyes for acetate, nylon, and such special materials as reeds, bark, and raffia. The staff is helpful and informative, and the prices are reasonable.*

Allcraft
45 West 46th Street
New York, NY 10036
(212) 840-1860
*Jeweler's supplies and tools.*

Alumilite
225 Parsons Street
Kalamazoo, MI 49012
(616) 342-1259
Or, to speak with a sales representative, (908) 531-4985
*Makes and sells easy-to-use, low-toxicity casting plastics. These plastics have an aluminum base, so they work well with metal powder fillers. The staff is helpful and nice to deal with.*

American Art Clay Co. Inc.
4717 West 16th Street
Indianapolis, IN 46222
*Makes Claycrete, a self-hardening clay often used by illustrators.*

America's Hobby Center
146 West 22nd Street
New York, NY 10011
(212)-675-8922
*A good source for all sorts of supplies for making models, including spring wire, enamel paints, aluminum tubing in different sizes, grinder bits, etc.*

B & H Photo
119 West 17th Street
New York, NY 10011
(212) 807-7474
*Offers low prices on photo equipment and supplies. Closes early on Friday and is closed on Saturday, but is open on Sunday.*

BJB Enterprises
13912 Nautilus Drive
Garden Grove, CA 92643
(714) 554-4640
*Casting plastics, including a clear, hard urethane and a clear urethane elastomer, can be found here. Other products, including casting foams, mold rubbers, primers, thinners, coatings, releases, and pigments, are available as well. The very helpful staff will send free literature and samples.*

Benner Medical Props
601 West 26th Street
New York, NY 10001
(212) 727-9815
*A good place to find fiberglass casting tape and plaster bandage, and all kinds of medical equipment that can be bought or rented for theatrical or television use. The store also features a stable of medically trained actors, if you need such a thing. Pleasant and helpful.*

C & B Fabrics
250 West 39th Street
New York, NY 10018
(212) 354-9360
*Offers a big selection of fabrics, catering largely to professional costumers and dressmakers, as well as to sewing enthusiasts. Prices are reasonable.*

Central Art Supply Co.
62 Third Avenue
New York, NY 10003
(212) 473-7705
*Medium-priced art supplies, mostly for painters, illustrators, and graphic designers. Very good paper section.*

Cerulean Blue
P.O. Box 21168
Seattle, WA 98111-3168
(206) 323-8600
*Offers a good selection fabric dyes and paints, specializing in dyes that are safe for home and studio use. Also sells tools, fabrics, books, and protective gear, and has a nice catalog available for purchase. Helpful and informative.*

Charette
215 Lexington Avenue
New York, NY 10016
(212) 683-4425
*Very fancy modelmaking supplies and drafting supplies. Good for basswood modelmaking strips in every kind form and size. Also sell professional-quality hot-wire foam cutters.*

Chavant Inc.
42 West Street
Red Bank, NJ 07701
(908) 842-6272
*A good source for all kinds of modeling clays in different degrees of hardness and softness, and sulfur-free plasticene for use with silicone or other RTV rubber molds. Chavant also makes and sells very fancy clay modeling tools for industrial prototype makers. The staff is helpful and willing to discuss products in detail.*

Cinderella Flower & Feather
60-64 West 38th Street
New York, NY 10018
(212) 840-0644 or (800) 992-0009
*All kinds of artificial flowers and feathers, including boas, ostrich feathers, and even birds' bodies. Pleasant and helpful, but busy.*

Dimensional Illustrators Inc.
362 Second Street Pike, Suite 112
Southampton, PA 18966
(215) 632-8238
*This organization, dedicated to promoting the work of dimensional illustrators and model-makers, sponsors an annual show with awards for the best dimensional illustration produced internationally, and publishes a book containing the work. A good resource for those interested in promoting their work, as well as for those looking for good dimensional illustrators.*

Dollspart Supply Co. Inc.
The Teddy Works
492D50 54th Avenue
Maspeth, NY 11378
(800) 336-DOLL
*"Anything and everything for doll"—doll eyes, teeth, wigs, bodies, clothes, various colors and lengths of mohair, and lots more.*

Dow Corning Corp.
Midland, MI 48686-0994
(800)248-2461
*Manufactures various silicone mold rubbers, some capable of holding high-temperature casting materials like low-melting-point metals. These products have very small catalyst-to-mix ratio, and thus require precise measuring.*

Dura-Foam Products Inc.
63-02 59th Avenue
Maspeth, NY 11378
(718) 894-2488
*A good source for foam rubber and rigid and flexible urethane foam.*

Diamond Fabric Discount Center
171 First Avenue
New York, NY 10003
(212) 674-9612
—or—
34 Avenue A
New York, NY 10009
(212) 228-8189
*All kinds of fabrics, many theatrical and unusual. Shopping here is a bit of an adventure, as the stores are big and stuff isn't always where you'd expect it to be. The staff is helpful, the prices are great.*

Eastman Kodak Information Center
Dept. 841K
343 State Street
Rochester, NY 14650
(800) 242-2424
*Call the 800 number if you have questions regarding a Kodak product. They will test film and eventually replace it if it is not good.*

Economy Foam Center/AAA Foam Center
173 East Houston Street
New York, NY 10002
(212) 473-D4462
*A good place to go for foam rubber sheets, shapes, vinyl fabrics, futons, or batting by the bag or roll. Good prices.*

Eltraade Co. Inc.
313 Canal Street
New York, NY 10013
(212) 226-0575
*A good outlet for blowers, exhaust fans, supplies for making vacuum degassment units, vacuum motors, and display motors of all kinds.*

Fairfield Processing Corp.
88 Rose Hill Avenue
Danbury, CT 06813
(800) 243-0989
*Sells the kind of polyester batting favored by Lisa Lichtenfels for her soft sculpture figures.*

Fibre Glast Developments Corp.
1944 Neva Drive
Dayton, OH 45414-5598
(513) 274-1159
*Distribute epoxy, fiberglass, polyester resin, and a high grade of talc for mixing in modeling wax formulas.*

Gamzon Bros. Inc.
21 West 46th Street
New York, NY 10036
(212) 719-2550
*A good source for jeweler's tools, supplies, equipment, with a big, free catalog full of useful tools.*

Graphic Artists' Guild
11 West 20th Street
New York, NY 10011
(212) 463-7730
*This professional organization supports the rights of graphic artists and illustrators, and also publishes the excellent* Pricing and Ethical Guidelines *handbook. In addition, the GAG gives courses on negotiation, pricing, and marketing artwork, as well as on various art techniques. A wonderful, kindly bunch that deserves support.*

Kreative Liquid Color
4780 Cheyenne Way
Chino, CA 91710
(714) 627-8486
*Makes colors for thermosetting plastics and color pastes for wax formulas. Will match color samples, has lots of colors.*

M & J Trimming
1008 Sixth Avenue
New York, NY 10018
(212) 391-9072
*Offers a huge selection of trimmings of all kinds, antique-looking and modern, plus ribbons, braid, sequins, buttons, etc. Usually rushed and busy.*

Maid of Scandinavia
3244 Raleigh Avenue
Minneapolis, MN 55416
(800) 3286722
*Cake and cookie decorating supplies, and many other home and kitchen products—even kids' books. A free catalog is available only to professional cake decorators.*

Metropolitan Impex Inc.
966 Avenue of the Americas
New York, NY 10018
(212) 564-0398
*Trimmings, bridal gown accessories, rhinestones, lace filets, etc. Good selection.*

New York Theatrical Sourcebook
Broadway Press
120 Duane Street, #407
New York, NY 10007
(212) 695-0570
*Probably the most complete source of suppliers of everything an artist or theater person could possibly want. It is absolutely great, and will direct you to sources for just about anything.*

The Paper Source
1506 West 12th Street
Los Angeles, CA 90015
(213) 387-5820
*A paper shop for the connoisseur (or for the paper sculptor interested in archival papers). Very fine selection.*

Pearl Paint
308 Canal Street
New York, NY 10013
(212) 431-7932
*Four floors' worth of art supplies for the graphic designer, illustrator, and craftsperson. A small sampling: gold leaf, many papers, airbrush sets, modeling clays, aluminum and brass tubing, model wood strips, etc. The huge store is fun to browse in, and they ship, too (ask for a catalog). The busy, rushed staff is usually pretty helpful, and prices fairly good.*

Plastic Adhesion Technology
P.O. Box 1365
Eatontown, NJ 07724
(201) 542-2320
*Makes and sells Form Fast, a display casting material that works like the late, lamented Celastic. Ask for Tom Peterson.*

Polaroid Technical Assistance
784 Memorial Drive
Cambridge, MA 02139
(800) 225-1618
*Call them for technical help. They will test film and replace it if it is not good.*

PRO Chemical & Dye Inc.
P.O. Box 14
Somerset, MA 02726
(508) 676-3838
*A large selection of fabric dyes and paints, at reasonable prices. Noteworthy offerings include textile pigment inks, other supplies for coloring costumes and scenery, and cold-water dyes. The staff is informative, friendly, and helpful on the phone, and a free catalog is available.*

Rita's Needlework
129 East 90th Street
New York, NY 10128
(212) 427-2557
*Has about 400 colors of embroidery floss, Aida and Hardanger cloth for cross stitch, many other supplies, and books on all kinds of embroidery—crewel, needlepoint, or whatever. Helpful and pleasant.*

Jiffy Mixer
4120 Tigris Way
Riverside, CA 92503
(714) 272-0838
*The source for the Jiffy Mixer, a non-aerating mixer for preparing molding and casting materials without incorporating air bubbles.*

Kindt-Collins Co.
12651 Elmwood Avenue
Cleveland, OH 44111
(800) 321-3170
*All kinds of waxes for prototype casting, plus pattern shop foundry supplies, including abrasives, adhesives, cements, coatings, releases, plastics, and plasters. The helpful staff will gladly send a free catalog.*

Rogers Foam Corp.
2580 Main Street
Hartford, CT 06120
*A place to find foam—Scotfoam, mostly.*

Sculptors' Supplies Co.
222 East Sixth Street
New York, NY 10003
(212) 673-3500
*All kinds of sculpture supplies and tools—armature wire, chisels, mallets, carving and modeling materials, etc. Very pleasant and helpful.*

Sculpture House
30 East 30th Street
New York, NY 10016
(212) 679-7474
—and—
Sculpture House Casting
155 West 26th Street
New York, NY 10010
(212) 645-9430
*These outlets sell complete lines of supplies for the sculptor. They have a catalog, as well as casting facilities that can be useful for model-makers.*

Silicones, Inc.
1020 Surrett Drive
High Point, NC 27261
(919) 886-5018
*A source for RTV silicone mold rubber, both the pour-in and butter-on varieties. The very helpful staff is willing to explain about products and send literature.*

Smooth On Inc.
1000 Valley Road
Gillette, NJ 07933
(908) 647-5800
*Flexible RTV rubber molds, component foams, and epoxy resins. The excellent catalog has excellent diagrams showing how to use rubber molds in casting. Very helpful and knowledgeable.*

Unnatural Resources
14 Forest Avenue
Caldwell, NJ 07006
(201) 228-5384
*Steve Eisenberg is the owner of this maker of innovative casting and display products. Leave a message and he'll get back to you. The materials are really interesting, and safe to use.*

US Gypsum/USG
101 South Wacker Drive
Chicago, IL 60606
(312) 606-4000
*All kinds of casting and sculpting plaster, made for every imaginable purpose. The plasters are sold through distributors, like art and sculpture supply places. The USG staff is helpful, and will send a catalog describing USG products.*

Utrecht Linen
111 Fourth Avenue
New York, NY 10003
(212) 777-5353
*Art supplies for the painter, illustrator, and graphic designer. A good paper selection, though not exhaustive. No craft supplies. Prices are really good, the staff helpful. A catalog is available.*

Van Aken Int'l
9157 Rochester Court
Rancho Cucamonga, CA 91730
(800) 262-1948
*Makes Van Aken modeling clay, a low-sulfur product that is excellent for clay animation, comes in many colors (which can be mixed together), and can be mixed with oil colors. Excellent stuff.*

Van Dyke's
P.O. Box 278
Woonsocket, SD 57385
Orders: (800) 843-3320
Questions: (605) 796-4425
*Taxidermy supplies, glass animal eyes, rigid foam animal forms, false animal teeth (I'm not kidding), driftwood and fake rocks for mounts, and also boxwood modeling tools, horn and bone saws, scalpels, airbrushes, sprayers and compressors, and even mounting plaques for animal heads and horns. You name it, they've got it. Friendly and helpful.*

Volunteer Lawyers for the Arts
1285 Avenue of the Americas
New York, NY 10019
(212) 977-9271
*If you are an artist, have little or no money, and think you have been or are about to be ripped off by a client, these guys are for you: kindly lawyers interested in artists, musicians, and theater people. The office has a list of lawyers that you can look at. You practically have to be a homeless person to qualify for their free legal assistance, but you can call one or two lawyers and briefly speak to them about a problem even if you're not a bona-fide starving artist.*

Wallis Mayers Needlework
30 East 68th Street
New York, NY 10021
(212) 861-5318
*A large selection of embroidery floss colors and other embroidery supplies. Helpful.*

Woodcraft
210 Wood County Industrial Park
P.O. Box 1686
Parkersburg, WV 26102-1686
Customer Service: (800) 535-4482
Technical Assistance: (800) 535-4486
*A wonderful source of woodworking supplies and tools, especially Swiss-made chisels. The staff is very helpful, and a gorgeous catalog is available.*

Zeller International
Main Street
Box Z
Downsville, NY 13755
(800) 722-USFX
*Makes and sells enormous number of casting and molding products geared to artists who are safety- and health-conscious, including casting plastics, resins, hard and soft foams, display casting materials, and many wonderful special-effects materials. The helpful, informative staff will send literature about what they make. An excellent source.*

# INDEX

3.16.93 AEI 65.00 53606